Romance Readers
GUIDE TO
HISTORIC LONDON

SONJA M. ROUILLARD

FOREWORD BY SABRINA JEFFRIES

ROMANCE READERS GUIDES

San Francisco, California

Published by Romance Readers Guides
P.O. Box 564
Alviso, CA 95002
www.RomanceReadersGuides.com

First Edition
ISBN: 978-0998740904

Editors: Caz Owens, Jude Simms
Copy Editor: Sandy Stark
Designer / Production Director: Steven Glapa

The information in this book is accurate to the best of our knowledge at the date of publication. It's always advisable to confirm details before booking. Romance Readers Guides and the author Sonja Rouillard cannot accept responsibility for outdated facts, or for inadvertent errors or omissions. Your experience is important to us: please share your travel stories—positive or negative—on our Facebook page: RomanceReadersTravelGuides.

Cover photos Amberley Castle Hotel and stock photography.
Back cover photos St. Pancras Renaissance® Hotel London.

DEDICATION

*To my kids — Ruben, Eddy, and Izzy — and to my husband
for putting up with me over the countless hours
they had to fend for themselves while I was buried in research.*

ACKNOWLEDGEMENTS

Thank you to the superb authors who allowed me to use excerpts from their delightful novels: Victoria Alexander, Mary Balogh, Lynne Connolly, Tessa Dare, Elizabeth Hoyt, Erin Knightley, Johanna Lindsey, Delilah Marvelle, and, through The Ampersand Agency, Georgette Heyer. And where would we be without Jane Austen, too!

An extra special thank you to Sabrina Jeffries for writing the foreword and especially for her wonderfully sensual scene set in The British Museum, which sparked my desire to include romance excerpts to bring to life these historic places.

Lastly, I'm grateful to my friends and family, always there to support and help me: Laurie, Joan, Kristi, Sandrine, Anna, Jennifer, Juanita, and Las Amigas!

BURLINGTON
ARCADE

Tel: 020 7493 2961
TRUEFITT & HILL
EST
1805
Gentlemen's Hairdressers
and Perfumers

TABLE OF CONTENTS

FOREWORD

Sabrina Jeffries

A few years ago, my husband and I took our first trip to London together. One stop I insisted upon us making was at the British Museum to see the Elgin Marbles (pieces of the Parthenon brought back to England by Lord Elgin during the Regency period). I had included a particular metope in one of my historical romance novels, *The Forbidden Lord*. So imagine how thrilled I was to be able to see that very metope in something other than a picture on the internet!

My husband photographed me standing next to it . . . and then photographed me standing on Rotten Row in Hyde Park and sitting in Grosvenor Square and strolling down the streets of Mayfair. Our visit was magical . . . because all of these places were integral to some book I'd written.

Until then, I'd been limited to research on the internet. Having an autistic son had made it difficult for us to travel, so that first trip (made possible by an incredibly wonderful caregiver willing to give a week of her life to watching my son) was such a thrill.

The only down side was that I had to piece together my own tours—find the places that interested me as a romance writer, figure out how to access them, and determine whether they would be useful to visit. Only think how much easier it would have been for me if I could have had Sonja's guide!

What could be more fun than experiencing London through the eyes of a fellow romance reader? I confess, the minute I heard about her project, I was captivated. So many of us readers (and authors) immerse ourselves fully in the periods our books are set in, yet we discover that the settings aren't something we can find easily or learn more about, if we're so lucky as to have the chance to travel to the center of many historical romances—London, England.

Sonja has set out to correct that omission.

What a thrill it was for me to discover Whitehall (which appeared in my Deborah Martin book, *By Love Unveiled*) in the same guide with Newgate Prison (in my Sabrina Jeffries title, *Only a Duke Will Do*), the British Museum (*The Forbidden Lord*), and Vauxhall (*The Study of Seduction*). Some of my favorite authors to read often include scenes from Hyde Park, Mayfair, and Almack's in their books, so I found it great fun to travel through those familiar settings with a guide who could inform me of what a romance reader would love to know.

I research my books thoroughly, yet there were nuggets of information in this guide that I had never heard—from things as simple as how the Mayfair area got its name to who was the youngest female convict ever to be deported to Australia, something that might have been useful to me for my novel, *The Pirate Lord*, about convict women sent abroad.

The extensive coverage of gentlemen's clubs is bound to fascinate any reader, since White's and Brook's and countless others are central to the plots of many a romance novel. In particular, any reader of Regency historical romances visiting London would absolutely want to visit those clubs, even if just to look at them from the outside (they are exclusive gentlemen's clubs, after all, and not likely to let a bunch of strange women wander through them). Sonja conveniently provides not only details about the most venerable clubs but descriptions of other more eclectic ones that might pique the interest of romance lovers.

Indeed, that's the best part of Sonja's *Romance Readers Guide to Historic London*—her awareness of what would most appeal to her audience. She talks about the invention of afternoon tea and then goes on to explain the various kinds of teas, any of which a reader could encounter in a Victorian romance. Then she goes on to explain how to find an authentic one in London—or a modern version, if the reader so chooses. (I can't wait to try the special Gluten-Free tea at the English Tea Room at the Brown's Hotel—I didn't even know such a thing existed!)

And if you're looking for a hotel, look no further. Sonja's descriptions of hotels and their historical background will have you salivating. I may not spring for a stay at The Ritz, but I'm not sure I can resist Amberley Castle. It sounds endearing. Plus, it's a castle. What's not to like? I can't help it—I'm a romance writer. Castles always suck me in.

Honestly, if you're a romance reader, most of the places mentioned in this guide will suck you in. So if you want to experience London the way one of your favorite romance heroines has experienced it, you can't go wrong with this guide to London through a romance reader's eyes.

What would Emma say?

A short story

CHAPTER 1

What would Emma say? ~ *a short story*

See modern London through the eyes of one of Jane Austen's most opinionated characters

"My dearest Mr. Knightley," spoke Emma, continuing to use his formal name, as she had warned she would always do, even though they were now married. "I know that you do not believe me, but I was there in London in the year two-thousand and seventeen, truly I was there. In some ways it was so very much the same and in others, well, even I know that what I am telling you utterly defies belief."

Mr. Knightley took a solid breath, and with a calm asperity that he most certainly did not within possess, attempted to gently guide Emma into seeing reason.

"Dearest beloved Emma, whose lifelong care you have so wondrously placed in my tender protection, can you not understand the skepticism I must endure in the face of your rather fanciful tale? It is just not plausible, my dear, that you were somehow transported two hundred years into the future while you were visiting your sister in London for two months."

"How could you think that I would purposely tell falsehoods?" cried Emma, turning her glowing cheeks away from him. "I thought you knew me better than that!"

Inwardly, Mr. Knightley was growing deeply apprehensive. The long-awaited and much-planned visit to Emma's sister Isabella had clearly proved too stimulating. London in 1816 was a colossal metropolis, and it had clearly overwhelmed his new young bride, who was at heart a country girl unused to the lavish excesses of the great city. Having finally found his happiness in holy matrimony with the young lady he had long secretly admired, he had wanted to indulge his sweet wife in her heart's desire for a visit to Brunswick Square so that she could finally partake of a full London season. Of course, he'd wanted to accompany Emma, but she absolutely refused to go unless he promised to stay behind to care for her poor dear father.

It had all been handled with utmost carefulness. Emma had travelled there and back with close friends, and he had stayed behind to assure Mr. Woodhouse that all was well with his beloved daughter and ensure that he would not be lonesome in the evenings, with Mr. Knightley now living at Hartfield House to keep him company.

Clearly, what had seemed the perfect plan had been unwise, with too much excited merriment for his sweet Emma. He realized that he must show her, yet again, the error in her thinking, and smart lady that she was, he was sure she'd quickly come to a reasonable state of mind. Mr. Knightley, therefore, concluded he must give her his full attention, demonstrating both his concern and his clear-thinking logic.

"My dear Emma, I apologize most humbly. I certainly do want to hear all about it with my promise that I will not again criticize your intellect."

Emma was not fully mollified, but she felt that it was her duty to relay her understandings of what was to come. Mr. Knightley would benefit from this knowledge as he planned for the future of their estates, she reasoned. Continuing with her account, she quickly got caught up in the excitement of all her discoveries forgetting that she had been annoyed with him for his lack of faith.

"Oh my! Oh my. London has changed in the future! But in some ways it is just the same," she told him earnestly, leaning in and placing a hand on his arm for emphasis. "St. James's Palace, Westminster Abbey, and many other famous buildings are still there, and I was even able to tour *inside* Buckingham Palace. In the future they let visitors inside, you know. So many things are the same!" she said again, smiling enthusiastically. "Hyde Park is still there as is the Tower, and one can even see the crown jewels so beautifully displayed. Simply wonderful, really!

"But some things made me sad too. There is no longer a 'London season' with endless balls and soirees, but really, in truth, there is something to do every single night with concerts, plays, operas, the ballet, and more. However, I think the most amazing change is how people get around now. There are these carriages without horses that go on their own power, and not only that but people descend underground and emerge elsewhere in London, like magic!" (taking a quick breath), "But I must say, all the multitudes of people and fast moving automobiles and the tube—that's what they call it—to all over the place was entirely overwhelming and I felt, at times, quite lost without you there beside me."

"Dearest Emma," interjected Mr. Knightley, highly motivated to insert logic into the exchange. "All of this must have cost a great deal, and I would think navigating such a changed city would be highly confusing. That is, if it were real, of course," he added, gently patting her hand that still rested on his arm.

Ignoring his aside, Emma exclaimed, "Perfectly, perfectly right you are! Every single time I emerged from the underground I got lost – every single time! I do not know how I contrived as well as I did. Street maps are posted down below in each station, but by the time I walked up the stairs I would get all turned around. One really *must* have a very good map to go about the London of the future. It's unquestionably the most essential item in one's reticule. The second most vital would be an Oyster Card, and I don't mean something to eat." (giggling slightly in private humor), "It's the way you pay to ride on those underground carriages."

"Yes, but how did you buy the…Oyster Card and map, and pay for all those outings," he tried again, carefully keeping the doubt from his voice.

"Oh, my dear George, I probably should not even tell you, but I awoke in my sister's house which still belongs to the family; our descendants are living there still! There was confusion at first, of course, and concern on my part that I could not return, but quickly it all worked out. I think they would have doubted who I was if it weren't for the fact that I so very much resemble the family in old photos, and—"

"Old what?" he interjected.

Emma blinked and laughed lightly. "Oh, of course, another novelty. They're…like paintings. Anyway, they were eager to learn about us and then very much wanted to show me all the wonders of the twenty-first century. It was kindness indeed! Heavens, I would have felt terribly beholden to them, but, in truth, they have inherited a great fortune from us, so really I was just spending our own money, don't you see."

Mr. Knightley felt perturbed but refrained from saying anything. Perhaps letting her finish her story would be the quickest way toward promulgating his plan to make her see reason.

"Now where was I?" Emma paused. "Yes, of course, the many changes. I so badly wanted to go to Almack's Assembly Rooms in the future, but it's no longer there. Just a boring office building, while the many gentlemen's clubs are as popular as ever, and they still do not allow women inside White's. A fact that seems to *really* bother the women of the future."

"Go on, my dear," he murmured, just wanting her to finish so he could begin to help her.

"Let's see, the best things about the future are that even though it is so very noisy and modern, new buildings everywhere, it is also cleaner too. No more is there horse manure everywhere—no more horses either, sadly—and the air is much cleaner since coal isn't used anymore, but of course it still rains *all* the time. It is still England after all. 'Bring an umbrella with you always,' my great great great—there are just too many to count—future niece Bella admonished me.

"Also, the noisy traffic from the horseless carriages is horrendous, and this is very important, one must look very carefully in *both* directions *every single time* one crosses the street. I was told that the American colonists come over and get hit by cars because the traffic goes in the other direction from the United States. Also, the pedestrian traffic can be dreadful, so many people pushing and crowding that one must take care even on the pavements.

"But then I would turn a corner and suddenly be on a quiet, quaint street lined with terraced houses just as in our time, beautiful and in perfect condition. But would you believe Bella calls these perfectly ordinary buildings 'historic' as if they're something special!"

"If not for the parked automobiles, it would look and feel just like our merry old England. There were many places like this, quiet little parks and charming walks or mews that one just needs to search out to feel like one is back in the Regency era—that's what they call our time. Anyway, there was one charming little park," (smiling inwardly), "that I went to repeatedly to sit quietly by myself and watch the people."

"Emma! Do you mean to tell me you went about walking alone?" he cried loudly and with heat. "I had thought you had better sense than to go out alone in London without even a maid along."

"Please rest assured, Mr. Knightley, that I took a footman with me always—while in our time of course. However, in modern times London is safer in some ways. Women can go out by themselves in most parts of London and dine alone too! It is still a big city, well *much* bigger really, with eight million people, but in the daytime a tourist should feel quite safe there, provided they hold on tight to their reticules, of course. Sadly, I suppose there will always be thieves and pickpockets no matter what the century.

"Oh!" Emma smiled brightly. "It never felt more like home than when I partook of 'afternoon tea,' although, to be sure, it won't be invented for another forty years or so. Our descendants took me to a charming salon, and there were wonderful little sandwiches, scones with clotted cream and jam, delicious tea, beautiful bone china, and pleasant tinkling piano music. We whiled away the afternoon so pleasantly. This new tradition will become as synonymous with England as hotdogs and apple pie are to America."

Mr. Knightley looked the question, and Emma responded: "Never mind about that; hotdogs are yet one more new, rather tasty invention of the future. Oh, but there is another rather bold addition in modern times; they actually serve champagne in the afternoons now, and I should not tell you, perhaps, but I indulged a wee bit myself. I hope you are not offended at my lack of propriety?" she asked, looking slightly chagrined.

Mr. Knightley was increasingly troubled about his new bride. Her fanciful imagination had always been a delight, but she seemed undeniably sincere in her retelling of this tale. Even so, he felt obliged to reassure her about the afternoon champagne; after all what harm, really, could there be in her imbibing something that was a figment of her imagination?

Patting her hand, he murmured in flat affect, "Do not trouble yourself about this, dearest. Believe me, there are other aspects to your tale that concern me more."

Feeling reassured that his opinion of her was not lessened, Emma continued, "As I was saying, so much is different but so much is the same. I found this handy little guidebook in Hatchard's Bookshop, which is still there on Piccadilly after two hundred and twenty years, if you can believe it. It was called the *Romance Readers Guide*, or something like that, and it showed me where many old places still existed, so that even a lady in the distant future can experience, if only for a brief time, the life of a Regency heroine. Imagine that! I wonder where I left the book, or perhaps it didn't return with me." Emma fretted, looking about her.

This was just too much. Mr. Knightley was forcibly struck by the irrationality of her utterances, and concluded it was time to end this madness.

Taking both of Emma's hands into his own, he said, "My darling, dear sweet Emma, you mean the world to me, so to hear you abusing the abundant reason you have is beyond what I can endure. You know that I cannot stand to see you acting or thinking wrongly without remonstrance, and surely you can see how your tale does not bear belief!"

Emma found her arm drawn within his, and pressed against his heart, and heard thus, in a tone of great authority: "I would like to suggest that it was a dream—would you consider that possibility, especially since you said you woke up in your bed at your sister's house? With all the excitement of finally having your London season, and the flowing champagne, it is no wonder you had such a dream. A nightmare really," he added, shuddering slightly at the many strange images she had conjured in her mind.

Emma started to speak, but he was not finished. "I know it must seem so very, very real, and it is such an inventive, marvelous fable. Emma, I think you could be a novelist with your fanciful ideas. Truly!" He meant the compliment sincerely, but it didn't change his very real concern for her well being. "But if you cannot see your way to believing it was a dream then I must admit that I am exceedingly worried about you, because I love you so much, dearest."

Again, Emma opened her mouth to argue for her own rationality, but staring into his deeply concerned visage she felt a moment of doubt. It was true that her story defied belief, not only that she had travelled through time but also that London and the world could have changed so very much in such a relatively brief span of time. *It had felt so real!*

Was it possible she was losing her mind, she anxiously wondered? Well, she thought, whether it was a dream or not, this here and now was her reality…making a life with the man she loved and most admired in the year 1816. So she answered with what any dutiful wife would in such a situation. Squeezing his hand reassuringly, she offered, "Of course, Mr. Knightley, it *must* have been a dream. What other explanation could there possibly be? I am so grateful for your counsel, as always."

"Oh, sweet Emma, let us reconcile and say no more about it."

Relief flooded through him that his beloved wife was not going insane, and in the quiet of their sitting room he pulled Emma close to him, enveloping her in a long embrace. He kissed her lightly on the lips, and they both thought about a time later that day when a greater privacy would allow for more than just a kiss.

"Mr. Knightley, I am so very glad that we are aligned again. You are my anchor, to be sure, and in this I know you will always return me to a proper state of mind."

"Of course, my dear," he replied, with a smile that only hinted at the superior conceit and manly pride he was surely feeling.

"My dearest," she said looking lovingly up at him. "I almost forgot, I brought you a special gift from the trip." She reached into her reticule and retrieved a small object wrapped in brightly colored paper. "I bought it at Harrods…" She paused realizing that the store didn't yet exist and wouldn't for a few more years. "It's a…new store in London, a little like Fortnum and Mason." Emma waited then, hoping he'd not question her further.

Murmuring his gratitude, he took it from her and carefully opened it, seeming to note the unusually crinkly but sturdy nature of the shiny wrapping.

"Mylar," she murmured, and left it at that.

Then he stood there deeply transfixed, staring at the odd, nearly flat, rectangle and turning it over and over in his hands.

"Emma, how fascinating. This has a look and feel unlike anything I have encountered before. What is it?"

"My darling, it is what they call a solar-powered cal-cu-la-tor. I was assured that it would work even without the new-fangled electricity that has not yet been invented, but soon. May I?"

Emma stretched out her hand and he placed it in her palm. She pushed the "on" button. "Let's see…we were married in 1815." She tapped in the numbers.

He'd watched intently, but she turned the screen anyway so he could see the full number on the small glass rectangle.

"Interesting! But what is it?" he asked, leaning in.

"Just one more moment, and you'll be able to divine its purpose. Dear Sir, what was the year of your birth?"

Mr. Knightley replied, "seventeen-hundred and seventy-eight, but you know this."

Emma nodded and smiled. She tapped the four numbers on the device and then pushed the subtraction button. "That's 37 years of your life without me by your side. A long time isn't it?"

She winked at him playfully, then handed the small contraption back. "Here, maybe you can play with this magical machine for a little while."

His eyebrows rose, then he nodded, seeming surprised at his own curiosity. "Well thank you again, dearest Emma. How fascinating," he murmured not looking at her, his focus consumed by the object in his hand.

Emma rose onto her tiptoes and gave him a quick, sweet kiss on his cheek, before turning merrily on her heel and walking briskly from the drawing room.

Let him puzzle that out, she thought, smiling to herself as she went outside to take a leisurely turn about the gardens on a rare sunny June afternoon.

Cliveden House, a Grade 1 listed mansion
now a hotel, outside London

CHAPTER 2 🌿

How to Time Travel

Instructions for taking a walk in the footsteps of your favorite romance heroine

Whether you just want to learn more about the places from your favorite novels or begin planning a grand excursion, this book is here to help. But first some quick how-to's to set the scene.

HOW OLDE: ♣♣♣

Most listings are accompanied by a scale designed to show how close the place or experience comes to the real deal—how authentically historic it is or feels, even if the place is relatively new. This is an American point of view from the perspective of a lifelong romance fan. The five criteria are:

Age ∼ Is it actually old? Grade listed?

Décor ∼ Do the public areas have period furnishings or decoration?

Presentation ∼ Do the hotel rooms have period décor, too, or is the presentation historical (tour guides in period dress or waiters in tails)?

Historical Offerings ∼ Are there period services (afternoon tea or carriage rides) or authentic English cuisine?

Feel ∼ Lastly, a bonus point if the overall impression took the author back to a time of Merry Old England.

GRADE LISTED ∼ what's that?

It seems like every other building in central London is "listed." This means that the structure is deemed to be of historical importance and, while it might be privately owned, will come under the protection of the Historic Building and Monuments Commission for England. Anything built prior to 1700 is automatically listed, as are most structures from 1700 to 1840. The grading is I, II*, or II, with I being the highest level of "exceptional interest." Only 2.5% of the more than 500,000 listed buildings are Grade I. So if you're sleeping or dining in a I, that's something special.

The downside of Grade listing is that all modifications require approval that is sometimes impossible to obtain. For the traveler, this translates into such problems as no elevators or air conditioning in the many authentically ancient buildings. While these are just inconveniences for some, for others that might ruin a trip, so I note these types of issues whenever possible. That said, if mobility or other health problems are a concern, please double-check directly with the property just to be safe before making any non-refundable reservations.

HISTORICAL PERIODS ⟿ *what time is it?*

This guide focuses mostly on the Regency and Victorian periods, but some listings date back much farther to the Medieval and a few to as recent as the Edwardian. For the novice romance fan, these periods usually refer to the ruling monarch or house.

Medieval	5th–15th Century	
Tudor	1485–1603	(Elizabethan 1558–1603)
Stuart	1603–1714	
Georgian	1714–1837 *	(Regency 1811–1820)
Victorian	1837–1901	
Edwardian	1901–1910	
Windsor	1910–Present	

*American Connection: Throughout the guide, where there's a connection to the US, it's noted. In this case, the 3rd of the 5 royal Georges, King George III oversaw the beginning of the end of the vast British Empire, when he lost the struggle to keep the colonies (us) in his grasp.

HISTORICAL MONEY ⟿ *what did it cost?*

From Almack's vouchers to gentleman wagers at White's to upgrading that old pile—what the aristocracy called their manors—it all cost money. Lots of money. To give a sense of just how much, online inflation calculators were used to estimate today's dollars.[1] For example, what would the £50,000 that King Edward III spent in 1370 to upgrade Windsor Castle equal today? Given that no two calculators give the same answer, three were used and the amounts averaged. It's not exact, but it will give an idea of what the value to us would be. Oh, and Edward's refurb would cost about $32 million today.

PRICE SCALE ⟿ *just how much will this cost me?*

Within lodging and dining there are different categories ranging from the modest "Governess on Holiday" to the truly exorbitant "For a King's Ransom." Prices are mostly listed in English Pounds to avoid exchange-rate fluctuations that would make the guide immediately obsolete. Just type "exchange rate calculator pound" into your favorite search engine, and you'll quickly get a calculator that will allow you to convert to your local currency.

FINDING DEALS ⟿ *again, how* **much** *will this cost me!?!*

Prices are for the least expensive double room from each hotel's summer rates—peak travel time and therefore the highest. However, you don't have to settle for the first price you find. Depending on how much time you have, I suggest trying this to find the best deals: 1) see what specials are offered at the hotel's website, logging-in first if you're a member of the brand's loyalty program, 2) check your favorite online booking site or www.HotelsCombined.com for a quick look at all the deals offered through third parties, 3) if far in advance, sign up for the hotel's loyalty program and wait for email specials, 4) approach the hotel directly by email or phone to ask if they have any special rates. If really far in advance, make a refundable reservation to hold a room and check back periodically for better deals.

Other savings include: travelling in off-peak periods, booking early or very last-minute (best for off-peak seasons), reserving a non-refundable pre-paid room, or reserving a special rate with free extras that can save you money, such as breakfast. Lastly, if you have loyalty points these can be used creatively; often they can be applied to pay for a portion of the room—cash & points—if there isn't enough for the whole stay. For some, this extra effort is all part of the fun (it is for me), but for others, especially those with time constraints, simply choosing the price range appropriate for your budget and getting a reservation booked quickly is best. A last note on discounts: at museums and tourist sights, discounts, called "concessions," are offered for families, elderly, disabled, etc.; check websites for details.

INTERNATIONAL CALLING ⟿ It's a bit confusing, so here's a basic primer. 1) get an international plan or you'll pay huge roaming charges (it must be GSM so ask your carrier). 2) bring a power voltage adaptor so you don't fry your phone. Each country has a code: US is 1 and England is 44. London area code is 020 (but drop 0 within UK). After is number in 5-7 digits. For the Guide, I've included the country code (44) and suggest email is used before departure; listed numbers are for use in UK. More info: www.HowToCallAbroad.com. Examples:

Landline in US → UK: 011 44 20 xxxx xxxx (011 is int'l access code)
US Cell in US → UK: +44 20 etc. (cells use + for int'l access)
US Cell in UK → UK: 00 44 20 etc. –or– +44 20 etc.
　(note: drop local London 0 prefix in all cases)
US Cell in UK → US (also texting): +1 (xxx) xxx-xxxx

ENTERTAINING YOUR XY TRAVEL COMPANION
⌁ for the guys

Dragging hubby along on your fairytale adventure might require offering a boon, so throughout the book sights are highlighted that might pique a gentleman's sense and sensibilities (such as Sherlock Holmes or WWII exhibits). Watch for these and then sprinkle a few of them throughout conversations about the trip, which should help improve his interest in travelling back in time with you.

LAST WORDS ⌁ well, not really

Through the *Romance Readers Guide to Historic London* you'll learn about the histories of places common to this romance genre. There's also authentic old world dining and lodging. *Ever want to sleep in a 400-year-old four-poster bed?* You'll learn that here. What you won't find are all the basics of a general travel guide, since that kind of information is readily available and more up-to-date on the web. Chapter 4's Maps show where most of the center city sights are located, although for greater London I heartily recommend the purchase of a good quality map or better yet a mobile app.

Another must for modern London is an **Oyster Card**. It's Britain's version of a subway card, used by tapping it on the reader when entering/exiting the Tube and entering buses. It can also be used on all public transport, some National Rail, and even the MBNA Thames Clipper river bus. The plastic card is £3, and you top it up with as much as you want. It saves time buying tickets at every station and the fare is cheaper than individual tickets. Plus, you can even get a refund on leftover cash before you depart. There's also the Travelcard for shorter durations/less distance. Learn more: www.VisitBritainShop.com

In the last chapter, Emma Woodhouse journeyed forward in time to experience some of the wonders of modern London. Now it's your turn to travel backwards—with a little effort and a fanciful imagination, you can learn about and even experience many of the wonders of Merry Old England.

So sit back and relax with this guide and a warm cup of delicious English tea. Nothing else will do, as Emma's talkative acquaintance Miss Bates would say...

"No coffee, I thank you, for me—never take coffee. A little tea if you please, sir, by and bye,—no hurry..."

CHAPTER 3

Then and Now

Famous historical sites from romance novels (mostly) and what they are now

Historical romance novels come to life for readers partly because they are set in places that were a real part of the culture of the period. When I first started reading them, I wondered whether these settings were genuine historical places or just representational—and mostly they are, or were at one time, real. More recently, I've wondered which ones still exist and whether I can visit them. The answer to that is yes and no—read on to find out which ones are still around. Here are the stories of these fascinating places, in alphabetical order:

THE ALBANY

1774–present

THEN: Built originally as a three-story mansion in the Palladian style, it was twice sold when the owners, first Viscount Melbourne and later Prince Frederick, Duke of York and Albany (supplier of the building's moniker) fell short of money.[1] In 1802, it was converted into 69 "sets," and thus was launched what is believed to be the first apartment block in London. It has a place in literary history,

The Albany
by Thomas Shepherd,
c. 1830

serving as bachelor residences to many writers, artists, and later photographers over its 250-year life. Fictitious gentlemen—by Dickens, Wilde, and the lesser-known Hornung—have resided here as well. The "place for the fashionable thrifty," wrote Marmion Wilard Savage in his 1848 *The Bachelor of Albany* and, as such, it has been home to a number of aristocratic men, both wealthy and not: in total, 2 earls, 1 baron, 6 knights, 5 lords, and even a prime minister. "Men" is the operative word here, as women weren't allowed inside the front door until after 1880. Sounding like the plot of a romance novel, Lady Caroline Lamb snuck into the Albany dressed as a pageboy to get around the no-women rule hoping to see her former lover Lord Byron, c.1815.[2] She didn't. In response to the note she left, pleading, "Remember me!" Byron wrote this enchanting ditty:

> *Remember thee! Aye, doubt it not.*
> *Thy husband too shall think of thee:*
> *By neither shalt thou be forgot,*
> *Thou false to him, thou fiend to me!*

There are real-life connections to romance fiction as well. Jane Austen's favorite brother Henry had his banking concern there for a time. But most exciting for me, Georgette Heyer—the author often credited with creating the Regency romance genre—lived in flat F.3 from 1942 to 1966. During these 24 years, Heyer penned 19 novels—among them, such famous works as *Arabella*, *The Grand Sophy*, and *Frederica*—while literally walking in the footsteps of Regency bucks who had roamed there more than a century earlier.

NOW: The Grade I listed Albany is occasionally referred to in current romances as the abode of an impoverished noble, and in actuality continues to exist as an apartment complex of the "utmost gentility and refinement," literally. A board of trustees enforces the requirement that tenants comport themselves to this high standard. While nowadays women may live there, rules forbidding children and pets remain, along with, reportedly, no whistling and no publicity. Rarely a "set" sells on the open market for £2 million plus, but the truly fortunate live there at rent-controlled rates that would turn any big city dweller green with envy.

Lucky is the guest that is invited inside to visit a friend in this peaceful oasis in the heart of London, complete with a garden in the center and a 100-foot covered walkway called the Rope Walk. This author had the pleasure of a very brief visit—upon hearing about my research mission a kindly porter gave me a quick tour through the mansion's lobby and down the famous Rope Walk. It was exciting to make it past the front door, but alas no photos could be taken. So, intrepid travellers, you can certainly walk into the front courtyard on Piccadilly Street and climb the stairs to peer in the door as I did—who knows, perhaps someone will allow you a quick trip inside as well.

𝓗OW OLDE: 🏆🏆🏆🏆🏆

Hours: not open to the public–unless you can beg your way in | **Tube:** Piccadilly Circus | **Map:** B

Location: Albany Court Yard, off Piccadilly (almost directly across from Fortnum & Mason)

A

ALMACK'S ASSEMBLY ROOMS
1764–1871

THEN: It is the goal of every *fictitious* heroine to get a "voucher" to Almack's. It was also the goal of every *real* Regency or Victorian debutante. The cost of the non-transferable annual subscription (10 guineas or about $1,000 in today's dollars) wasn't the hard part. Getting one of the six or seven Lady Patronesses to approve of you was. It could be said that they were the female Beau Brummells of society, the arbiters that manufactured exclusivity at Almack's. Admittance proved you were at the highest levels of society, the top of the *ton*, and the rules, etiquette, and refreshments are precisely as described in our novels. The

A Ball at Almack's Assembly Rooms drawn by George Cruikshank, 1821

rules were strictly enforced; for example, the ingénue could not begin dancing without permission from one of the Patronesses, and usually the dancing partners were also assigned. No admittance unless properly dressed. The real-life Duke of Wellington was refused entry for wearing trousers rather than knee breeches. He complied from then on. And, as is often referenced in novels, the doors closed precisely at 11pm with no one admitted afterwards.

Only tea and lemonade were served to avoid drunkenness, along with the oft-mentioned day-old thin-sliced bread with butter and for dessert, dry cake (as opposed to stale, this means unfrosted or un-iced in England). This was done to differentiate the club from the lavish private balls—although why anyone would want this distinction I do not quite understand.

> All on that magic List depends;
> Fame, fortune, fashion, lovers, friends;
> 'Tis that which gratifies or vexes
> All ranks, all ages, and both sexes.
> If once to Almack's you belong,
> Like monarchs you can do no wrong;
> But banished thence on Wednesday night,
> By Jove, you can do nothing right.
> — Irish poet, Henry Luttrell, 1822[3]

It was indeed the "Marriage Mart" as it is called in the novels (eventually more important than being presented at court). It was the place to come and be seen—to show off that you were of the highest social rank, worthy of an aristocratic husband. In truth, the entire London season was geared toward the goal of matchmaking, as Johanna Lindsey points out in The Heir:

> ... "As it happens, and it can't be disputed, London is the place that all the marriageable young women flock to each Season. It's a well-known marriage mart. If Englishmen have managed just fine finding their wives there for years, myself included, why then wouldn't Duncan be able to?"

Of course it must be noted that the "Englishmen" in question were all of the aristocracy or nobility searching for wives of equal stature. That said, a favorite romance plot is the lady or gent who "marries up"—she for great looks and he with great wealth. It was, and is, a real-life trope too. Perhaps the earliest form of 'trophy' wife. In truth, this did happen, but such unions usually started in the bedroom instead of the ballroom (see Curzon Street).

Now back to where it all started...the first incarnation of Almack's. It was a coffee house on Pall Mall founded in 1759 where gentlemen would gather, drink coffee or wine, and read their newspaper. It reopened later as a mixed-sex version of a gentlemen's gaming hell, quite the opposite of Almack's later role as arbiter of proper behavior and cultured society. This early version was a moneymaking casino—very high-stakes—with a light supper served by Mr. and Mrs. Almack. Just as in many romance novels, young men sometimes lost a great deal of money there, such as the two famous brothers, Charles and Stephen Fox—both under age 25—who between them lost £32,000 (about $5.5 million today) in just three days playing Hazard (similar to American craps).

In 1765, Almack's was transformed into the version we know and love in our novels. The club opened in a purpose-built building in the Palladian style, which in this case means big and boxy, on King Street. Run by a group of seven Patronesses (mostly countesses) who were the *de facto* queens of London society, they kept a tight rein on the vouchers and Wednesday night dances—now the club's sole activity.

After more than one hundred years of Wednesday night dances, Almack's was sold in 1871 and renamed after the new owner, Willis's Rooms (Map C already shows it thus). Sadly, this hallmark of Victorian London was completely destroyed in 1944 by German bombs.

NOW: Go to 26-28 King Street today and you'll find a rather boring office building bearing the title 'Almack House' carved above the entrance. It's worth a look as you visit other old sights still in existence on the compact St. James's Street area.

How OLDE: 🏛🏛🏛🏛🏛 ~ *it's gone, sadly*
Tube: Green Park | **Map:** C | **Location:** 26–28 King Street

---

ARUNDEL CASTLE
1068–present

This castle is uber romantic! It's the kind of magical place where pretty princesses get locked in towers and handsome heroes save them. Or where 21st Century heroines on a tour of it find themselves flung back in time to meet the knight of their dreams. Romance authors agree with me—check out Lauren Royal's *The Duke's Reluctant Bride* (Cainewood Castle is loosely modeled on Arundel) or Eliza Knight's *A Lady's Charade* (Hardwyck Keep is based on it). There's even a contemporary rom-com set in Arundel village: *United States of Love* by Sue Fortin. All fun reading for your easy Sleep Like a Princess overnight excursion to West Sussex, about two hours south of London (Ch. 9).

THEN: Situated magnificently on a hill overlooking the River Arun, this castle is the second largest in England. The nobles that built this fortress over the past millennia were intricately linked with the convoluted history of England and its rulers. So, for this entry only, we'll step *all* the way back in time to chronicle the human story and a nation's rise that set the stage for the historical periods of our favorite romances.

As far back as 500,000 years ago there is evidence of hominin occupation in this area, particularly along the coastline. Jumping forward to the late Mesolithic period (10,000–4,300 BC) there are signs of more advanced activity—clearing of woodland and coastal chalk found in excavation sites some ten miles north of where it was mined. By the Neolithic (4,300–2,200 BC) there are significant land alterations that can be detected by laser scanning and aerial photographs—such as the Neolithic causewayed enclosure, The Trundle, northwest of Arundel. And so it goes through the Bronze and Iron Ages. By the end of these eras, remains of "hill forts" provide evidence of defended settlements, complete with elite residences for the leaders.

The ancient inhabitants of the Arundel area were a Celtic tribe, the pagan Atrebates. In the Roman period (43–410 AD), the territory was divided, and the Celtic kingdom of Regneses was established (its capital is today Chichester). By the end of the Romans' rule, there were permanent agricultural systems in place, trading roads, and villas that can still be seen in ruins throughout the South Downs area. So, if you find yourself walking on a strangely straight hill ridge or other odd formation in West Sussex, assume you are hiking on ancient history.

The early medieval period (410–1066) sees the decline in the Roman occupation and a shift away from urban/villa economies back to rural subsistence farming. Into the vacuum migrated Germanic tribes from continental Europe mixing with the local Celtic-Belgic-Gaul population to create Anglo-Saxons. Not much is known due to the lack of major building projects, until their conversion to Christianity in the late 700s— with that came written records of land charters documenting land holdings belonging to the English Crown, important loyal noblemen, and the Holy Roman Catholic Church. The nearby Amberley Castle (now a hotel, see Ch. 6) was held by the Bishops of Chichester. Then came the French Norman Conquest across the English Channel and the *Doomsday Book* of 1086 (see listing below).

And finally...the first Earl of Arundel.

So while it's ancient history to us, when Roger de Montgomery (originally the more French Montgomerie) was awarded the Arundel holding and Earldom by William the Conqueror in repayment for his loyalty, he gained a well-established, profitable, feudal system over vast fertile lands—nearly all of what is now the county of West Sussex. Along with many other properties awarded him, the "living" from these estates was about £2,000 annually (very roughly about $3 million today).[4] It was more than enough at the time to build a colossal fortress, on William's behalf, to guard Sussex against invasion via the River Arun.

The Norman Conquest came about because Edward the Confessor died without an heir and the Duke of Normandy, also called William the Bastard, saw an opportunity. This is one of many examples of the problems that arise, big and little, when a king didn't do his begetting, and I begin to see why Henry VIII was so preoccupied with siring a strong male heir.

As for Arundel, the first feature Montgomery built was the "motte," an artificial mound more than 100 feet high that arises from the dry moat, followed by a gatehouse in 1070. After his death, Arundel reverted to the English crown, now held by William's fourth son, King Henry I, who in turn left Arundel as a dower for his second wife Adeliza of Louvain. She married William d'Aubigny II, and eventually King Henry II awarded him the Earldom in 1154.

But before that the castle's nobility inaugurated a long history of political intrigue and attempts at grabbing power—some of which yielded benefits, while others beheadings. In 1139, Empress Matilda, the daughter of Henry I but raised in what is now Germany, moved into Arundel Castle for her plot to take the crown during the anarchy that followed her father's death. She ultimately returned to Normandy, leaving her eldest son to continue the campaign, and he succeeded in becoming Henry II in 1154.

From then, until now (with a few more reversions back to the crown) Arundel Castle has descended through female heiresses from the d'Aubignys to the Fitzalans (13th C.) to the Howards, who brought with them the Dukedom of Norfolk (16th C.). Quite the dower power.

ROMANCE AND HEARTBREAK ~ The Dukes of Norfolk have controlled Arundel Castle ever since—more than 850 years. They've been major political players, including fighting on both sides in the Wars of the Roses (the 1st died on the battlefield) and through the Tudor period (the 3rd was manipulative uncle to both Anne Boleyn and Catherine Howard, and we know how that ended). However, the 3rd turned out to be very lucky—having fallen out of favor with Henry VIII he

A view of Arundel from the river in 1827, by J. P. Neale

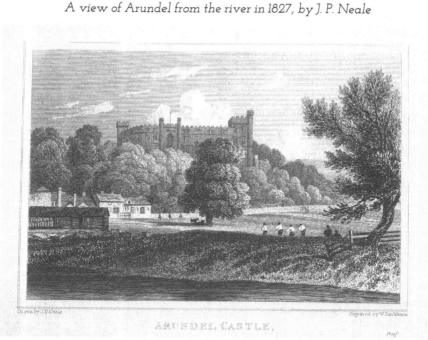

ARUNDEL CASTLE.

was awaiting execution in the Tower of London, but the night before his scheduled beheading the old king died. Whew! The 4th wasn't so lucky—he was beheaded for plotting to marry Mary, Queen of Scots. During the English Civil War (1642–1651), Arundel was besieged twice, first by the Royalists and then by the Parliamentarians, both hoping control of the fortress would secure their victory.

SPIRITUAL BEINGS OF THE RELIGIOUS KIND ~ They were a devout Catholic dynasty, with two cardinals among them, and they sometimes suffered for their faith after Henry VIII's break with the church. Others happily renounced their beliefs, such as the 3rd Duke who sided with the King over the issue of divorce. However, the 13th Earl of Arundel refused to convert and died a martyr in the Tower of London in 1595. In 1970, Pope Paul VI canonized him. The earl's father, also a devout catholic, executed for treason in 1572, did not receive sainthood.

Recently, the Dukes of Norfolk have worked to reconcile Catholic followers within English rule. As a result, Arundel Castle has today an anomalous arrangement—two religions under one roof. St. Nicholas Church and the attached Fitzalan Chapel, built in 1380, was Catholic until the establishment of the Church of England, then it became Anglican. But in 1879, the High Court determined that the Chapel was not part of the Protestant parish and instead an independent ecclesiastical structure (Grade I listed). Today a glass wall divides the building and only rarely, for celebratons, is the grille door separating them opened.[5]

SPIRITUAL BEINGS OF THE GHOSTLY KIND ∿ With such a long, bloody history, thousands of high and low born people having called Arundel Castle their home, it's not surprising that some former inhabitants have refused to leave...ever. Five seem to be the most active, but reports suggest there are many more lingerers. The oldest apparition is believed to be the 1st Earl of Arundel—unable to let go of his creation, Roger is a watchman that forever roams the keep. The friendly Blue Man dates to the 1630s. It's presumed he lived in the castle and his foppish garb is that of a King Charles I cavalier. Blue is spotted floating around the library and reading one of the thousands of books on the shelves—*my kind of ghost*. So strong is the apparition that witnesses can read the title of the book in his hands, and it's always a different one!

The Kitchen Boy haunts the castle scullery scrubbing pots and pans, possibly an abused servant child who was beaten to death. Never finished with his chore and fearful of another thrashing, witnesses hear the clanging and see him endlessly and frantically working late into the night. The fourth phantom isn't of human demise. Rather it resembles a white bird, similar in size and shape to an owl, and is most often seen flapping its wings in one of the windows. It's considered a harbinger of death because someone always dies after it appears, either a castle inhabitant or someone closely tied to a resident. Interestingly, one of the Dukes kept American white owls.

Another ghastly ghostly occurrence was in 1958 when a footman in training reported seeing something as he crossed the ground floor on his way to turn off the drawbridge lights late one night. He followed the wavering apparition, which consisted of only the upper half of a man with long hair and a grey tunic. When the strange man vanished into thin air, the servant panicked and fled. Lastly, there is a tragic story of unrequited love—a young woman named Emily committed suicide by leaping from the Hiorne Tower when her love affair ended tragically. Always crying, she appears in a long white dress on moonlit nights wandering the top of the tower in search of her lost love. While I enjoy a ghost story as much as the next, either Emily was a very busy girl or this phantom is a twice-told tale (Amberley Castle, Ch. 6). Or perhaps Emily was a common name, because there is one difference—Amberley's Emily lived prior to the 1530s (when the Bishops lost ownership of the castle), while Arundel's can exist only from the 1790 erection of the Hiorne Tower. Since all these sightings occur late at night, it will be hard for any day-tripper to be so lucky as to meet one.

The Duke of Norfolk is the oldest extant dukedom and therefore the "Premier"—or highest ranking—in the peerage. The Earl of Arundel, a title the heir uses until he inherits the dukedom, is the oldest Earldom too. The hereditary position of Earl Marshal of England comes with it as well, with duties that include overseeing state ceremonies such as royal coronations and funerals. So, today this illustrious noble family continues to hold great prestige, but they no longer involve themselves in palace or political intrigue.

THE RISE AND FALL OF FAMILY FORTUNES AND THEIR FANTASTIC FORTRESS[6]

✦ **1068: Roger de Montgomery created 1st Earl of Arundel** and awarded most of West Sussex

✦ 1068–70: Roger constructs "motte," timber keep, and Pulborough stone gatehouse (the hill and bottom 2 stories of the gatehouse survive; look for round-arched entrance)

✦ 1130: King Henry I erects first stone keep and two baileys

✦ 1138: William, married to Henry I's widow, builds stone shell around motte, increasing his defenses and status (corbels and mural fireplaces within some buildings survive)

✦ 1139: stone apartments built for extended stay of Empress Matilda (apartments survive)

✦ **1155: William d'Aubigny II confirmed as 2nd Earl of Arundel**

✦ 1170–80s: King Henry II makes fortress more livable at great expense, including improving his chamber and garden[†]

✦ **1243: John Fitzalan of Clun becomes 6th Earl of Arundel by de jure matris**—meaning "by right of his mother" who was daughter to the last d'Aubigny Earl of Arundel

✦ 1285: King Edward I grants Richard, 10th Earl of Arundel, the power to levy taxes on locals and hold lucrative fairs to fund repairs of the deteriorating castle and add a well tower

✦ 1380: Richard's will bequeathed funds for a new chapel which is finally built and holds the family tombs (pretty Fitzalan Chapel survives and is open to the public)

✦ 1380: the marriage of the future Henry IV of England to Mary de Bohun takes place at the castle

---

[†] *How do we know such detail? There are 800-year-old records of "payments," and thanks to the marvels of the world-wide web, this lowly researcher can access them.*

✦ 1580: **Philip Howard inherits earldom through his mother,** daughter of the 19th Earl and wife to the 4th Duke of Norfolk—so Philip brings with him the Norfolk Dukedom although it wasn't restored to the family for four more generations[†]

✦ 1642–45: In the English Civil War, Arundel is besieged by both sides and badly damaged (cannonball marks are still apparent on the barbican outer walls; see also Amberley's war problems in Ch. 6)

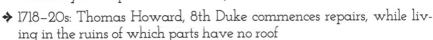

✦ 1718–20s: Thomas Howard, 8th Duke commences repairs, while living in the ruins of which parts have no roof

✦ 1783: Charles Howard, 10th Duke, secures £5,000 for restoration by the Act of 1783

✦ 1786–1815: Charles Howard, 11th Duke, and friend to Prinny, continues lavish restoration and new building until his death for an estimated £600,000 or $53 million today (the library survives today as he designed it)

✦ 1846: for Queen Victoria and Prince Albert's 3-day visit a royal suite of six rooms is created (while the suites are private family rooms today, visitors can see the Queen's Victorian-style bedroom furniture, plus the guest book signed by them)

✦ 1800–1875: some medieval sections are still in ruin—the keep, gatehouse, and barbican are covered inside and out with ivy, and large horned owls, an eagle, and other birds live there

✦ 1875–1909: Henry Fitzalan-Howard, 15th Duke, tears down unfinished work of earlier dukes, repairs medieval sections, and conducts a major rebuild of the newer livable parts of the castle in 13th Century style. Electric lighting is added to the entire castle at a cost of £36,000 ($5 million today), as was an integrated fire fighting system, service lifts, central heating, and a gravity fed water supply that also serves the village.

✦ 1976: **Miles Fitzalan-Howard, 17th Duke, inherits from his second cousin once removed** (*so important to have male heirs, you know*). His Grace establishes an independent charitable trust to ensure the castle's continued financial viability.

[†] *It's fuzzy here in that various monarchs rebooted the Earldom, so Philip is either the 1st, 13th, or 20th Earl of Arundel, depending on who you ask.*

HOW MUCH DOES IT COST? ～ Maintaining ancient castles like Arundel is astronomically expensive—everything from heat and electricity to major repairs must be funded, and today there are no serfs working the land or peasants paying rents. Estimates put operating costs at 2%[7] of the value of a manor-house or castle, so that's something to keep in mind before you bid on that adorable little "pile." Arundel Castle Trust's 2015 financial statements show that upkeep is around £1.5 million annually, including about £400,000 on essential repairs. This doesn't include the cost of running the tourist functions, with total operations running nearly £3 million. Admission fees account for 66% of this, with the rest covered by various endowment interest, gift shop/café sales, and car-park income.[8] This is big business, with a single goal of keeping this thousand-year-old masterpiece maintained in perpetuity.

Incidentally, now that it's a charity, it requires that the Duke pay modest rent when staying there (reported to be £10 a night). While a great many properties have been given to the National Trust, this new arrangement inaugurated by the Duke, which both saved the castle and kept it the family seat, has since been copied at the Chatsworth, Harewood, and Wilton estates.[9] And we lovers of all things historical and romantic get the pleasure of visiting them now as tourists.

And the practice of 'visiting' large estates and castles when the lord is away has a long history in England. Today's version is just more formalized, with fees charged and tourist services provided. It's also less prone to embarrassment…

Anyone familiar with Jane Austen's *Pride and Prejudice* remembers Elizabeth Bennet's distress when her aunt wishes to stop by Pemberley, Fitzwilliam Darcy's Derbyshire estate, on their vacation journey, it being "not in their direct road, nor more than a mile or two out of it." It's a normal thing to do, and the housekeeper is only too pleased and proud to show them around the grand house that she oversees. Forced to accompany them, Elizabeth finds herself wistfully enjoying the chance to see the home of her nemesis/love-interest. That is until she runs into Darcy while perusing his possessions.

They were within twenty yards of each other, and so abrupt was his appearance, that it was impossible to avoid his sight. Their eyes instantly met, and the cheeks of both were overspread with the deepest blush. He absolutely started, and for a moment seemed immoveable from surprise; but shortly recovering himself, advanced towards the party, and spoke to Elizabeth, if not in terms of perfect composure, at least of perfect civility.

She had instinctively turned away; but, stopping on his approach, received his compliments with an embarrassment impossible to be overcome. ... [The Gardiners] stood a little aloof while he was talking to their niece, who, astonished and confused, scarcely dared lift her eyes to his face, and knew not what answer she returned to his civil enquiries after her family. Amazed at the alteration in his manner since they last parted, every sentence that he uttered was increasing her embarrassment; and every idea of the impropriety of her being found there recurring to her mind, the few minutes in which they continued were some of the most uncomfortable of her life. ...

The others then joined her, and expressed their admiration of his figure; but Elizabeth heard not a word, and, wholly engrossed by her own feelings, followed them in silence. She was overpowered by shame and vexation. Her coming there was the most unfortunate, the most ill-judged thing in the world! How strange it must appear to him! In what a disgraceful light might it not strike so vain a man! It might seem as if she had purposely thrown herself in his way again! Oh! why did she come? Or, why did he thus come a day before he was expected? Had they been only ten minutes sooner, they should have been beyond the reach of his discrimination; for it was plain that he was that moment arrived— that moment alighted from his horse or his carriage. She blushed again and again over the perverseness of the meeting. And his behaviour, so strikingly altered,—what could it mean? That he should even speak to her was amazing!—but to speak with such civility, to enquire after her family! Never in her life had she seen his manners so little dignified, never had he spoken with such gentleness as on this unexpected meeting. What a contrast did it offer to his last address in Rosings Park, when he put his letter into her hand! She knew not what to think, nor how to account for it.

Austen's plot device is perfect on so many levels—we can feel Elizabeth's wistful interest in Darcy's elegant home, her utter mortification when he finds her there, confusion at his changed manner, and finally the melting longing that grows as she gets to know the real man beneath his aloof, haughty facade. None of which would have happened, had Elizabeth been successful in dissuading her relatives from stopping by to tour a historic estate.

While the likelihood of you running into a romantic hero while touring Arundel Castle is probably somewhat low, there's always a chance. It's such a magical place!

NOW: Rather than a museum or a ruin, this ancient fortress is a working castle—home to the 18th Duke of Norfolk and his Duchess for five months of the year and a major tourist sight for the other seven. With more than 170,000 visitors each summer, the Trustees do it right with all the services one would expect—gift shop, café, and various tour options. They keep the excitement going with special events throughout the season—jousting tournaments and the like.

ARUNDEL CASTLE ～ *How* **OLDE:** ♔ ♔ ♔ ♔ ♔
See Amberley/Arundel Excursion in Ch. 9 | www.ArundelCastle.org
+44 19 0388 2173 | Arundel, West Sussex, BN18 9AB

◇―❧―――――――――――――――――●

THE ATHENAEUM CLUB ～ see White's Competitors listing

◇―❧―――――――――――――――――●

BANNS OF MARRIAGE
1215–present (abolished in Catholic law in 1983)

THEN: First formally decreed in Catholic Canon law, the purpose was to announce an impending marriage so that anyone with knowledge of a canonical or civil objection could raise them before an illegal wedding was conducted. Originally the "banns" were read publicly by priests from the pulpit for three consecutive holy days, and later also posted in the weekly parish bulletin. The law continued under Henry VIII's Church of England.

As an aside, the word "bann" does not relate to "banning a marriage" but rather is from the Middle English word *ban* meaning "proclamation," an adaption of the earlier Old English *gebann*. While it's likely that information on banns and marriages was picked up and reported as gossip in early printed newssheets, as far as I can tell the practice of placing an official announcement by the gentry in Victorian newspapers beyond the church bulletin was not common—although many a romance character discovers this way that his or her beloved has become engaged. The banns are the reason that the Victorian hero must secure a "Special License" if he needs a quick wedding to the heroine—perhaps she's already pregnant or she needs rescuing by marriage—or as sometimes happens he might kidnap her to Gretna Green where the posting of banns was not required.[10]

Now: Banns were abolished in the Catholic Church in 1983. In England and Wales, they are still legally required for a Church of England wedding (Marriage Act of 1949, amended in 2012). While banns are not a legal requirement in the United States, voluntary engagement announcements in newspapers are a modern equivalent, and the more blue-blooded the personages, the larger the listing. Of course, most states do require a marriage license to establish that the parties are free to marry.

BANQUETING HOUSE (PART OF THE PALACE OF WHITEHALL)

1619 – present

THEN: The original York Place estate—dating to the mid-1200s—was owned and improved upon by various influential Archbishops of York, the last of which was the powerful and wealthy Thomas Wolsey (1475-1530). By 1512, King Henry VIII, whose palace had burned down, began to covet York Place. Later, when the King removed Wolsey from power for failing to secure Henry an annulment from his first wife, the deed came with the bonus of claiming York Place for himself. From there, Henry acquired more land surrounding the mansion and renamed the complex the Palace of Whitehall where it remained a prominent royal residence for nearly two centuries. For real-life romance, King Henry married both Anne Boleyn and Jane Seymour there in 1533 and 1536, respectively. Of course, that didn't end well for either lady. Henry died there in 1547. His daughter, Queen Elizabeth I built the first communal entertainment space—or Banqueting House—there in 1581. Additional royalty that resided at Whitehall included King Charles I who was executed there, and lastly James II.

Besides formal state dinners and receptions, Banqueting House was also used for performing court masques—theatrical productions that combined music, song, poetry, dance, elaborate costumes and sets, and even special effects. Later, a bigger banqueting house was built on the same site, and here there is an early American connection—in 1617 Pocahontas and Tomocomo (an emissary of Chief Powhatan) were brought before King James I and Queen Anne in the Banqueting House, and they observed a masque performance.[11] Tomocomo did not even realize he'd met the King because of James's unimpressive size and presence until Captain John Smith convinced him later. This second structure burned down in 1619.

James I immediately rebuilt Banqueting House and it is this exceptional building that remains today. He hired the famed architect Inigo
Jones, who designed it to look like a piece of ancient Rome transported
to London. It was in direct contrast to the rest of Whitehall done in the
medieval Tudor style. Today, Jones is credited as the founder of the classical renaissance in English architecture. For the inside, Charles I commissioned huge ceiling murals from the Flemish artist Sir Peter Paul Rubens.
Considered the "crowning glory" of this building, Rubens had to wait
two years to receive his £3,000 payment and gift of a heavy gold
chain. With continued expansion, the Palace of Whitehall eventually
covered 23 acres and 1,500 rooms, becoming the largest royal palace
in all of Europe, bigger even than Versailles and the Vatican. Sadly,
Whitehall burned to the ground in 1698 leaving only the Banqueting
House still standing. Plans to rebuild the palace never came to fruition.

NOW: The Grade I listed Banqueting House is considered a masterpiece of Palladianism, the first classical structure of what is today a
common London style. Inside, the grandeur reflects Palladianism with
mathematical dimensions and clean lines. And thankfully Rubens'
masterworks were protected early on—when it was realized that
smoke from torches used for the masques was darkening the paintings,
the performances and parties were moved to other facilities, thus pre-
serving the paintings for future generations. This is a minor stop on a
romance fan's London tour, but as the only remaining building of the
Palace of Whitehall it is the setting for many historical novels, such as
the 1940 best seller, *Forever Amber* by Kathleen Winsor,[†][12] the Tudor
Court novels by Philippa Gregory, and *Girl on the Golden Coin* by
Marci Jefferson. It's worth a stop if you have the time.

How OLDE: 🏵🏵🏵🏵🏵
Price: £5.50 (or £48 for all 6 Historic Royal Palaces; see Ch. 4)
Hours: Daily 10am–1pm | Check website for private function closures
Tube: Charing Cross, Embankment, Westminster
www.hrp.org.uk/BanquetingHouse | +44 20 3166 6000
Corner of Horse Guards Avenue and Whitehall

[†] *While tame by today's standards, Forever Amber was banned as pornography in 14 US
states. Reasons cited included 70 references to sex, 10 descriptions of women undressing in
front of men, and 49 miscellaneous objectionable passages, among other things.
One caveat: romance fans might find Amber unlikeable, an anti-heroine lacking personal
growth or self-awareness and comparable to Scarlett O'Hara.*

BEDLAM

1247 – present

"*We are both candidates for Bedlam!*" cried Whitney, in Judith McNaught's *Whitney, My Love.* This is a common sentiment in romance novels; however, it is usually the hero who is concerned with his sanity, rather than the heroine.

THEN: Not many romance writers actually send their characters to Bedlam—well I haven't found any yet—but the term is often used when any character, usually a man, is doing something crazy. What characters are really referring to is Bethlem Royal Hospital, one of the world's oldest hospitals for the treatment of mental illness. First founded as part of the St. Mary of Bethlehem priory (where Liverpool Street Tube station is now), it was originally a fundraiser for the church and hostel for the poor. However, by the 14th Century they were treating the insane, although not very effectively and often with "inmates" chained and manacled. It became a Royal hospital after the Reformation, and throughout this time was the only public institution for those with mental disorders. In total, the hospital was rebuilt and relocated four times.

Perhaps the most ghastly, scandalous phase was from 1676–1770 while the hospital was housed in a reportedly magnificent baroque building in Moorfields, then the last open space in London (now Finsbury Circus, a park, near Moorgate Tube). During this period, sightseers could pay a fee (variously a penny or 10 shillings), which allowed them to walk around and watch the chained and sometimes naked inmates, male or female, in their cells. As evidence of the institution's "charitable" mindset, entry was free to the public on the first Tuesday of each month. It is also reported (although not verified) that visitors could bring sticks to poke the inmates who were now called patients (a term adopted sometime in the 1700s). This display of madness as a public show was a popular pastime for the masses. The aristocrats were also invited in the hopes of soliciting a charitable donation to the hospital. However, by the 1790s the building had become over-crowded, crumbling, and sinking, due to having been built without a foundation over the old "town ditch" (garbage dump). It would be a most unfortunate Regency novel character that found him or herself incarcerated here.

The Bedlam of the Victorian era was located at St. George's Fields in Southwark (south of the Thames) in a grand neoclassical structure—the pride of London at the time—that operated from 1815–1930. This building was bigger but not always an improvement for the patients—only one toilet per gallery, the new-fangled steam heat didn't function properly, and the upper floors initially lacked glass windows (shutters either darkened the rooms, or when open allowed cold air inside). Eventually more than 350 male and female patients were held there, but mercifully by the 1850s the use of restraints was abandoned. An aristocratic romance novel character in this period would find their stay much improved as these "unfortunates" could undertake productive work, visit the in-house library, and even enjoy music and mixed-gender dancing in the ballroom.

As for why it was called Bedlam, in Old English, Bethlehem was 'Betleem,' which evolved in Middle English to 'Bedleheem' or 'Bedleem,' to finally the term we know today. Because of its earlier entertainment value for sightseers as well as its use in plays, c.1620, the word entered the popular lexicon to eventually become synonymous with a "state of wild uproar and confusion."

NOW: THE IMPERIAL WAR MUSEUM ∼ *for the guys* and FREE. In 1936, the museum took over the building, and the grounds surrounding it became a public park. The IWM also manages the Churchill War Rooms and HMS Belfast. While the façade remains Victorian, the interiors are solely devoted to the conflict of war from WWI and WWII to the present. War history buffs will be very happy here. Information below is for the IWM London.

*𝓗*OW OLDE: ♟♟♟♙♙ ∼ *perfect "for the guys," but for Bedlam enthusiasts there isn't a single manacle*
For details on all 3 museums: See Museum Quick Guide, Ch. 4.

ALSO: **BETHLEM MUSEUM OF THE MIND** at the Bethlem Royal Hospital (relocated in 1930) in London's southeastern Borough of Bromley focuses on the history of Bedlam. In addition to artwork (often by patients) there are extensive archives available to researchers and the general public **by appointment**; even better us for non-Londoners, some documents can be accessed online.

*𝓗*OW OLDE: ♟♙♙♙♙
∼ *for the history buff or Bedlam-focused romance*
Price: FREE | **Hours:** W-F & first/last Sat of the month 10am-5pm
Closed holidays | **Location:** see website for directions; about 20 min by train from London Bridge or London Victoria stations
www.bethlemheritage.org.uk | +44 20 3228 4227
Monks Orchard Rd, Beckenham, Kent, BR3 3BX

BERKELEY SQUARE AND BERKELEY HOUSE

1698–present

THEN: Berkeley Square (pronounced 'barkley') was ◌◌ **B** one of several fashionable residential blocks often sited in romance literature, along with Grosvenor (pronounced 'grove-ner') and St James's Square. Located in the upscale Mayfair neighborhood, the square's pretty park was not the result of forward-thinking city planners but because of a deal made when John, Lord Berkeley of Stratton, sold his house in 1696 to the 1st Duke of Devonshire.[13] The Duke wanted to retain his pretty view, so Lord Berkeley agreed not to build on the remaining land. Berkeley House became Devonshire House, but sadly this grand mansion was torn down after it was sold to pay death duties (taxes) in 1920.

Residents of this neighborhood included Regency dandy Beau Brummell and six Prime Ministers, most of whom lived in another famous mansion, Lansdowne House (of which only part remains).

American Connection: Lansdowne's formal dining and drawing rooms can be seen in New York's Met Museum[14] and the Philadelphia Museum of Art, respectively. These were rescued from the part of the mansion that was torn down in 1931, and lucky for us they were snapped up by these institutions. It's fitting that they reside in the US since Lord Shelburne, who completed the mansion, was also a strong advocate for US independence and helped negotiate the end of the Revolutionary War in Paris. For his service to the crown, he was made 1st Marquis of Lansdowne. There were also famous Americans who were at times residents there: William Waldorf Astor (then richest man in the US) and Harry Gordon Selfridge (of the department store). Today the remaining portion of Lansdowne is a private club with the same name.

Berkeley Square's most important resident to young unmarried ladies of the Regency lived at No. 38—Sarah Child Villiers, Countess of Jersey and one of the seven patronesses of Almack's. Lastly, we can't forget a Regency favorite—Gunter's Tea Shop, known for their ices, a sort of mix between ice cream and sherbet. It was housed at No. 7–8 until the east side of the Square was demolished, c.1936. Also important to the Regency maiden, Gunter's was one of the first places where a single woman could share a treat with a man un-chaperoned. The lady would remain in the open carriage with the gentleman standing near her, and Gunter's hardy waiters dodging traffic to serve them in Berkeley Square.[15]

NOW: A charming park remains with fanciful statues, park benches, and many very tall London Plane trees providing shade in the summer. Planted in 1789, they are among the oldest trees in London. While nearly all surrounding buildings now house businesses rather than aristocrats (only No. 45 remains a private home), the west side of the Square retains most of the original architecture complete with the historic Link extinguishers (metal cones once used to put out street gas lamps[16]).

How OLDE: ♟♟♟♟♟ ~ *The park may be 100% authentic, but the modern office towers detract*
Price: FREE | **Tube:** Green Park, Bond St | **Map:** B
Web: For a detailed history complete with excellent photos (including the Georgian-era double staircase inside No. 44) go to LondonDiary-Blog.wordpress.com and search Berkeley Square.

◇◦✥◦———————————•

BOODLE'S AND BROOK'S (GENTLEMEN'S CLUBS)
~ see White's Competitors

BOND STREET ~ see Shopping in a Bygone Era

◇◦✥◦———————————•

BOW STREET RUNNERS
1739–1829

The bodice rippers of the last century didn't often contain stories with main characters that were Bow Street Runners, but today historical romantic suspense is popular and as a result they are oft mentioned.

THEN: Early London policing was a haphazard affair, often requiring victims to hire "thief takers" on their own. In the 1730s, the City of London wanted to encourage the official reporting of crimes, so they established "rotation offices," the "rotation" referring to fixed operating hours on different schedules so a victim could always find an open office to report a crime. "Thief takers" were still hired to solve the crime. One of the most successful of these new government offices was located near Covent Garden at 4 Bow Street (named such because of the curved shape of the road). Within ten years, this particular office began hiring agents on retainer and thus the Bow Street Runners were born (although they preferred their official title of Principal Officer). Extremely successful, these agents became famous and enjoyed a comfortable living…and later, exciting roles in popular fiction.[17]

NOW: Thankfully today's citizens and visitors are protected by a highly-trained force of approximately 700 officers in the City of London Police (the oldest heart of the city, about 1 square mile) and 30,000 officers in the Metropolitan Police Service (serving the rest of the 609 square miles). The Met "bobbies" are based at world famous New Scotland Yard. As for the Bow Street Runners of yore, there is a plaque commemorating the most famous of them, but otherwise it's now just a street.

How OLDE: 🏆 ♜ ♜ ♜ ♜ ♜
Price: walking down the street, FREE | **Tube**: Covent Garden

◇❧◦—————————————————————◦

BRIGHTON PAVILION (AKA ROYAL PAVILION)

1786–present

While located on the coast 55 miles south of London, Brighton became a hotspot during the Regency with the Prince of Wales making it his home away from home—on a scale fit for a future king (see Ch. 9 Easy Excursions). The terms 'Prinny' and 'Regency' that infuse historic romance fiction derive from this period. The Brighton Pavilion, even if not often mentioned in novels, is a prime example of the opulence and excesses of the period. Author Georgette Heyer, whose stories often included royalty in supporting roles, sets scenes inside the Pavilion in *Regency Buck*, and Prinny even tries to kiss the heroine Judith Taverner in a drawing room there.

The reason this tiny fishing village became one of George IV's royal residences is that doctors advised that swimming in the sea might help his painful gout. So in 1786, he rented a modest lodge facing the promenade. This became the home where he resided with the love of his life, the Catholic (and therefore unmarriageable, although he tried) Maria Fitzherbert. A year later, he hired famous Carlton House architect Henry Holland to expand the building into a neo-classic "Marine Pavilion." George furnished it lavishly with Chinese art, furniture, and hand-painted wallpaper.

Royal Pavilion by Augustus Pugim Sr., 1824

Appointed Prince Regent in 1811 due to his father King George III's madness, he considered the lodge too small for royal entertaining. Thus, in 1815, he began the last expansion. Playing on Prinny's love of the Orient, architect John Nash built a fanciful pleasure palace of Indio-Islamic onion domes and colorful exotic interiors. Redubbed the Royal Pavilion, it wasn't completed until 1823 and by that time, King George IV's ill health only allowed for two visits before his death in 1830. But his building largess had by then transformed Brighton from a modest fishing village of 3,600 residents to a popular seaside city of more than 40,000.

However, neither King William nor the next monarch, Queen Victoria, found the palace appropriate to their tastes or need for privacy and more space. Victoria sold it to the City of Brighton in 1850 for £50,000 and stripped the interior of its lavish fittings and art for use in other royal homes. It was presumed that the now outmoded and unfashionable palace would be demolished, but the advent of the railway in 1841 brought increased tourism to Brighton. The gutted insides were refurbished in a gaudy Victorian style with the Queen returning some of the fixtures, and the city started charging sixpence for tours.

WWI saw it turned into a soldier's hospital, resulting in much damage, but luckily the Royal Pavilion had become a tourist destination by then. So renovation began anew and has continued ever since with the goal of returning the pleasure palace to its original oriental splendor for future generations.

NOW: Today, unlike the rough ten-hour bumpy carriage ride the sick Prinny had to endure, a quick one hour rail trip from London makes

Brighton a fun day trip or easy overnight. Booking a guided tour is required to enter the Royal Pavilion, but it is well worth it. This palace is unlike anything else—a fairytale fantasy of Far East meets Royal West. One wishes that overnights could be booked, because it would be sure to inspire some wonderful romance novels. However, almost as nice, one can reserve an After Hours Tour (£40, ○◎↺ **B** limited to 20 guests) that concludes with a drinks reception in one of the magnificent rooms. Your chance to play princess for two hours, and maybe your prince will do better than Prinny did with Miss. Taverner…and he'll succeed in kissing you!

*H*OW OLDE: ♟♟♟♟♟
Price: £12.50 (see Ch. 4 for discounts) | Hours: Daily 10am–5:15pm; longer in summer | Closed Dec 25–26 | Location: 15 min walk from Brighton railway station and 5 mins from the sea
http://brightonmuseums.org.uk/royalpavilion | +44 30 0029 0900
4/5 Pavilion Buildings, Brighton, BN1 1EE

◇━✲━━━━━━━━━•

THE BRITISH MUSEUM
1753–present

THEN: The oldest national public museum in the world, it was founded on the idea of free admission to all "studious and curious Persons." The initial collection was established by the will of Sir Hans Sloane, a physician and scientist who collected more than 71,000 objects over the course of his life. Desiring that the collection be preserved intact, he bequeathed it entirely to King George II for the British people in return for a payment to his heirs of £20,000 (today that is roughly $6 million—clearly a bargain then and now). Thus, on June 7, 1753, by Act of Parliament, The British Museum was established and in early 1759 opened to the public in the converted 17th C. Montagu House in Bloomsbury.

Over the years, the museum has been rebuilt and expanded on the current site in order to house an ever-increasing collection. It now has more than 8 million objects spanning all areas of human history and culture. Early major acquisitions included King George II's Old Royal Library of books, the actual Rosetta Stone, and the Parthenon sculptures—often referred to as the Elgin Marbles. With the exception of two world wars, the museum has never closed in more than 260 years, with attendance rising from an initial 5,000 to 6 million annually.

NOW: The British Museum remains one of the preeminent institutions of its kind in the world. This is not without controversy, however. Its large collections were in part obtained as a result of British colonial expansion, and some artworks were obtained without permission from the country of origin. Today, many nations are demanding the return of their antiquities—a situation faced by nearly all large museums, especially since these newly developed countries now have their own institutions capable of adequately caring for and displaying these priceless objects.

This brings us back to the Elgin Marbles which Greece wants returned (during Victorian times these referred to all statues housed in the museum's Elgin Room). Obtained controversially by the Earl of Elgin from the Ottoman Empire in 1812, these marble sculptures depicting centaurs and other naked forms were very popular in Victorian times providing the general public a first chance to see such artwork—they were also deemed *highly* inappropriate for maidens. This scenario pops up occasionally in romance novels when the heroine sneaks out to view the scandalous nudes, but perhaps the most stimulating fictional depiction is in Sabrina Jeffries' *The Forbidden Lord* when the Earl of Blackmore dangles the chance to see them as an excuse to get the heroine Emily alone. The tables are turned, however, when she displays an un-maidenly interest in the anatomy that leaves the hero feeling slightly jealous and deflated.

> *She stretched her hand out over the table to press it against the centaur's marble flanks. "So real. You can see the ribs beneath the skin, as if he were an actual creature."*
>
> *…While she examined the metope, he drank in the sight of her. Talk about fine craftsmanship—she was about as fine a piece of work as a man could want. Her skin rivaled the marble for smooth creaminess, and the curves apparent beneath her gown made his mouth water and his fingers itch to touch her…*
>
> *She stroked the sculpture again with a gentle touch, and he felt a jolt of lust so intense he nearly groaned aloud. He wanted those fingers to touch him, to caress him. He wanted it as badly as he'd ever wanted anything.*

By the way, if you do seek out the Elgin Marbles, as I did when visiting the museum, they're now housed in the Duveen Gallery, Rm 18. Also of interest to the historical romance fan are galleries on Medieval through Victorian Europe (Rms 38–51). And, when viewing the Elgin Marbles (now labeled the Parthenon Sculptures), please know that "Do

Not Touch" is *de rigueur* these days. Modern visitors would find themselves in considerable trouble if caught caressing any part of the anatomies on display. Ahh, but thanks to Jeffries' delectable prose we can imagine doing just that in private with our own personal hero.

How OLDE: ♛ ♛ ♛ ♛ ♛ ~ *although the en-* ⊙⊙ **B**
tranceway is quite modern looking/feeling
Hours: Daily 10am-5:30pm; Fri to 8:30pm | Closed Jan 1, Dec 24–26 | **Price:** FREE | **Tube:** Tottenham Ct Rd, Holborn, Russell Sq, Goodge St | www.britishmuseum.org | +44 20 7323 8000 Greet Russell Street

◇-❦❀-⎯⎯⎯⎯⎯⎯⎯⎯⎯⎯⎯⎯

BUCKINGHAM PALACE
1703-present

THEN: As a working royal residence, Buckingham Palace is not a setting used much in fiction. Royalty and romance and history—from commoners marrying up to bereft widows in mourning—are nonetheless as much a part of this place as the off-white Portland stones that make up its famous façade. For this reason, I've included a brief history, and for the author looking for inspiration a visit here is a must, especially the Royal Mews with its fairytale gold carriage.

Earliest estates on this site date to the Middle Ages when it was the Manor of Ebury (also called Eia) on marshy ground along the river Tyburn (which today still flows under parts of the palace and courtyard). Early owners of the undeveloped property included Edward the Confessor[18], William the Conqueror, Westminster Abbey, Henry VIII, and James I who attempted to raise silk worms there (c.1607). Sir William Blake built a home on the site in 1624, but the current building (greatly expanded over time) dates to 1703 when John Sheffield, Duke of Buckingham, demolished the dated house to create "Buckingham House." From George III's time, the mansion housed royalty, and was almost continually expanded until its current size and façade was achieved in 1913. This is where the world famous balcony is located, the one from which the royals greet the masses on special occasions. It has been one of the "official" royal residences since 1837, appointed such by Queen Victoria.[19]

NOW: Today it is a working palace with 775 rooms covering 830,000 square feet and the largest private garden in London. A grand ballroom added in 1854 still serves today for state dinners and investitures (knightings and dame-ings, you know). It's not the largest palace in the world, but most big ones, like France's Versailles or China's Forbidden City, are now just museums, lacking the beehive activity that gives Buckingham Palace life and a sense of exciting purpose. Visitors can tour the State Rooms (when the Queen is not in residence), the Royal Mews, and The Queens Gallery (rotating exhibitions from the Royal collections).

How OLDE: 🦀🦀🦀🦀🦀
Hours: Open Aug-Sept (occasionally other dates) | Mews and Gallery all year | **Price**: from £21.50 for palace to £37 for all 3 | **Tube**: St James's Park, Victoria, Green Park, Hyde Park Corner
www.royalcollection.org.uk | +44 303 123 7300
Official address: London

BURLINGTON ARCADE ~ see Piccadilly Shopping, Ch. 8

COCKPIT STEPS AND COCKFIGHTS
Prehistoric–present

THEN: While I've yet to read a full-on cockfight in romance fiction, there are sometimes references to the scoundrel or blackguard who attends such notorious events or worse loses his fortune betting on one. In practice, cockfights were not considered criminal or evil. Certainly not after the King, Henry VIII, built a Royal Cockpit. Further, its popularity as a quick way to make a buck...no, strike that...a guinea, actually, led to regulation of the sport and those new gaming rules eventually extended to other sports. So this practice, abhorred today, might actually have contributed something lasting and positive.

Due to paintings and obscure mentions in text, it's believed cockfighting dates all the way back to the beginning of recorded history, some 6,000 years.[20] It's probably older than that. It's unclear when it arrived in London, but early mentions date to the 1500s. Most of these early events were egalitarian in that the social classes mixed, if not the sexes, but with the advent of a second Royal Cockpit (the first being Henry's at the Palace of Whitehall) a place was reserved for the wealthy, the five-shilling price tag keeping out the riffraff. This cockpit was built up a hill from St. James's Park, so steps were built in a passageway between buildings, becoming known as the Cockpit Steps.[21] Gentlemen arriving at the top along Old Queen Street (one presumes it was called just Queen Street then), often arrived by sedan chair in the 17th Century, so a public house across the street grew in popularity with the two sedan-chair workmen waiting for the contests to end. Hence the funniest pub name I've ever heard was created: Two ⒸⒸ **C** Chairmen Pub, which dates to 1729.

NOW: While illegal in the UK, US, and most developed countries, it's still popular throughout much of the world. The Royal Cockpit was razed c.1816 to make way for new structures, however the Cockpit Steps remained. If you're leaving Buckingham Palace, you can find them on the right hand of the street walking east on Birdcage Walk. The stairs will land you practically onto the doorstep of the Two Chairmen Public House where you can enjoy a pint of ale and soak in the authentic ambiance (see listing Ch. 5).

How OW OLDE: ♟ ♟ ♟ ♟ ♟ ♟ ～ *because, really, they're just stairs*
Stair Hours: open 24/7 | **Pub**: see Ch. 5 | **Tube**: St James's Park
Price: stairs are free but a pint of ale will set you back some pounds

◇❡✍⟶⟶⟶⟶⟶⟶⟶⟶⟶⟶⟶⟶⟶⟶⟶⟶⟶⟶●

CORINTHIAN
700 BC–present

A man, a place, and an architectural style.

He was a very notable Corinthian. From his Wind-swept hair (most difficult of all styles to achieve), to the toes of his gleaming Hessians, he might have posed as an advertisement for the Man of Fashion. His fine shoulders set off a coat of superfine cloth to perfection; his cravat, which had excited George's admiration, had been arranged by the hands of a master; his waistcoat was chosen with a nice eye; his biscuit-coloured pantaloons showed not one crease; and his Hessians with their jaunty gold tassels, had not only been made for him by Hoby, but were polished, George suspected, with a blacking mixed with champagne. A quizzing-glass on a black ribbon hung round his neck; a fob at his waist; and in one hand he carried a Sèvres snuff-box. His air proclaimed his unutterable boredom, but no tailoring, no amount of studied nonchalance, could conceal the muscle in his thighs, or the strength of his shoulders. Above the starched points of shirt-collar, a weary, handsome face showed its owner's disillusionment.

Georgette Heyer's description from her novel, *The Corinthian*, is all you need to know about this type of gentleman, epitomized, and perhaps created by, the real-life Beau Brummell.

As for the design term, it pertains to Greek architecture arising from the 700-338 BC city-state of Corinth—think slender stone columns capped with a flow of drooping leaves. Corinth was notorious for its extravagance and decadence as well as having skilled fighters, and while Corinthian was used since the 1650s to describe an architectural style, its use as a descriptor of certain types of men came into fashion around the early 1800s. The Corinthian lifestyle was most prevalent in the Regency to early Victorian periods; however, there are still modern day versions of rich, accomplished men renowned for seeking athletic thrills. Sir Richard Branson comes to mind with his planes, trains, and automobiles... and hot air balloons, catamarans, motorbikes, and if that isn't enough, spaceships too.

◇☞────────────────────────•

COURT (THE ROYAL KIND, IN ENGLAND)
Circa 300-present

THEN: Throughout ancient history, there was a court system where the leaders, usually hereditary, ruled from their seat of power— their "court"—and were surrounded by a retinue of staff and supporters, but the system really took off in the middle ages. It was both an idea and a physical place, the location being wherever the monarch was in residence. With instantaneous communication inconceivable, the idea of a court was to provide a place where anyone with business to conduct could go in the hope of gaining an audience with the king who would hear their problem or proposal. Besides the royal family, the court system included their households, and everyone from courtiers (nobility who had the king's ear or his bed, and ladies in waiting to the queen) to other nobility seeking favors, to entertainers, to high level staff, and on down to the servants and guards. These people, sometimes in the thousands, were there "officially" to serve His or Her Majesty, but often worked behind the scenes for their own purposes. While this system continued until Queen Victoria's reign, as political power was democratized the nature of the royal court changed. In terms of romance fiction, stories placed within a royal court are found most often in those set in the medieval period.

NOW: There is still a royal court in England, currently presided over by a queen. Its purpose—to support The Sovereign and family—is still roughly the same, even if the monarch's role has changed from ruler to Head of State. Today's royal household mostly consists of paid staff, but roles like the "lady-in-waiting" remain. While these ladies no longer dress their mistress, they do continue to provide counsel and companionship to the female royals.[25] As for the physical royal court, Buckingham Palace's 19 'State Rooms' serve in a ceremonial fashion in the same way that the Great Rooms did in the medieval times. See Buckingham Palace listing for visiting details.

⬦◦❦◦────────────────────●

COURT (THE JUDICIAL KIND)
1305–present

All of the historical sights listed below are mostly unchanged from their initial incarnation. While rarely referenced in romance fiction, they're here because of their historical importance. These kinds of buildings are what we think of today as a "court," a place where the law of the land is implemented and judgment passed. The term is derived from the earlier usage as the place where monarchs ruled, but since those leaders also ruled over disputes or crimes—"Off with his head!"—it transformed to mean a legal system presided over by judges. Given the roots of this early legal system, it's not surprising that monarchs still have a role here—appointing barristers to the Queen's Counsel and judges to Her Majesty's High Court. Incidentally, a knighthood goes along with the judicial appointment.

ROYAL COURTS OF JUSTICE ∿ Opened by Queen Victoria in 1882, the façade of this stunning Victorian Gothic building is so exotically fanciful, with its towers, turrets, spires, and arched windows, I half expected to see a game of Quidditch in action inside its awe-inspiring Main Hall (*yes, I know, the age-old game is played outdoors, but that's just how very big is this cavernous space!*). Once past the modern security, the space is lavish and authentically cool with a towering 80-foot-high arched stone ceiling (like a cathedral), intricately tiled floor, and oak-paneled courtrooms. Anyone is free to visit and even at times sit in on a court hearing, where you can watch barristers in their long black robes and goofy white wigs. It's also impressively large, with approximately 1,000 rooms and 3½ miles of hallways. Highlights include the Bear Gardens, Painted Room, Crypt, and a sculpture/legal dress exhibit.

TIP: In the Main Hall you can see a list of court cases in session posted on the big wooden cabinet. Also look for a leaflet at the reception desk for a map and information on the building. Visitors may

Fantastically Gothic ～ The Royal Courts of Justice

only sit in the courtroom's last two rows. Dress conservatively. Bow your head to the judge when entering/exiting the courtroom. Don't enter if marked "In Camera," or "In Private" or when windows are covered. No children under age 14 allowed in the courtroom. No cameras allowed inside and mobile phones switched off. A café is located in the Crypt corridor. One-hour Architectural Tours may be pre-booked for a £12 pp fee; see website. All persons pass through airport-style security when entering.

How Olde: ⚖⚖⚖⚖⚖
Price: FREE entrance to building; tours £12 | **Hours:** M-F 9:30am–4:30pm | **Tube:** Chancery Lane, Temple, Holborn | **Map:** D
http://theroyalcourtsofjustice.com | +44 20 7947 6000
The Strand

OLD BAILEY ～ This separate building is also called the Central Criminal Court of England and Wales. This court dates back to 1585 and was named after the street where it was located, a lane that ran along the City of London's ancient fortified wall (also called a bailey). The court was conveniently close to the infamous Newgate prison. Destroyed in the Great Fire of London in 1666, the building was rebuilt and used through the 19th Century. In 1907, King Edward VII officially opened the current courthouse. To make room for the much larger structure, Newgate Prison, by then dilapidated, was demolished. Even this modern courthouse has been reconstructed following severe WWII damage.[26]

Because the most serious criminal cases in London ⚞Ⓒ⚟ **C** were tried here over the centuries, the Old Bailey is oft referenced in fiction, including Dickens' *A Tale of Two Cities* and Gilbert and Sullivan's *Pirates of Penzance*. In total, more than 200,000 criminal trials have been held here, and that's not counting those in the original building. The public is free to visit here as well, however it does not have the character of the Royal Courts. I do like the inscription above the front door: "Defend the Children of the Poor & Punish the Wrongdoer." Due to security issues, there are many additional restrictions: absolutely no electronic devices, sharp objects, backpacks, etc.; no one under age 14; public restricted to upstairs galleries (check website for full list).

How **Olde:** ⚜⚜⚜⚜⚜ ~ *historic in practice but building not old*
Price: FREE | **Public Gallery Hours:** M-F 10am–12:40pm & 2-3:40pm | **Tube:** St. Paul's, Blackfriars | **Map:** D | www.cityoflondon.gov.uk/about-the-city/about-us/buildings-we-manage/Pages/central-criminal-court.aspx | www.old-bailey.com/visiting-the-old-bailey (unaffiliated but useful) | +44 20 7192 2739 Old Bailey and Bishop's Ct

INNS OF COURT ~ From 1154, King Henry II is credited with establishing basic legal principles through his series of Assizes (meetings with powerful barons that issued binding decrees). He transformed criminal trials from physical ordeals, where God was expected to reveal judgment, into trials by jury (and in some cases by 12 free men, a standard still used today in the UK and the US). Surprisingly, it was the Church that instigated this change, disapproving such practices as trial by combat or water or hot iron (although "wager of battle" was not officially abolished until 1819). Henry also decreed that only "royal courts" could try criminal cases. By 1250 royal judges had amalgamated the various local customs into one Common Law for the whole country and absorbed much of the legal powers of the local baronial and ecclesiastical (religious) courts.[27]

Around that time separate "Inns" started to be founded that literally served as inns for the barristers and clerks, providing "chambers" for lodging and legal education. Today, they no longer offer housing or formal education but do provide office space, dining, lectures, and fellowship. Only four remain of these storied institutions and the public is not admitted inside. However, if you can find a friend with connections to sponsor you, then you might have the pleasure of dining in one of their Great Halls. I can only speak for one—Middle Temple—and eating in the same room where Queen Elizabeth occasionally dined and Shakespeare's *Twelfth Night* received its first performance in 1602 was an amazing experience.

The Inns' grounds and parks are open to the public, along with select buildings as noted, and walking this oasis of quiet in the heart of London is both calming and a step back in time—because these large complexes don't have all the modern noise and bustle (i.e. neon lights, car traffic, horns). While exact founding dates are unknown, they all have continuous records dating back centuries. Dates are listed thus: (approximate founding / earliest records / earliest surviving structure)

LINCOLN'S INN: (c.1388 / 1422 / 1490 Old Hall) Located on Chancery Lane, this is the largest of the Inns. There are numerous buildings constructed over three centuries sitting on 11 acres. WWII bombing seriously damaged some of the ancient structures, but they were rebuilt with the same external appearance. The glorious Old Hall, a fine example of Tudor architecture, was used as a court as well as for revels and feasts. From 1737, it was the Court of Chancery until the 1882 opening of the Royal Courts of Justice, nearby. It is also the setting for the start of Dickens' *Bleak House*. The 1620 Chapel is open to the public, M-F 9am–5pm (closed holidays). Grounds open M-F 7am–7pm year round and picnics may be taken on the North Lawn between 12–2:30pm. Major refurbishment is taking place through 2017, which may restrict access. www.lincolnsinn.org.uk

INNER TEMPLE: (c.1339 / 1381 / 1600s) The name for this and Middle Temple, derives from the Knights Templars that had their headquarters on this site for some 150 years, before they were dissolved in 1312. While Inner Temple is as old as the rest of the Inns, most of the buildings are 20th Century. The Blitz of WWII hit this inn hard, destroying most of the medieval buildings, including the Hall, the Temple, and many sets of chambers. They have all been rebuilt in period style, but now date only from 1959. The pleasant grounds are open 12:30–3pm M-F.

TEMPLE CHURCH: (1185) One of the oldest churches in London, it sits next to Middle Temple Hall. The Templars built it in the round after the Church of the Holy Sepulchre in Jerusalem, considered the most sacred place in the Holy Land. A chancel with organ and choir copes was added in the following century, and music has played here for more than 700 years. Temple Church is open to the public for services M-F 9am, Sun 8:30am & 11:15am. Otherwise visitors may enter generally 10–4pm M-F for a fee of £5. Confirm times: www.templechurch.com Needless to say, appropriate dress is required. Enter via Temple Lane/Fleet St gate.

MIDDLE TEMPLE: (c.1339 / 1501 / 1573) Middle Temple comprises 43 buildings with the pinnacle being Middle Temple Hall, considered one of the finest examples of an Elizabethan banqueting hall in the country. While WWII bombing damaged one wall, the famous oak roof—an architectural feat in 1573—survived and remains today as a fine example of a double-hammer beam construction that spans the 101 by 41 foot ceiling. This hall also features two important furnishings—the 29-foot-long bench table, reputedly made from a single oak tree from Windsor Forest and gifted to them by Queen Elizabeth I, and a "Cup-board" (a very old table, really) made from the fore-hatch of Sir Frances Drake's flagship, the Golden Hind (c.1600). Drake was not a member of Middle Temple but dined there often. The Hall's function then and now is similar to the other Inns. One-hour group tours of 10 people minimum can be booked for £8 pp. Grounds open M-F 12–3pm May-Sept. www.middletemple.org.uk

New Great Hall, Lincoln's Inn, 1846

GRAY'S INN: (1370 / 1391 / 1558—although parts of it are probably older and some stained glass dates to 1462) Most of it was severely damaged by WWII bombings, which resulted in reconstruction that dates from the late 1950s, and many buildings have a modern appearance. The great Hall was also damaged but the interior decor and beautiful stained glass windows had been stored for safety, so it was possible to almost perfectly reconstruct it. The Gray's Inn gardens, called The Walks, are an oasis of tree-lined parkland. Covering 5.8 acres they are one of the largest private gardens in London and among the oldest, their layout created by Sir Francis Bacon in 1606.

Although I've yet to find a romance fiction set here, this is a place of romance and intrigue. Notes Samuel Pepys (1660), "to Gray's Inn where I saw many beauties," and on The Walks, a "great store of gallants." On the darker side, in 1701 there was a duel between a Captain Greenwood and Mr. Ottway, which ended with Ottway dead and Greenwood convicted of manslaughter. Gray's Inn also has a storied past when it comes to fiction. Shakespeare's *Comedy of Errors* received its first known public performance here (1594). And finally, the 1825 Raymond Buildings housed the solicitor's office where Charles Dickens clerked (his actual high desk can be seen in the Doughty Street Museum). Gardens open to public M-F 12–2:30pm year round. www.graysinn.org.uk

How OLDE (FOR ALL THE INNS): ⚜ ⚜ ⚜ ⚜ ⚜
Price: FREE to walk the grounds | **Hours:** see each listing
Tube: Chancery Lane, Holborn, Temple | **Map:** D | Although unaffiliated, two inexpensive walking tours provide a good introduction: Old Bailey Insight & Legal London Tours explore the courts inside and out; London Walks offers tours of the Inns' grounds (www.Old-Bailey.com and www.Walks.com)

C

Covent Garden

1631–present

"*Ah-aw-oo!*" a downtrodden woman cries in dispair. "*Look wh' y' gowin, deah.*"

For millions of Americans, this is our first introduction to Covent Garden, when cockney-accented flower girl Eliza Doolittle (played by Audrey Hepburn in the movie) runs into Freddie Eynsford-Hill in the pouring rain in *My Fair Lady*. Based on George Bernard Shaw's *Pygmalion*, the musical begins under the portico of St. Paul's Church (not to be mistaken with the cathedral of the same name). This is the Inigo Jones' designed parish church anchoring Covent Garden square. *Pygmalion* is a story as romantic as they come, although feminists today might have a problem with the ending where Audrey Hepburn's Eliza docilely returns to a seemingly uninterested Professor Higgins who orders her to find his slippers. But one knows that theirs will be a happily every after, even if not the one we'd choose for ourselves. It also wasn't the one Shaw chose, wanting a more feminist Eliza to go it on her own, but for the romantic there is nothing like standing under the portico of this more than 340-year-old church and looking out to imagine life here during the Regency or Victorian eras.

Then: Take yourself farther back in time to the Dark Ages, the 700s, and envision open fields and the first Saxon village of Lundenwic, which thrived for nearly 200 years before being abandoned.

Covent Garden's current name derives from the fact that Westminster Abbey walled the land off (c.1200) for farming and orchards, becoming "the garden of the Abbey and Convent."[22] Some 350 years later Henry VIII dissolved the monasteries in his quest for a son and took it back (along with the land that eventually became Buckingham Palace). He gave the now-called Covent Garden lands to the Earls of Bedford. The 4th Earl commissioned architect Jones in 1552 to build fine houses, an Italianate piazza, and the above mentioned church.[23] This "planned" housing around a square was a new idea and became the model for other developments as London expanded. By this time there was no remnant left of any gardens—it was all stone and filth in a city lacking sewers and plumbing.

Over the course of the next hundred years a fruit and vegetable market developed in the square, and the next hundred brought decline with disreputable but popular taverns, coffee-shops, gaming-hells, and brothels. Due to nearby theatres, it was also popular with actors, writers, and artists, and the area became a fashionable bohemia for the well-heeled

to play at night so long as they sported a Y chromosome.[24]

Now we're deep into romance territory. For more than 200 years, this area was virtually off limits to ladies of quality (except to alight their fancy carriage and be escorted into the Covent Garden Theatre, now the Royal Opera House). It was, however, a hotspot for men on the prowl while the lower classes attempted to shop for necessities and otherwise live their lives. While many Regency gentlemen kept sophisticated courtesans ensconced in town houses (or wished they could), the bad-boy rakehell might find himself in a Covent Garden brothel or if really desperate soliciting the myriad streetwalkers that serviced clients in dark alleys. However, in romances, of course, the hero stops himself before following through—his honor as a gentleman at stake, just like Sir Ian Moore in Laura Lee Guhrke's *She's No Princess*. In other stories, the hero ends up rescuing the young urchin, only to discover she's really a princess or lost heiress or…you get the idea. (Rags to riches tropes are one of my favorites, hence my love of Eliza Doolittle's story.)

But back to Covent Garden. By 1757, prostitution was so much a part of the area that a salacious book was printed annually for almost 40 years: *Harris's List of Covent Garden Ladies*. Selling for only two shillings and sixpence, it had an estimated annual print run of 8,000 copies. As you might guess, these were "Ladies of Pleasure" with listings of about 150 working women and covering everything from their looks, to manners, to where they could be found, to most important what services they provided. Perhaps a bit salacious, but I couldn't resist a 1788 excerpt on Miss H-ll-nd of No. 2, York-Street, though it does seem a bit contradictory in its description:

Those who choose to sail the island of love in a first rate ship, or to enclose an armful of delight, must be pleased with this lady; who, tho' only seventeen and short, is very fat and corpulent; yet, notwithstanding, she is a fine piece of frailty; her face is handsome and her nut brown locks, which are placed above and below, promise a luscious treat to the voluptuary. Her temper is agreeable and pleasing, and she is so far from being mercenary, that a single guinea is the boundage of her wish.

The publication was shut down and its sponsors jailed by 1795, but it took until 1980 for Covent Garden to begin its transformation from seedy dump to glitzy tourist destination  that draws millions annually.

NOW: The Covent Garden Area Trust works to conserve the historic architecture and unique atmosphere of the 97-acre area in the heart of London. If you happen to be there toward the end of June you might be lucky enough to witness the "weird and wonderful" Rent Ceremony, where the Town Crier and a jazz band lead a march around the Piazza so Trustees can pay rents on Trust buildings of 5 red apples and 5 flower posies (www.CoventGardenTrust.org).

If you miss that, you can still stand under the world famous portico of St. Paul's Church and hum your favorite *My Fair Lady* tune—I promise no one will stop you. You can also visit the signature Apple Store and visit Apple Market (no relation), featuring British-made crafts in the North Hall, and enjoy numerous fine restaurants and pubs. In summertime, there are "loverly" outdoor cafés right on the square and plentiful street performers for entertainment. If you desire more historic dining, the colorful Lamb & Flag (c.1688) is just two blocks away (Ch. 5).

ℋOW OLDE: ♧♧♧♧♧ ~ *except it's cleaner and nicer now*
Price: Singing in the Rain is FREE | **Hours:** 24/7, but be safe and don't go late at night alone. | **Tube:** Covent Garden, Leicester Square
www.coventgarden.london

. . . and in 2015

◇❦⬭⬭⬭⬭⬭⬭⬭⬭⬭⬭⬭⬭⬭⬭⬭⬭⬭⬭•

COVENT GARDEN THEATRE ⌇ see Theaters in Ch. 7

◇❦⬭⬭⬭⬭⬭⬭⬭⬭⬭⬭⬭⬭⬭⬭⬭⬭⬭⬭⬭⬭⬭⬭⬭⬭•

CREWE HOUSE
1899–present

THEN: One of the few remaining original Mayfair houses, this mansion is set back in a green yard, complete with a carriageway in the front. Called Wharncliffe House since the end of the 18th Century and referred to as such on old maps, it was built in 1730 and altered/expanded twice by the early 19th century. It was purchased by the 1st Marquis of Crewe and renamed in 1899.

⌇ **for the guys** During WWI, the Marquis placed the mansion at the disposal of the war effort, and it became the campaign headquarters for Viscount Northcliffe's appointment as Director of Propaganda in Enemy Countries. Throughout 1918, the house was a beehive of activity, both writing and producing propaganda literature aimed at the enemy. Employed in this secret work was a mixed group of military leaders, journalists, and authors "of distinction," including the renowned H.G. Wells. *Secrets of Crewe House* by Sir Campbell Stuart offers a dry but thorough exposé about what was accomplished during this brief period as a secret government bureau.

NOW: It can be viewed from the outside through a fence, but I wouldn't advise taking photos as it is now the Royal Embassy of Saudi Arabia (official address 30 Charles St), which purchased it in 1984 for 37 million pounds. With that, any chance for us regular folk of visiting the inside of this hallmark of Regency splendor disappeared forever. The Saudis extensively restored the interiors and gardens after they acquired the mansion, however, the oldest surviving interior feature is the double-height front hall dating only to 1911.

How OLDE: ⚜⚜⚜⚜⚜
⌇ *priceless, if you could wrangle an invitation*
Hours: not open to the public | **Tube**: Green Park | **Map**: B

CURZON STREET

Circa 1700–present

THEN: Previously called Mayfair Row, this street in the heart of Mayfair starts at Hyde Park and terminates at Berkeley Square. It was renamed Curzon Street, c.1760, after an early landholder there. Many notable members of the peerage and other colorful characters have been residents, and for a time even MI5 (England's CIA) was located on Curzon Street. Its colorful history has made it popular with authors—among the many who used this street in their stories are Oscar Wilde, Roald Dahl, William Makepeace Thackeray, Sir Arthur Conan Doyle, and John Le Carré. Sadly, apartment blocks or businesses have replaced nearly all the historic mansions, with the exception of Crewe House.

Real life romance thrived on Curzon Street because of the quirky little Keith's Chapel that once stood across from Crewe House. Prior to the Marriage Duty Act of 1695, which penalized clergy for performing marriages without banns or license, it was the site of many "clandestine marriages"—which simply meant, marriages without the aforementioned banns and licenses and taking place outside the lovers' home parish. This was useful if there might be royal or familial obstacles to their union. Needless to say, these were usually love matches, and for Reverend Alexander Keith and his army of morally-flexible clergy it was a thriving business providing as many as six thousand weddings annually before the Marriage Act ruined it.

Among the most romantic was the second marriage of Henry Brydges, 2nd Duke of Chandos to a pretty chambermaid, Mrs. Anne Wells Jeffrey. Now that is certainly marrying up! Even more bizarre, supposedly said Duke first met her at a country inn, The Pelican in Newbury, having stopped there for dinner. When he heard it proclaimed, "A man is going to sell his wife, and they are leading her up the yard with a halter round her neck," Henry went to have a look. It must have been love at first sight, because the Duke bought Anne immediately from the feckless husband. It was several years before her spouse died, and then Henry married her on Christmas Day in 1744 at Keith's Chapel.[28] Other reports say the Duke saw the inn's ostler beating his wife "in a most cruel manner" (*is there an un-cruel manner?*) and bought Anne for half a crown, then educating her, and finally marrying her upon her husband's death. This report is supposedly from the Duchess herself on her deathbed to her assembled household staff.[29] Imagine going from beaten-sold-wife-for-mer-chambermaid to the Duchess of Chandos all because a nobleman was hungry and happened to stop for dinner. This sounds like a romance novel waiting to be written!

Amongst the most salacious of these "clandestine marriages" was the union of James, 6th Duke of Hamilton to the impoverished, untitled, but extraordinarily beautiful Elizabeth Gunning, formerly of Ireland. Elizabeth, at the ripe age of 19, was by then a celebrated beauty in London. She and her sister were quickly dubbed "THE diamonds of 1752." The "debauched, extravagant," and oversexed young Duke wanted Elizabeth so badly that when her mother was away, he "made violent love at one end of the room" (one supposes that this means entreaties of affection) in the middle of a large party at Lord Chesterfield's new mansion. He succeeded in marrying her within an hour of proposing. When the first parson refused to do the deed *sans* license or ring, James took his intended to Keith's Chapel where they made do with a "ring of the bed-curtains" at 12:30am. Thus the Duke was finally able to slake his insatiable lust on her by two that morning—and that's how Miss Gunning became Duchess of Hamilton. Alcohol, it is reported, may have had something to do with his ardor.

When the hard-drinking, hard-gambling dissolute James died merely six years later, 25-year-old Elizabeth was still at the top of her game, remarrying and becoming Duchess of Argyll. So enamored of her beauty was King George III that he elevated Elizabeth to the title, Her Grace, 1st Baroness Hamilton of Hameldon in her own right. She also served in the prestigious role of Lady of the Bedchamber to Queen Charlotte for 23 years. More of a social-climbing story than Chandos's rescue of the beaten wife, but still Elizabeth, a nobody from nowhere, ended up a member of the *haut ton* for the remainder of her life. And I should not forget to mention, Elizabeth married her duke on St. Valentine's Day.[30] Now *isn't that romantic?*

Charming, little Keith's Chapel was described in their advertisements as a "corner house…And that it may be better known, there is a porch at the door like a country church porch." It remained until 1894 before it was torn down to make room for Sunderland House (built by American Vanderbilt money and destroyed in WWII).

NOW: Mostly office and apartment buildings all around. If you're viewing Crewe House, use your imagination to picture Keith Chapel on the eastern corner of Curzon and Trebeck streets and dream of the multitudinous marriages of yore. Oft referred to as the "Gretna Green of Mayfair," its 16 marriages a day would rival in speed and efficiency the modern chapels of the current "Marriage Capital of the World"…Las Vegas.

*H*OW OLDE: 🌳♛♛♛♛♛
~ *mostly modern now except for Crewe House*
Price: FREE | Hours: 24/7 | Tube: Green Park | Map: B

◇—❧~◟—————————————————————◆

DOMESDAY BOOK

1086—present

THEN: Not a place, but a survey ordered by King William I after he conquered England. Initially it was called *Liber de Wintonia* (*Book of Winchester*), because that's where he established his new capital, and his *Liber* was stored there until the early 1300s.

Because of William's mass redistribution of land holdings—from Saxon to Norman nobles—following his conquest of England, there was a knowledge void about the extent of his new wealth and therefore how much tax (called geld) he could demand in the name of the Crown.

> So, William sent *"his men over all England into each shire; commissioning them to find out 'How many hundreds of hides were in the shire, what land the king himself had, and what stock upon the land; or, what dues he ought to have by the year from the shire'... 'What, or how much, each man had, who was an occupier of land in England, either in land or in stock, and how much money it were worth.' ... So very narrowly, indeed, did he commission them to trace it out, that there was not one single hide, nor a yard of land...not even an ox, nor a cow, nor a swine was there left, that was not set down in his writ..."*
>
> As recorded in the *Anglo-Saxon Chronicles*, c.1085[31]

•————————————————————⟨⊱◇⊰⟩————————————————————•

Domesday Book excerpt that records
Amberley Castle (sic Amerelie), now a hotel (see Ch. 6)

There is, of course, documented evidence of this type of tax accounting dating back even further:

And it came to pass in those days, that there went out a decree from Caesar Augustus that all the world should be taxed. And all went to be taxed, every one into his own city.

As for the Domesday Book, from across England with ruthless efficiency, every accounting was brought back to be transcribed, mostly by one hand, in Medieval Latin using black and some red ink onto treated sheepskin parchment. It was stored in an ironbound chest. The assessors' estimation of each man's wealth was final and without appeal, which led to the English referring to it as "the Book of Judgment" because its declarations were as unalterable as God's Last Judgment. As a result, by the 12th Century, the common name for it had changed to Domesday (Middle English for Doomsday).

The survey recorded a total of 13,418 places. Strangely no assessments were made of the City of London, Winchester, and some other important towns, but it's hypothesized that this is because they were given independent charters and/or were tax-free.

While the survey is incomplete, leaving out numerous areas, especially in the north and Wales, it's utterly astounding to know that there is a census recording minute details about 268,984 people living in the year 1086. At the top were the Norman nobility with Anglo-Saxons appearing as under-tenants of their new lords. 40% are listed as *villani* (loosely translated as villagers), and 10% were *servi* (slaves) who could be bought and sold and were often listed alongside the number of ploughs owned.[32]

It also uses ancient Anglo-Saxon terms that this travel guide has refrained from using to avoid confusion. Among them, "Hide" which back then meant a plot of land sufficient to support one household, incorporating how fertile the land was in combination with the acreage. Domesday assessors generally accorded land that produced £1 of income per year equal to 1 hide. "Rape" is another unusual term, used for the six subdivisions of the county of Sussex. Each with its own Castle center, the "Rapes" retain their names today (Arundel, for example). Other similar terms included the "Lathes" of Kent and "Ridings" of Yorkshire.[33] And then there's "Shire," a term interchangeable with county, and still somewhat in use today.

The Domesday Book was eventually moved with King John to the Palace of Westminster in London, and it continued to be valued as an important legal document down through the ages. As recently as the

1960s it was still referred to in court cases regarding ancient property rights.

NOW: The nearly 1,000-year-old manuscript resides in The National Archives at Kew, along with its ironbound chest. Excitingly, as of 2011 anyone can view this important document in both searchable English and the actual Latin photographed pages (as on page 57). Check out: www.OpenDomesday. org (translations plus originals) or www.DomesdayBook.co.uk (easier to search, but with less information).

DRURY LANE ～ see Theaters in Ch. 7

DUDLEY HOUSE
1730–present

THEN: Like many of the great old houses, if the walls could talk… Our historical romance novels give us a sense of what they were like, both upstairs and downstairs. But most of them are gone now, replaced for something newer or destroyed in WWII. Here is the tale of one that survived.

The aristocratic Ward family acquired this mansion facing Hyde Park in 1742 and greatly expanded it, eventually adding an 81-foot long picture gallery with marble columns and a mirrored, gilded, 50-square-foot ballroom. The family held many titles, including Baron, Viscount, and later Earl of Dudley. As was the practice of the times, this town house was their base during "the season," and it was run just like in our novels, with a full staff from head butler and housekeeper, ladies maids and valets, and on down to footmen and scullery maids. Its convenient location and grand opulence made it the favorite spot for the Prince of Wales (Edward VII) to meet his mistress, actress Lillie Langtry.[34] Hard to imagine telling a friend that you're going to stop by their home on a regular basis to use their bedroom for adulterous sex, but who's going to turn down the future king of England!

Sadly, just as with all the rest of these city mansions, the exorbitant cost of running it led to its ultimate demise. It was sold and sold again, then severely damaged in WWII, before deteriorating into near ruin. Only its use as offices for sixty years kept it from being demolished. Then in 2006, the 44,000 square foot mansion was purchased by Qatari Sheikh Hamad bin Abdullah Al-Thani for £37 million, becoming once again a private residence. While it is a bit of a sore spot for many Londoners that much of the prime-est real estate in London is now foreign owned (it's estimated that the Qatari alone own more than £1 billion worth, nearly a quarter of Mayfair's 279 acres).[35] But at least prince Hamad worked meticulously to return the 17-bedroom manse to its former magnificence and period décor. He also runs it in the grand style of old with a full staff that supposedly don white tie and tails each evening.

NOW: Today, this Grade II listed building, one of the few remaining London private "palaces" left, is estimated to be worth upwards of £400 million, making it one of the highest priced homes in Britain. While the present owner enjoys entertaining with lavish dinners, it's unlikely that the average Joe will get to see the inside. However, we can sometimes see the art that adorns his walls, because the prince is generous in lending it to museum exhibitions in New York and London.

By the way, it seems that having Midas-level money doesn't just buy one prime real estate, it can also buy invisibility—at least electronically. Searching for either Dudley House or 100 Park Lane on some online maps can yield "current location disabled" or it takes you to a completely different address. So, if you want to take a look at the restored façade, go to 99 Park Lane, which does usually appear, and it's next door. Look up to see the original Ward coat of arms with the phrase *Comme Je Fus* (As I was), and you've found the right place. To see the inside, *Vanity Fair* magazine has a photo spread. One can easily imagine a Regency heroine taking a turn about the great picture hall on the arm of her beau.[36]

How OLDE: ♗♗♗♗♗ ∼ *sadly, not open to hoi polloi, ever*
Tube: Marble Arch | **Map**: B | Park Lane at Culross Street

◇❦◯────────────────────────•

FLEET PRISON
1197–1846

THEN: Among the most infamous of the London prisons, Fleet operated for six centuries and housed from 150–300 prisoners and their families at a time. It was built just south of Fleet Lane on the east side of the Fleet River (today this is the largest subterranean river in London running roughly under Farringdon Street down to the Thames). The prison was destroyed and rebuilt twice. First it burned to the ground in the Great Fire of London in 1666, and second it was torn down in the Gordon Riots of 1780. Fleet Prison was a cesspool of disease made worse by the cesspool of a river that ran next to it, stinking so badly that as early as 1355 the first of several government inquiries were made about the prison's conditions. It was used primarily for debtors, political prisoners (those problematic folks that the king or queen wanted out of the way), and religious dissidents. Everything bad you can think about applies to the Fleet (for general informa- tion on these ancient, inhumane, for-profit institutions see Prisons).

Two things made Fleet Prison unique. First, it wasn't the level of your crime that defined your treatment, but the amount of money you could pay the gaolers. For instance, if you had sufficient coin upon entering you could pay not to have manacles. With more funds, you got better housing, food, and other creature comforts. This in itself was not unusual at the time, but at Fleet if you had enough money—and it was notori- ous for having the highest "fees" in England—you didn't even have to stay in the prison. The area around the compound was an unofficial special district that the warden controlled. Pay enough to compensate for the loss of earnings for actually housing said prisoner, and one was free to take lodgings in the neighborhood outside the jail until cleared of whatever crime for which one was accused. The keepers didn't really care, as long as they got their take.

Fleet Marriages were the second reason it was notable. Like the aforementioned Keith's Chapel on Curzon Street, this area—both in and out of the prison—was renowned for its clandestine marriages. Throughout the 17th and 18th centuries, there were thousands of them, all of which added to the warden's profits. While the Church of England worked to end irregular marriages in its parishes, clergymen—both inmates or not—operating within the "Liberty of the Fleet" were outside the church's jurisdiction. In the 1740s more than half of all London wed- dings took place in the Fleet, as many as 6,600 annually (roughly 1 in 7 in all of England).[37] The 1753 Marriage Act effectively ended this prac- tice, the clergy's punishment being "transportation"—and by that I don't mean free rides in a stagecoach, but rather forced, usually permanent, relocation to penal colonies in Australia or the Americas where convicts toiled in indentured servitude for terms of 7 or 14 years or life. While a few other prisons also had clandestine marriages, Fleet was notorious for them. After they were outlawed, Gretna Green, of romance fame, became the next best option for quickie unions in the days before Vegas.

Who were the inmates? Everyone from lowly laborers to lords were sent to the Fleet. Notables include Sir Richard Grosvenor, 1st Baronet, William Penn founder of Pennsylvania, and the author John Cleland who bought his freedom by writing the erotic novel *Fanny Hill:*

Memoirs of a Woman of Pleasure (1749). There is an American connection here in that after being censured everywhere for more than 200 years, *Fanny Hill* was again published in 1963 in the UK, but in the States it was again banned and wound up in the court system, eventually making it to the US Supreme Court (Memoirs v. Mass), which in a 1966 landmark decision declared that it was not obscene. Though not a traditional romance, there is a central love story and a happily ever after...and a lot of sex.

Back in Britain, Dickens immortalized Fleet Prison in his 1836 *The Pickwick Papers*. The most famous warden was Thomas Bambridge; so immoral were his extortion practices that he was sentenced to Newgate Prison and a special act was passed to ensure that he didn't gain further from his position of warden at Fleet. The infamous Fleet Prison was demolished in 1846 and nothing of it remains today. If you find yourself at the corner of Farringdon Street and Old Fleet Lane (a block north of Fleet Street), you'll see a modern office building, but know that for 649 years it was the site of immense misery and torment along with such outrageous extortion that modern criminals could learn a thing or two.

FORTNUM & MASON DEPARTMENT STORE
~ see Chapter 8

THE GEFFRYE MUSEUM OF THE HOME
1714–1911 (almshouses) and 1914–present (museum)

THEN: This large complex was built by the Ironmongers' Company with a bequest from Sir Robert Geffrye, who was a former Master of Ironmongers and former Lord Mayor of London. For nearly 200 years these connected, brick, two-story townhomes housed 50 poor pensioners at a time. By the late 1800s, the area of Hoxton had become unsavory and the Ironmongers wanted to sell the valuable land and buy new almshouses farther afield in Mottingham, Kent. If it weren't for the near 20 year fight by such groups as the Society for the Protection of Ancient Buildings and the National Trust, the place would have been torn down and replaced by tenement housing to make money. The fight went all the way to the Court of Chancery, a buck-stops-here equivalent to our US Supreme court. In the end, the London County Council bought the property, hoping to tear it down for a park. A second campaign by leading members of the Arts and Crafts movement successfully petitioned the Council to convert the buildings into a museum about the local furniture industry, which opened in 1914.[38] Its purpose was to educate the local workforce about the artistry and quality of the furniture they were employed to make. Ironically, while the now Grade I listed almshouses escaped WWII damage, the new ones in Mottingham were badly bombed.

NOW: Today this charming, modest museum can bring to three-dimensional life the interiors from our favorite novels with furnishing and designs from 1600 to present. The 1830 Regency

Almshouses in 1906 and The Geffrye Museum today

"withdrawing room" is particularly delightful. As an added plus, there are even four replica chairs visitors can try out, one for each century, that grow more comfortable as one travels through time—perfect for a selfie.

Becoming an independent charitable trust in 1991, the institution has since greatly expanded and improved its facilities. The museum is unique in focusing on the London middle classes—merchants, doctors, and other professionals who could afford comfortable town houses with quality furniture. The layout is like a walk through time—moving from room to room, the visitor is taken on a quick 400 year journey through the different historical periods, illustrating the changing style and tastes of the urban middle class. Additionally, one of the almshouses has been carefully restored along with furnishings, clothing, tools, and cooking equipment to offer visitors the chance to glimpse the living conditions of London's poor and elderly, in two distinct periods—the 1780s and 1880s. There is also a restored almshouse chapel (where pensioners were required to attend services weekly), a reading room, historical paintings room (depicting home life through the ages), and a pleasant little gift shop and modern café (avoid the busy lunch period, but a lite afternoon tea with scones, clotted cream and jam can be had for about £6). Lastly, in the warmer months there are four period gardens to explore.

How Olde: ♕♕♕♕♕

Museum ～ **Price**: FREE | **Hours**: including gardens 10am–5pm Tues-Sun & Bank-Holiday-Mon | Closed major holidays | Ask about their Educational Mobile Website feature for 3G devices which uses free WiFi to take you beyond, virtually, the rope in each room.
Almshouse ～ **Price**: £4 timed ticket (first-come, first served; no advance booking) | **Hours**: Limited Sat/Tues/Wed dates throughout year | Check website for details
Tube: Old Street, Liverpool (20 min walk) or Overground: Hoxton Station (directly behind museum)
www.Geffrye-Museum.org.uk | +44 20 7739 9893
136 Kingsland Road, Hoxton

Gentleman John Jackson
1769–1845

Founded by a champion bare-knuckle pugilist, Jackson's Saloon was both a thriving boxing academy and *haut ton* meeting place for wealthy men. Already a popular spectator sport in the early 1700s, by the end of the century boxing had codified rules along with the enthusiastic participation of both commoners and gentlemen. And, of course, there was plenty of gambling.

Twenty-six-year old Jackson, an amateur boxer, made a name for himself by winning the Champion of England title on his third public fight in 1795. His takedown of the reigning champ in only ten and a half minutes with hardly a scratch to himself made him instantly famous among elite men. Rumor has it he did this by grabbing hold of his opponent's long hair with one hand while pummeling him with the other—spurring a new shorter hairstyle for boxers, if not immediately for the general public.

Jackson used his celebrity to launch his self-defense school at Number 13 Old Bond Street. It was well situated for Regency sportsmen with his friend Angelo's Fencing Academy next door. And, Jackson's gentlemanly manner and elegant dress recommended him to the nobility. For the younger set, it was a meeting place for socializing, a gymnasium for maintaining fashionable physiques, and for the "artistic" sort a chance to watch buff half-naked men dance about the floor, their toned bodies slick with sweat, their chiseled chests heaving, their... *But I digress.*

The poet, Lord Byron was a devotee. In his March, 1814, diary entry about his workout with Jackson, Byron wrote, "exercise is good, and this the severest of all; fencing and the broad-sword never fatigued me half so much."[39]

By request, boxing demos were provided for the Emperor of Russia, King of Prussia, and the Prince of Mecklenburg. So respected and well liked was Jackson that the Prince of Wales asked him to provide security for his 1821 coronation as king, which the boxer did by assembling 18 burly and intimidating prize fighters. There were other clubs, including Daffy's, Limmer's, and Offley's, but Jackson's was the premiere establishment, and it was considered an honor to be invited to spar with the founder himself. He was also instrumental in forming the Pugilistic Society, which brought increased respectability to the sport. Buried in Brompton Cemetery in Kensington, one can still see the giant Lion-topped stone monument placed there by his friends.

Gentleman Jackson and his Saloon make frequent appearances in historical romance novels written in recent times, but his first literary appearance happened just a year after his champion fight, when Sir Arthur Conan Doyle wrote him into his Gothic mystery and boxing tale *Rodney Stone*. Regency author extraordinaire Georgette Heyer often included mention of him in her novels, among them *Cotillion, Frederica, Pistols for Two,* and *The Nonesuch*. In *The Grand Sophy,* Heyer describes well the type of man who frequented such places:

> *After stabling the chestnut that afternoon, he had first gone off to Bond Street, to work off some of his fury in a sparring-bout with Gentleman Jackson, and had then repaired to White's, where he had spent an hour playing billiards…*

For wealthy young men of the period, especially second sons, life was clearly a rocking good time.

◇-❧∕❀────────────────────⧫

GLOBE THEATRE
Old: 1576–1642 | New: 1997–present

THEN: Prior to Queen Elizabeth I's reign, English plays were performed in spaces not purpose-built for theater: private homes, great halls in castles and the Inns of Justice, and for *hoi polloi* in the stable yards of inns. These posting inns were built in squares around a center stable yard with walkways along the inside on all levels (think American motel if the building was a rectangle and the parking lot was in a courtyard along with the outdoor stairs and walkways). A small stage might be placed at one end of the yard, and the audience stood either on the ground or on the walkways. Then actor-manager James Burbage got the idea to create a real theater in Shoreditch using this arrangement from posting inns. Shakespeare soon joined this troupe and it flourished for 20 years. Many additional theaters were built in this time. In 1599, Burbage's son rebuilt it across the Thames in Southwark, literally dismantling and carrying the timber across the river to create the Globe Theatre, a round amphitheater with a thatched roof. It thrived for 14 years and many of Shakespeare's greatest plays debuted there. Then in 1613 during a performance if *Henry VIII* a stage cannon caused the thatched roof to ignite and the theater burned to the ground in less than two hours. Reportedly, no one died in the inferno. It was rebuilt yet again, with a tiled roof, and operated until the closure of all theaters under England's Puritan rule in 1642. By 1644, it was demolished to build tenement housing. This version is referred as the Old Globe.

NOW: With the new Globe we go straight to an American Connection: The US actor Sam Wanamaker performed in London in 1949 and was inspired to recreate the theater. This is reportedly because of his first professional theater experience: performing Shakespeare in a temporary Globe Theatre in the 1936-37 Great Lakes' Exposition (a world's fair) in Cleveland, Ohio. After returning to the UK to perform in 1951, he initiated the Shakespeare Globe Trust, and after 23 years of fundraising, researching the original, and planning, he died in 1993—but his lifelong project was now a done deal with a site secured and building underway.

For hundreds of years the Old Globe's exact location was lost to time until the original foundation was discovered in 1989 in a car park, and amazingly it's only 750 feet from the site secured for the New Globe. There were no blueprints or plans of any kind to make an exact replica, but things they learned from excavating parts of other theaters and researching first person accounts were that the Old Globe wasn't an exact circle, that is was a 20-sided building, and that it had a diameter of 100 feet. It is estimated that it could hold 3,000 spectators. Today's Globe is as accurate as possible while also incorporating modern safety and fire laws. The new Globe was opened in June 1997 by Her Majesty the Queen and has been presenting Shakespeare and other plays ever since.

Tours may be taken of the theater, but for a truly historic experience, see a play. **TAKE HEED!** The Globe is open air (hot in the summer, cold in the winter), and the show goes on in the rain (no umbrellas allowed). How more authentic can one get! There are also local Bankside tours about this notorious medieval entertainment district.

NOTE: There are other historic theaters that are sometimes referred to in romance fiction. See "Theaters" for a brief list.

How OLDE: ♣ ♣ ♣ ♣ ♣ ~ *a reconstructed time travel to medieval times*
Tour Hours: M-Sat 9am-12:30pm | Sun 9am-5pm | Multi-lingual tours start every 30 min | Closed Dec 24-25 and during performances | **Price:** £16
Theater Season: year round | Winter indoors in the candlelit playhouse | Summer outdoors in the round | **Price:** Pit Standing £5; Gallery Benches £20-45 | **Tube:** St. Paul's, Mansion House, London Bridge (all 10-15 min walk) | **Thames Clipper Ferry:** Bankside Pier (2 min walk) | www.ShakespearesGlobe.com | +44 20 7902 1400 | 21 New Globe Walk, Bankside

HAMPTON COURT PALACE
Circa 1300–present

This palace, 13 miles from London, saw many important moments in England's history. A medieval manor predates it, but power-building forces—starting with Cardinal Thomas Wolsey—greatly expanded the structure into a lavish palace. King Henry VIII seized ownership of it in 1528 and continued the work, enlarging it to accommodate his court of more than 1,000 lords and ladies. It was here that Henry sent the letter that first threatened Rome with the dissolution of the Catholic Church in England. Henry's son Prince Edward was born here in 1537 and baptized with royal pomp in the chapel, but Queen Jane Seymour died soon after from childbirth complications. This was the site of much of his wifely intrigues—1 divorce (Anne of Cleves), 2 marriages (Catherine Howard, Kateryn Parr), and 1 house arrest for adultery (Howard).

Later, Shakespeare performed many of his works in the Great Hall for King James I, and that same James held a conference that ultimately brought the world the *King James Bible*. Parts of the older castle were demolished and rebuilt—the Tudor façade replaced by a baroque exterior. After King George III was crowned in 1760 he abandoned Hampton Court as a royal residence. In 1838, Queen Victoria opened the state apartments and glorious English gardens to the public free of charge (sadly, no longer free).

For a period of time the palace was divided into "grace-and-favor" apartments and being granted one was a sign of high favor. Although not all were large or even comfortable, competition for them was fierce. Among the heroines that lived there was Princess Sophia Duleep Singh, daughter of a Maharaja and goddaughter to Queen Victoria, who with her sister became famous suffragettes, campaigning for votes for women and joining the march on parliament in 1910. Princess Sophia famously refused to pay her taxes—her logical reasoning holds some resonance today for citizens where their vote doesn't count equally: "When the women of England are enfranchised I shall pay my taxes willingly. If I am not a person for the purposes of representation, why should I be a fit person for taxation?"

AMERICAN CONNECTION: General Eisenhower planned the invasion of Normandy from Bushy Park, which adjoins Hampton Court parkland. You may have already seen the palace and didn't know it, because three American movies used it for scenes: *Pirates of the Caribbean: On Stranger Tides*, *Sherlock Holmes: A Game of Shadows*, and for us romance fans, Disney's live action *Cinderella*.

HAMPTON GHOSTS: After being accused of adultery and locked in her rooms, Catherine Howard escaped and ran down the gallery hoping to plead for her life to Henry. Captured by her guards, she was dragged screaming back to her chambers, and today Catherine continues to cry for her life in the Haunted Gallery. Verification includes 19th Century residents claiming to hear screams, two women fainting on the same 1999 evening in the same spot, and many reports of eerie feelings within the gallery.

But that's not all—Dame Sybil Penn was nurse to baby Prince Edward and later to Elizabeth I when the princess had smallpox, which Sybil then contracted and died from in 1562. She remained happily buried in an impressive tomb at a nearby church for 267 years until said church was rebuilt in 1829 and the tomb moved. Shortly after, the troubles began—people heard the sounds of someone working a spinning wheel through the walls at Hampton Court and a search revealed a previously unknown chamber...and an antique spinning wheel. An unknown chamber in a palace. *Really?* Well, sections of Hampton Court were torn down and rebuilt, and expanded, and remodeled, and again rebuilt, over seven centuries, and today there are more than 1,300 rooms. So, yeah, it seems possible there might be a spare chamber or two, long forgotten, but the question is, why was it walled shut in the first place?

More recently, there's Skeletor. Not only did he open a fire escape door three times late at night in the winter of 2003, but CCTV footage showed the doors flying open and no one there. On the second night after the doors flew open, a specter in period dress is seen emerging to close them. And, in the palace guest book on that same day, a visitor wrote that she'd seen a ghost in the area. *Eww. Spooky!* You can see the image yourself at the Hampton Court website.

Just 35 minutes by train from London, combined with Windsor Castle and maybe a carriage ride, this makes a great day trip (Ch. 9). You can even take a boat to arrive just as King Henry and other royals did. Entrance fee includes costumed guided tours, electronic audio guide, various exhibitions, the Cumberland Art Gallery, and the beautiful gardens and maze.

*H*OW OLDE: ⚜⚜⚜⚜⚜
Price: about £20.90 without voluntary donation | See Ch. 4 Museums Quick Guide for UK voluntary donation scheme explanation
Hours: Daily Winter 10am–4:30pm | Summer 10am–6pm
Directions: see Ch. 9 | www.Hrp.org.uk/hampton-court-palace
+44 20 3166 6000 | Surrey KT89AU

◇-❦/๏------------------------•

Harrods Department Store ~ see Ch. 8

◇-❦/๏------------------------•

Hyde Park
1536–present

> *"In the park?" she said. "Hyde Park?" It was the dream. It was the pinnacle. Everyone—even the merchant class of Bristol—knew all about Hyde Park in the afternoons during the Season.*
>
> *"None other," he [Lord Francis Kneller] said. "At precisely five o'clock, ma'am. At precisely the time when there will be so many carriages and horsemen and pedestrians there that only a snail could be content with the speed of movement."*

THEN: This excerpt from Mary Balogh's wonderful novel, *The Famous Heroine*, makes clear what Hyde Park meant to young Regency ladies in search of a husband. Nearly every romance novel set in London includes at least a mention of Hyde Park. Young ladies are courted on afternoon carriage rides, heroes succeed in stopping runaway horses and saving heiresses, governesses chase after children and run into handsome rakes, young men engage in pre-dawn duels, and lovers—or seducers—take secluded paths that allow for a quick stolen kiss. But did all this really happen? It does sound like it!

The partying really took off following the Restoration of Charles II—The Merry Monarch—in 1660, thus ending Oliver Cromwell's eleven-year military rein that included the somber guarding of public morality. Of this happy time, Samuel Pepys reports on Hyde Park in his famous diary: "Gaiety, jollity, and merry life" and in 1661, that "there was his Majesty and an innumerable appearance of gallants and rich coaches, being now a time of universal festivity and joy." In 1815, more than 150 years later, Captain Rees Gronow, an officer and a dandy, reports that "The company, which then congregated daily about five, was composed of dandies and women in the best society; the men mounted on such horses as England alone could then produce."[40]

As regards dueling, there are many reports of them both with swords and pistols, however the majority of duels had nothing to do with protecting a heroine's honor. Provocations ranged from nasty name calling, to fighting because two gent's dogs were fighting, to anger because one titled lady revealed the age of another (when pistols failed to hit their target, the ladies resorted to swords). In fact, there was only one duel over 'the love of a woman' that I could find, and in it the gentlemen politely removed themselves to a nearby tavern to fight with swords because they felt the park was too crowded; neither was seriously wounded. For real tragedy, suicides were common in the Serpentine Lake, and Harriet Westbrook, first wife of poet Percy Shelley, drowned herself there in 1816.[41] Percy had left her for his future wife, Mary (later author of *Frankenstein*), but it's believed that Harriet killed herself over another man she thought had abandoned her—he hadn't.

Riding in Hyde Park's Rotten Row and Hyde Park Corner, circa 1900

As for proof of stolen kisses and governesses secretly meeting their heroes, I have yet to find any absolute proof that it happened in Hyde Park, but the romantic in me just knows that it did—and probably still does.

HYDE PARK HISTORY: The earliest information dates to c.1100 when the area was called the Manor of Eia (later subdivided into three, one of which was called Hyde) and belonged to the monks of Westminster Abbey. The park was founded when King Henry VIII seized it from the monks in 1536 and turned it into private deer hunting grounds. Charles I opened the park to the general public in 1637, and during the Great Plague in 1665 many common Londoners camped there to escape the crowded squalor of the medieval old City in the hopes of avoiding the disease.

In 1689, William III built "The King's Private Road" or "Route du roi," which was a wide drive that led from Kensington Palace, along the park's southern edge, toward St. James's Palace. The name eventually transformed into Rotten Row. Renowned for horseback riding by the nobility in our novels, it's still used for that today, including by the Queen's mounted guards, but carriages no longer ply it. Incidentally, it was the first road with artificial lighting in England, as the king had it lit with 300 oil lamps beginning in 1690 as a precaution against the highwaymen that frequented the park after dark. In romance fiction Rotten Row is sometimes the place of reckless races, but regardless of what's going on, it was never a place for a young lady alone.

> *A shout and the whinny of several horses on the riding path before them summoned his focus. Up ahead, through the throng of endless carriages and people on their horses, he glimpsed a woman marching along the edge of the carriage path, ignoring the shouts flung at her and the passing horses and barouches that veered to get around her. ...*
>
> *Charlotte.*
>
> *Alexander yanked his horse to a complete halt in utter disbelief. His stomach flipped. By God. What the devil was she doing? Aside from causing an uproar for walking on the path the ton very much preferred to designate for themselves, she was likely to get herself trampled.*
>
> *And though his pride urged him to simply let her march straight into the Thames for all he cared, a much larger part of him roared at him to do something. Immediately.*

To find out just how far Alexander goes to rescue the young miss, you'll have to read Delilah Marvelle's *Lord of Pleasure.*

Another romantic spot is the Serpentine, one of England's first man-made lakes. Queen Caroline, wife of George II, created the water feature in the 1730s. Events in Hyde Park included a fireworks display organized by Prinny to celebrate the end of the Napoleonic Wars in 1814 and the Great Exhibition of 1851.

NOW: Hyde Park is much the same as it was two hundred years ago. Carefree strolls along tree-lined paths still lead to the Serpentine Lake where ducks, geese, and more swans than I could count, float elegantly by or come toward you in search of a free crumb. Looking toward the horizon one might see modern buildings, but there are also tree-lined places where the view is mostly or entirely of period structures. If not for the modern clothing, you could feel like you're in Victorian times here, which still features picnicking, boating, horseback riding, and kite flying. Sadly, carriage rides are no longer allowed.

How OLDE: ♔ ♔ ♔ ♔ ♔
Price: FREE | Hours: daily 5 am to midnight | Tube: Lancaster Gate, Marble Arch, Hyde Park Corner | Map: A | www.royalparks.org.uk +44 30 0061 2000 | 350 acres west of Mayfair

◇⟲◦————————————•

INNS OF COURT ～ see Courts

KENSINGTON AND KEW PALACES ～ see Royal Palaces

◇⟲◦————————————•

LONDINIUM
43–410 AD

The Romans founded this city on the banks of the Thames, roughly the same place where the original one-mile square City of London sprang up centuries later. In 61 AD Queen Boudicca, leader of the Celtic Iceni tribe (whose lands included modern East Anglia) attacked Londinium, burning it to the ground and killing 30,000 citizens. Rebuilt by the Romans, it thrived from 100–400, becoming the largest city in Britannia with roughly 45,000 people. Today, many remnants remain of the major temples, bathhouses, and roads erected by the Romans. At the Museum of London, you can see part of the three-mile defensive wall (20 feet high and 8 feet wide), and many of the major roads of today got their start in Londinium.

Commander Aulus Plautius, who was forced to halt his Roman advance on the natives when he reached the Thames, built the very first London Bridge. Recent excavations show it's only yards from the current bridge.[42] Over 400 years, the city rose and fell, until the collapse of Roman rule and the reduction of troops led to a drastic decline, the many buildings falling to ruin. In the rise of Constantine II and constant attacks from pirates and local tribes, the Emperor Honorius refused to send more troops and told the Britons to defend themselves, bringing about the end of the Roman Londinium. By 500 AD, the city was mostly an uninhabited ruin.

Over the following Dark Ages, various tribes started returning, and its name was variously Lundenwic, Lundenburh, Caer-Lundein, depending on who was in control. Modern day London really got its start circa 600s, becoming part of the Kingdom of the East Saxons. Its king, Saebert of Essex, converted to Christianity which brought London in 604 its first Catholic bishop, St. Mellitus, thus beginning the return of Roman influence that would last until Henry VIII ended it again in 1530.[43]

And going further back, there were earlier settlements in the area dating to 1100 BC. It's the stuff of prehistoric legend (look up the giant Gogmagog from the ancient land of Albion). There's much fodder here for fantasy romance authors to delve into, although the tragic story of the 1st Century warrior woman Boudicca, who tried to kick the Romans out, is my favorite. The Museum of London is a good place to see artifacts from these earliest periods and from Londinium. They've even created a free app (iPhone/iPad only) that shows you where all these Roman sites in London are located (www.MuseumofLondon.org.uk/Resources/app/Streetmuseum-Londinium/home.html)

LONDON BRIDGE
1831–present

This late Georgian-era bridge is *not* the inspiration for the child's song, *London Bridge is Falling Down*. That English nursery rhyme probably dates to the late Middle Ages. And this actual falling down bridge has no real place here in this guide because you won't find it anywhere in London. It's included just as an oddity—which it surely is! Perhaps it should go in Ch. 7, because it does offer a free, authentic walk down a Victorian roadway right here in the USA, although passersby may stare if you go with the full period dress/parasol thing.

THEN: For a little over 130 years, London Bridge provided horses, carriages, and pedestrians with easy passage over the Thames. This view of the bridge shows 1890s London City with Fishmonger's Hall (built by George Gilbert Scott in 1833; see St. Pancras in Ch. 6), St. Magnus the Martyr Church (built by Christopher Wren in 1676), and behind it the Monument to the Great Fire (also by Wren in 1677). All three buildings are still there today but are utterly dwarfed by modern high rises.

NOW: Those structures may still be there but the bridge isn't. After 1900, the weight of horseless carriages and later modern lorries was causing this large erection to sag. The 1,000-foot bridge was sinking at a rate of one inch every eight years, and by 1924 the east side was nearly four inches lower than the west side.[44] Defying belief, the City of London succeeded in selling it to an American businessman in the 1960s for $2.5 million. Moving all 10,000 granite tons of it to America, he installed it in his planned Lake Havasu community. After the rebuilding expenses, the total cost was $9.4 million ($56 million today), and London Bridge reopened 5,400 miles away in Arizona in 1971.

"It's all quite mad—it could only happen in America. Only an American would think of investing that much in something as crazy as this," said a British newsman, as quoted in the *New York Times*.[45]

London Bridge still in London!

However, audacity paid off—the hot, dry backwater of 4,000 residents now throngs with tourists and thrives with a population of 53,000.

◇‑❧‑‑‑‑‑‑‑‑‑‑‑‑‑‑‑‑‑‑‑‑‑‑‑‑‑‑•

MAYFAIR
1686–present

THEN: What is Mayfair? And why does it figure so large in historical romance novels? Quite simply, it's just a neighborhood, but in the Georgian and Regency periods it was *the* neighborhood if you were a merchant family with upper-class aspirations and the only ton-acceptable address for an upper crust's town house, rented or owned. For the well-heeled, Mayfair also offered fashionable shopping on Bond Street and St James's Street (see Shopping in a Bygone Era here and in Ch. 8).

The neighborhood got its name from an annual 14-day May Fair (1686–1764) authorized by King James. Prior to that, this area to the west of the ancient "City of London" was a barely-inhabited boggy marsh and open fields. Within a few decades the wealthy started building houses and estates there to escape the overcrowded cesspool that was old London. It was also conveniently located near St. James's Palace. Early notable families included the Grosvenors, Rothschilds, Berkeleys, Burlingtons, and Curzons, with Grosvenor Square and Berkeley Square remaining today as nice little parks. Most of the town houses and mansions were built between 1750 and 1850, with the majority in the Georgian architectural style. The 'nobs' had everything they needed here, with Hyde Park bordering to the west and fine shopping streets near the eastern edge along Regent Street. What started as open fields was soon the center of high society during the annual Season.

> Around them, the fashionable Mayfair throng ebbed and flowed. Young bucks loitered in doorways, gossiping and eyeing the grandly dressed ladies. A dandy strolled past in a pink-powdered wig, his long walking stick extravagantly employed. ...
> "How do you find our capital, Mr. Hartley?"

...asks Elizabeth Hoyt's heroine Emeline in *To Taste Temptation*. The hero escorting her on a day-long shopping expedition responds with just one word: "*Crowded.*" Well it's even more crowded today, with nearly 10 million people packing London's streets on a daily basis. Even so, the hordes seem to disperse across the city, so it rarely feels as shockingly crowded as the streets of midtown Manhattan at lunchtime.

On a side note, this novel features a favorite trope of mine, the out-of-place American in London, but with an unusual twist, this time the transplant is a man, a very rugged untamed one who informs Emeline that he was raised in the wilderness. "Were you raised by wolves, then, Mr. Hartley?" she asks, trying to put him off. Luckily for her, he's more amused than put off.

Now: Mayfair remains a premiere address with some of the highest rents in London and many five-star luxury hotels. While there are still a few residential mansions (see Crewe and Dudley entries), most of the stand alone buildings now house embassies and hedge fund companies. The old US Embassy is located in Mayfair too, but the architecture—1960s modernist concrete—is most decidedly not of the period. However, soon you too can boast a Grosvenor Square address; well, at least for a night or two, after the old embassy reopens as a luxury hotel, but the prices are sure to be as exorbitant as everything else in Mayfair. High-end shopping remains too, with Savile Row and Burlington Arcade, but Bond Street is more about art galleries than fashion these days. High tea can be enjoyed in one of the oldest hotels in London, Brown's, and these additional historic buildings house excellent museums: Handel House[46] (1720) and the Royal Academy of Arts (17th Century Palladian).

How Olde: ⚜⚜⚜⚜⚜
Tube: None within Mayfair, but bordering are Marble Arch, Bond St, Oxford Circus, Green Park, Piccadilly Circus | **Map**: B

MARRIAGE MART ~ see Almack's

NEWGATE PRISON
1188–1902

Newgate is both the most notorious and most romantic of London's ancient prisons. As the name implies, this prison was originally located at the "new gate"—a stone portal in the ancient Roman Londonium wall. It does look almost romantic in a medieval sort of way. This was *the* first official prison, built after King Henry II took control of the legal system in his Assize of Clarendon. Henceforth, prisons would be built to house the accused until royally appointed judges determined their guilt or innocence and imposed a punishment. Like other subsequent gaols, Newgate was a cesspool of overcrowding, filth, and sickness, so squalid that supposedly the floors crunched when walked upon due to all the lice and bedbugs underfoot.[47] They were mostly unlit, too. In one year alone 22 prisoners died of "gaol fever" (typhus). So bad were the conditions that officials temporarily shut down the prison in 1419. Over its 350 years, it was expanded and renovated many times, growing in size to hold 300 inmates (c.1550) until the Great Fire of London destroyed it in 1666, after which it was completely rebuilt.

Like other prisons of the time, genders were separated but classes of criminals weren't, so that petty thieves were housed alongside rapists and murderers. Rather than wardens, the prison was managed by two elected sheriffs, who in turn handed over the reins to private "keepers" for a fee. These keepers were the ones who charged prisoners for "services," and it was one of the most lucrative positions in London. While there were official, legal fees for some services, lacking direct oversight, the keepers were motivated to charge as much as they could for virtually anything they could think of, right down to taking money to *not* torture someone. Repeated attempts at reforming the system had little effect, and Newgate was considered one of the worst places to be incarcerated.

This did not improve with the construction of a new prison completed in 1775. Gone was the romantic exterior, and the inside was purposefully bad. It featured a new French design, actually called "Architecture Terrible" (*say it with French accent to sound fancier*). On purpose, the prison was dark, drab, and nearly windowless, with the goal of instilling terror in citizens so they would be discouraged from committing crimes.

In a time when women were still considered the property of their husbands, it was women's libbers who succeeded in achieving real prison reform. Concerned with the treatment of women and the children living in Newgate, Elizabeth Fry successfully presented evidence to the House of Commons in 1818 and

◇❀◟

Newgate Prison ~ Such a romantic building for such a dreadful place.

improvements were made. She was the first woman ever to present evidence in Parliament, and was recognized for her "angel of prisons" work on a £5 Bank of England note from 2001–2016. American Connection: At age 18, Elizabeth was deeply moved by the preaching of American Quaker William Savery, which led to her interest in helping the poor and prisoners.[48]

Author Daniel Defoe gives us a glimpse into the nightmare that was Newgate with his protagonist *Moll Flanders* (1722), a heroine who was born in the prison and later incarcerated there for thievery.

> ... 'tis impossible to describe the terror of my mind, when I was first brought in, and when I looked around upon all the horrors of that dismal place. I looked on myself as lost, and that I had nothing to think of but of going out of the world, and that with the utmost infamy: the hellish noise, the roaring, swearing, and clamour, the stench and nastiness, and all the dreadful crowd of afflicting things that I saw there, joined together to make the place seem an emblem of hell itself, and a kind of an entrance into it.

These are Moll's reflections, but given that Defoe, himself, was twice imprisoned in Newgate—accused of slander by his political opponents—I imagine this passage represents his feelings as well upon entering that hellish place.

Charles Dickens used Newgate in *Oliver Twist* and five other works, and American author Louis L'Amour has his hero escape from it in *To the Far Blue Mountains*. For historical romance fans, American author Kathleen Winsor's heroine Amber does time in Newgate too.

Among the famous non-fictitious inmates is John Bambridge (see Fleet Prison); William Kidd, a.k.a. the infamous pirate Captain Kidd; and Giacomo Casanova—yes, *that* Casanova, the romantic lover of women...many *many* women!

Then there was the well-mannered, polite thief James MacLaine, known as the "Gentleman Highwayman," who even wrote anonymous letters of apology to some of his victims. Sounds like a romance hero to me, especially given that after the rather fine-looking James was caught, merely six months into his career (along with his accomplice William Plunkett), courteously robbing from the rich to give to the poor (himself), polite society rallied to his side. Weeping aristocratic women gave him gold, an estimated 3,000 fashionable sympathizers visited him at Newgate, and petitions seeking clemency were signed aplenty. The only downside to this roguish tale being that he was promptly sentenced and hung on October 3, 1750, just 3 months after he was captured.[49] Perhaps this is more farce than tragedy, because his partner escaped with the money and his life—never to be heard from again (although some believe he's the same Colonel William Plunkett who founded Plunketts Creek, Pennsylvania, before dying of very old age in 1791).

Another romantic saga is that of young Mary Wade, who was convicted in 1789 of stealing a frock, cap, and tippet (early form of scarf, often fur, but in this case linen). Only 11 years old, she was sentenced to execution. Then, as luck would have it, King George III recovered from his madness—at least temporarily—and to celebrate, all women condemned to death were granted a stay of execution. Mary was then incarcerated in Newgate until she was transported to Australia in June 1789, becoming the youngest female convict ever to be deported. She remains renowned in her new country for almost single-handedly—or single womb-edly, I guess—settling Australia with a record 300-plus living descendants at the time of her death at age 82. Revered today as a "founding mother," her progeny are estimated in the tens of thousands, including one former PM.[50] She is 33 degrees of separation from Kevin Bacon and 27 from Queen Elizabeth II.[51]

From 1783 to 1868, Newgate was the locale for all London public executions, and all British executioners were trained there. The prison was demolished in 1904, and today the Central Criminal Court (Old Bailey) is located on the site. However, behind the Old Bailey, down a gloomy dark lane, at the back of Amen Court, there is one surviving two-story section of old prison wall. Find a Latin plaque with crossed swords on the building next door and you've found what's left of Newgate. However, I should warn you to watch out for the ghost of the Black Dog who lives in a tiny passage on the other side of the wall known from prison days as "Deadman's Walk" because it led the way for prisoners to their execution. Supposedly, the slithering, slavering, dark spirit still patrols the wall looking for revenge. You'll recognize him by the hideous stench (Google it...).

For more macabre fun, kitty-corner from the Old Bailey is the St. Sepulchre-Without-Newgate Church (meaning outside the wall). Inside on display is the Newgate Execution hand-bell. Rung for more than two centuries on the night before executions, the doomed were serenaded thus:

All you that in the condemned hole do lie,
Prepare you for tomorrow you shall die;
Watch all and pray: the hour is drawing near

That you before the Almighty must appear;
Examine well yourselves in time repent,
That you may not to eternal flames be sent.
And when St Sepulchre's Bell in the morning tolls
The Lord above have mercy on your soul.

The infamous
Newgate Execution Bell
on display at St. Sepulchre

AMERICAN CONNECTION: Captain John Smith, founder of Jamestown and saved by Pocahontas, was a member of St. Sepulchre's and was buried on the grounds in 1631. Although his precise location was lost in the Great Fire, he is commemorated with a stained-glass window in the south wall.

ℋOW OLDE ST. SEPULCHRE'S: ♟♟♟♟♟
~ *haunted wall fragment & executioner's bell*
Price: FREE | **Hours**: see website | **Tube**: St. Paul's | **Map**: D
www.StSepulchres.org | Holborn Viaduct & Amen Court

OLD BAILEY ~ see Courts

OLD GLOBE ~ see Globe

OLD VIC OR THE VICTORIAN THEATRE
~ see Theaters in Ch. 7

PICKERING PLACE
1734–present [52]

THEN: Now the parish of St. James, this ancient site was first a medieval leper colony for maidens until 1450, then becoming a convent. King Henry VIII seized control of the area c.1530 and built St. James's Palace as his country hunting-lodge—London being a much smaller city to the east back then. This exact location once housed Henry's royal tennis courts. Nearly 200 years later, James Pickering, son of the founder of Berry Brothers and Rudd wine merchants (Ch. 8), built a tiny little square here consisting of only four town houses behind their thriving business. There's even a brief American Connection commemorated by a plaque: the Embassy of the Republic of Texas was housed in rooms at Pickering Place, rented from Berry Bros., c.1840s until the US annexed Texas in 1845.

But what makes Pickering Place historically notable, beside its diminutiveness? Tucked out of sight and situated as it was so near gentlemen's clubs such as White's and Boodle's, it quickly became infamous for such disreputable activities as dog fighting, bear baiting, bare-knuckle boxing, and cockfighting. Georgette Heyer's *Regency Buck* recognizes this notoriety when the heroine Judith Taverner worries that her brother is frequenting a "house off St. James's Street." The hero of the story, Lord Worth, acknowledges he knows of the gaming hell located at No. 5 Pickering Place, but he's untroubled by her concerns. While no "official" clubs resided there, one can assume considerable gambling took place within these homes given the goings on outside in the little courtyard.

Perhaps most importantly, the secluded privacy in the heart of the city was ideal for many clandestine and illegal duels. Imagine a handsome Regency rogue emerging from White's at dawn, disheveled and slightly tipsy, to answer a challenge to his lady's honor in this tiny courtyard, the tight town houses blocking the sunlight and shrouding the participants in near darkness, the pacing footsteps clicking on flagstones, the solitary counting of a second before the sharp report of two pistols breaks the quiet of the early morning. In fact, it is believed the last public duels in London took place here: a swordfight to the death in the late 1700s and a pistol fight in the mid 1800s.

NOW: Pickering Place is London's smallest public square, and it remains almost exactly as it was when built in 1734 with gas lights, a stone sundial (now tipping slightly), and the four original Georgian town houses—three still owned by Berry Bros. Look for the oak paneled tunnel next to the wine store and take a walk into the past. Once inside take a moment to imagine the countless real-life heroes and heroines that have trodden these ancient stones, everyone from Lord Byron and Beau Brummell to rakehells to common street doxies. And now you.

If you go in the summertime, some of the tiny square now holds patio seating for Boulestin restaurant, so you can while away an afternoon there in the shadow of history. ⟨P⟩

𝓗ow Olde: ⚜⚜⚜⚜⚜
Hours: public space open 24/7 but sometimes gate locked
Website: www.Boulestin.com | **Tube**: Green Park | 3 St James's Place

---

PRISONS, HISTORIC AND INFAMOUS
1100–1952

Today only one former prison structure remains intact—the Tower of London—but in addition to the famous ones—Newgate and Fleet—there were at least fifteen more in central London.[53] With more than 300 offences carrying the death penalty, it didn't take much to land oneself in prison. Angering the King or high-level clergy or voicing dissent could do it. Finding oneself in debt was, perhaps, the most common. As with the Tower, some of these structures had multiple functions. Purpose-built prisons then were more like jails today where one waited until the trial, rather than places for serving out a sentence, since most convictions ended in execution. After the 1620s, penal colonies became the most common sentence, considered more humane than execution for those convicted of minor crimes (such as cutting down a tree).[54]

As noted earlier, these prisons were run for-profit with the crown handing down "letters patent" to wardens to run them. The wardens made their money by providing room and board for the inmates, although the payer for these services was not the state but rather the prisoners themselves. Extortion was the name of the game with fees, legal or not, for everything from having a bed (hay with a dirty cover) to coal for heat to not getting shackled. Inmates were docked for entering cases in the log and for noting their dismissal—*would you even be let out if you couldn't pay the dismissal fee?* Or, as noted, they could actually live outside the prison.

The conditions were atrocious, but for the wealthy, one might live in moderate comfort with furniture, a roaring fire, and even gourmet food. Many prisons were divided into the "Commons" (i.e. destitute; often encouraged to beg through the prison bars) and the "Masters" (those with funds to pay off the gaolers). Most were "open" prisons where different categories of offenders were mixed together and visitors could enter, bringing gifts and food. The wardens went further than extortion, sometimes opening prisoners' mail and stealing the funds sent by relatives to help the inmate. Beatings and bribery were common. The conditions were so deplorable that even in the age of Bedlam, then thought proper health care, the authorities sometimes ordered inquiries into the state of the prisons.

Most ironic, was the use of prisons for holding people in debt, although the purpose was not punishment of the debtor but security for the creditors, since fleeing the country was a common way out for the noble in debt. For even the smallest amount, a person could be locked up and then be unable to work to pay off the creditor while at the same time running up more debt for the room and board he was charged while locked inside. As a result, the only prisoners who could resolve this dilemma either had rich relatives or found lucrative work within the prisons (writing *Fanny Hill* or marrying people as at The Fleet). Later, accepting transportation to a penal colony and agreeing to work for 7–14 years to pay off the debt, prison fees, and sailing costs became another avenue to freedom. The paradox was not lost on many inmates who wrote stories or news articles about the irony of this catch–22 situation. Perhaps the worst aspect of this practice was that once the family breadwinner was locked up it left the rest of the family destitute, and as a result they often moved into the prisons with him and their children ended up being raised inside these filthy environments.

Each of these ancient prisons met their end either because local governments abolished them or because mobs tore them down. The last medieval gaol was also the longest operating: the Tower of London, which housed its first inmate in 1106 and its last, the Kray twins, in 1952. Arrested for failure to report for national service, they were taken there because that's where their military unit's barracks were. See separate listings for the Tower, Fleet, and Newgate, but here are some other notables:

MARSHALSEA: (1294–1842 | primarily debtors) Charles Dickens famously wrote about the horrible conditions in *Little Dorrit* after his father spent time inside for owing 40 pounds. One wall and two original gate arches still exist in the yard next to St. George the Martyr Church (**Tube**: Borough).

BRIDEWELL: (1553–1855 | mostly vagrants, homeless children, unruly women) Located at the intersection of the Thames and Fleet rivers, it was a prison, a hospital, and a charitable institution that apprenticed orphans into trade. A model prison in some respects, it offered the first ever medical care for inmates. Sometimes the poor would even seek incarceration in order to receive the free services. But it wasn't perfect—public viewing of half-naked women being birch-flogged was so popular that a gallery was built to house the audience, who could at times bribe the gaoler to strip and whip the girl's buttocks rather than their backs. Prior to serving as a prison, it was Bridewell Palace (built 1510) and home to King Henry VIII, so it's unfortunate that the structure was demolished in 1863. The former entrance, a rebuilt gatehouse (c.1805) and commemorative plaque are all that remains at 14 New Bridge Street (**Tube**: Blackfriars).[55]

CLERKENWELL: (1616–1890 | detention) As many as 10,000 people passed through its gates annually. Although demolished in 1890, underground tunnels built in 1844 and used as an air-raid shelter during the WWII Blitz can be visited from Clerkenwell Close, behind St. James Church (**Tube**: Farringdon, Angel).

KING'S BENCH: (1373–1877 | debtors) The Shangri-La of prisons, it was considered "the most desirable place of incarceration in London" notes *The London Encyclopaedia*, and its "courtyard thronged with life: there were tailors, barbers, hatters, piano makers" [*piano makers... really?*], along with 30 gin shops, and even a cook for the rich prisoners.[56] (*I could not confirm the use of pianos within this prison.*) Living outside the prison "at liberty" was also allowed here. Among notable inmates was Emma, Lady Hamilton, famous for her adulterous, passionate love affair with naval hero Lord Horatio Nelson. After he was mortally wounded at the Battle of Trafalgar, her storied rise from daughter of a blacksmith to maid to Lady and friend to a Queen (Maria Carolina of Naples) ended badly, including time in King's Bench for truly immense debt before later dying destitute in Calais. Nothing remains today of this prison, demolished in 1880 and immortalized by Dickens in *David Copperfield* (**Tube**: Borough).

THE CLINK: (1151–1780 | prostitutes, religious prisoners, debtors) This was a small prison owned by the Bishop of Winchester and connected to Winchester Palace (modern Southwark). Its main contribution was giving the world a nickname for prisons: "Put him in the clink." Today there's a small commercial museum located at the site, which contains an original wall. It gets mixed reviews but if you're in the area... (www.Clink.co.uk) The nearby Anchor pub is historic, charming, sometimes very crowded, and also has a room dedicated to the Clink Prison (**Tube**: London Bridge).

Ranelagh Gardens
1742–1803

THEN: Located in Chelsea, Ranelagh was created to compete with Vauxhall, and compete they did! Considered more fashionable, modern, and respectable than the by then 80-year-old Vauxhall, Ranelagh charged more than double the admission at two shillings and sixpence—to keep the riffraff out.

These two gardens strived to outdo each other in the refreshments, décor, and especially the music. While Vauxhall served the famous paper-thin slices of ham to go with plenty of hard spirits, Ranelagh went proper with tea, coffee, and scones. Decorations were grand and exotic at both, but Ranelagh went big with an immense, three-story rotunda—like a covered Roman amphitheater—where patrons could avoid the heat of the summer or the cold of winter.

They competed also in lights, first oil, then gas, used to turn a dark park into a decorated fairyland. Vauxhall holds the record for sheer numbers, while Ranelagh focused particularly on the glorious illumination of its pavilions, especially the rotunda that boasted 2,080 lights, a fourth of which lit eighteen huge, ornate chandeliers unlike anything seen before.[57]

Bringing orchestral music to the masses (or at least anyone that could afford the admission) was an important contribution to society. While Vauxhall gets credit for building the world's first purpose-built music hall, Ranelagh's later rococo rotunda included a chimney and fireplaces so concerts could continue in winter. There were no rows of seats like modern concert venues, and from paintings it appears patrons stood or strolled during the recitals.

These gardens provided additional avenues of income for composers of the time. George Frideric Handel reigned at Vauxhall, premiering many of his works there. His 1749 *Music for the Royal Fireworks*—commissioned by King George II—was offered as a dress rehearsal (*sans* fireworks) to an estimated 12,000 people.[58] Other noted composers there included Arne and Worgan. Ranelagh scores a special footnote in musical history by having presented the nine-year-old virtuoso pianist, Wolfgang Amadeus Mozart, performing his own compositions in 1765.

For a while Ranelagh reigned supreme—as Horace Walpole famously wrote, "Nobody goes anywhere else; everybody goes there. It has totally beat Vauxhall... You can't set your foot without treading on a Prince, or Duke of Cumberland."

Romance author Lynne Connolly, in her *Temptation Has Green Eyes*, illustrates this with fun detail:

> *Julius had acquired a booth by the Octagon, where they could watch the world go by, eat an elegant supper, and listen to the orchestra, who tonight were defiantly playing Italian music. Defiantly, because Ranelagh's main rival, Vauxhall, was a strong supporter of Handel's music.*
>
> *Due to the huge chandelier above, one of the marvels of London, and the lights in the booths, the light was almost as bright as day in this part of the Gardens. People promenaded, watching each other with avid or curious eyes, and Sophia drank in the vista from her new perspective of one of the highest in the Land. Or rather, the wife of one of them....*
>
> *If the Pretender ever set foot on England's shores, as rumor had it he did, he'd come here rather than Vauxhall. Probably feel quite at home.*

While Ranelagh's respectability initially helped increase attendance, it conversely contributed, in part, to its decline, with the younger crowd finding it too tame and seeking more adventure at Vauxhall. Ranelagh closed in 1803 and its amazing rotunda was demolished in 1805. (For more information on "pleasure gardens" see Vauxhall entry.)

NOW: Part of the grounds of the Chelsea Royal Hospital, Ranelagh Gardens today consist of pleasant shaded walks and grass. It hosts the world famous Chelsea Flower Show each May. Daily walking tours of the Hospital and Gardens can be booked in advance for groups of 10+. There's also a free museum and a coffee shop, complete with free WiFi and views of the gardens. It's the perfect place for a quick afternoon tea.

*H*OW OLDE: 🏛🏛🏛🏛🏛 ~ *pleasant, but nothing like the original*
Price: Park & Hospital Museum FREE; tours £12
Park Hours: Daily M-Sat 10am; Sun 2pm | Closes at sunset | Closed Dec 25 and during Chelsea Flower Show | Royal Hospital Road
Museum Hours: M-F 10am–4pm | **Tube**: Sloane Sq., Victoria St
www.chelsea-pensioners.co.uk | +44 20 7881 5493

ROTTEN ROW ∾ see Hyde Park

ROYAL COURTS OF JUSTICE ∾ see Courts

ROYAL OPERA HOUSE AND ROYAL HAYMARKET
∾ see Theaters in Ch. 7

ROYAL PALACES
Circa 1100-present

Look for these palaces with their own listing: Buckingham, Hampton Court,* St. James's, Banqueting House,* Windsor, and, of course, the Tower of London.* The Historic Royal Palaces (HRP), a charitable tust, operates all the starred ones, plus Kensington and Kew, described here.

Hillsborough Castle in Northern Ireland, also part of the starred collection, is too far away to be listed here. However, there's an interesting US connection: The aristocratic Hill family originally owned it, and son Wills Hill, the Earl of Hillsborough, was Secretary of the American Colonies during the early 1770s. His heavy-handed, oppressive approach to the Colonists' concerns fueled American unrest. Had he managed the task more successfully, it's possible the American Revolution might never have transpired—we might today be more like a southern Canada.

SAVINGS TIP: The HRP membership program is a good value if you plan to visit multiple palaces. See Museum Quick Guide, Ch. 4.

KENSINGTON PALACE: (1605-present) Built as Nottingham House, it was purchased for £20,000 and expanded by King William III and Queen Mary II in 1689. William needed to get away from the dank, damp air at Whitehall because of his asthma. They moved the court there and enjoyed the fresh air for a brief while. Unfortunately sickness and tragedy followed. Mary died of smallpox there at age 32 (1694), and William fell from his horse while riding at Hampton Court but insisted on returning to Kensington where he lay ill for two weeks before dying at age 51 (1702). Later, Queen Anne and her husband Prince George of Denmark lived there, and she built an Orangery, which can be visited today. King George I vastly rebuilt Kensington, but his successor, George II, was the one who got to enjoy it. He was the last monarch to make it his seat of power, and afterwards it again fell into disrepair.

Even so, Princess Victoria was born at Kensington Palace in 1819, and it was there, asleep in her bed at age 18, where she was awoken early on June 20, 1837, to learn she was now Queen of England. Eventually, the palace was in such bad shape that it faced demolition. It was only Queen Victoria's insistence that "while she lived, the palace in which she was born should not be destroyed" that stopped its demise. Parliament agreed to restore the state apartments if they would be opened to the public, ultimately resulting in its contin- ued dual purpose, both public museum and royal home.

Diana, Princess of Wales lived there for 16 years following her divorce. Recently, the Duke and Duchess of Cambridge lived there as newly-weds and now have returned to make it their permanent home with their two children, Prince George and Princess Charlotte. They'll be living in the modest sounding Apartment 1A, but make no mistake this is no small London flat, but rather an entire floor of the palace. Unlike other residences that aren't open when the nobility are residing there, this one is open year round, but don't expect to catch a glimpse of the family. They've got separate gardens and don't use the tourist entrance either.

This palace often has special exhibits, such as the 2017 "Diana: Her Fashion Story" which can result in entire days being sold out (check website). Entrance fee includes palace, gardens, and special exhibitions. This palace felt more touristy, with few furnishings and some odd displays, but the exhibitions were interesting. **TIP:** For mobility issues, there is Liberty Drives that offers free electric buggy tours around the 760-acre park in the summer (see 'Getting here' webpage for more information). Lovely Kensington Gardens is free to enter, as is the elegant 1704 Orangery, which is a fine dining restaurant (Afternoon Tea is £60 for 2; reservations advised).

How OLDE: 🌸🌸🌸🌸🌸
～ *100% authentic but doesn't feel like it*
Price: varies by time of year, roughly £15 excluding voluntary donation | Hours: Daily Winter 10am–4pm, Summer 10am–6pm
Closed Dec 24-26 | Special closures are noted on website
Tube: High St Kensington, Queensway, Notting Hill Gate; all 10-20 min walk | +44 20 3166 6000 | www.Hrp.org.uk/kensington-palace
Kensington Gardens, London

KEW PALACE: (1631–present) Originally a country retreat for a wealthy merchant family, the Fortreys, this palace has seen many uses, from royal school house, to royal residence, to royal incarceration for mental illness. It was there in the White House, that mad King George III was "recuperated" with straitjackets, leeching, and emetics for what many now believe was a hereditary blood disorder, porphyria. His Queen ended up dying there—on her way to Windsor Castle she became seriously ill with dropsy and ended up staying there for several months, before dying in November 1818. For nearly 100 years this small palace was ignored until Queen Victoria opened it to the public in 1898. Recently, it underwent a major ten-year restoration, and reopened to much pomp in 2006. Queen Elizabeth II even celebrated her 80th Birthday there. It was the first time in 200 years that a monarch had dined there.

The palace resides inside Kew Royal Botanic Gardens, which are not free and require a separate ticket. The extensive, lovely gardens include glass arboretums, an aquatic garden, a gallery. The Palace has restored apartments with furnishings. This excursion will probably appeal most to those especially interested in botany.

How OLDE: ❦❦❦❦❦

Price: £15 for garden entrance; discounts online | Historic Palace memberships gets a 10% discount | **Hours**: Palace open seasonally, late Mar-Sept | Gardens 10am-dusk | Closed Dec 24-25
Tube: Kew Gardens | Kew Palace: www.Hrp.org.uk/kew-palace Richmond Kew Gardens: www.Kew.org | +44 20 3166 6000

◇❦❧————————————•

SADLER'S WELLS ∼ see Theaters in Ch. 7

SELFRIDGES DEPARTMENT STORE ∼ see Ch. 8

◇❦❧————————————•

SHOPPING IN A BYGONE ERA

Georgian–present

THEN: One fun aspect of historical romance novels is the shopping or dressmaking needed to prepare the heroine for her debut at Almack's or a ball. Many of the nobility—and the characters in our beloved novels—never had to leave the convenience of their own boudoir to acquire a wardrobe for The Season, with the modiste bringing staff and fabric to her. But other young ladies enjoyed chaperoned trips to Bond Street. For the heroes, however, such chaperoning is often considered a fate worse than being "tarred and feathered," as one hero muses when his mother requests he accompany his sister to Bond Street. Although one must assume that this young buck has never actually experienced a feathered tarring. Still, Richard believes shopping a very dangerous business.

> *...Bond Street was a hornet's nest of eligible debutantes and their marriage-minded mothers—even more so than a ballroom, where they tended to be on their best behavior. If a gentleman wasn't careful, he could be easily be trapped. He loved women and their company, but his tastes ran toward the more sophisticated, unruinable variety. "I'll make you a compromise. I will purchase every green ribbon on the whole street if I may go alone. Clearly I am not to get any sleep this morning, so I would rather go before the fashionable hour, if you don't mind."*

As it turns out Richard is rewarded for his great sacrifice by meeting his future love, even if things don't go smoothly at first...and you'll want to read Erin Knightley's *A Taste for Scandal* to find out just what a mess he makes of it.

Another popular trope is the poor Cinderella heroine gazing longingly at something in a shop window, perhaps a confection of feathers and flowers in a hat shop—or, more accurately, women's chapeaux would be purchased in a *millinery*. Regardless, it's always some frivolity she can't afford but desperately desires—and lo and behold the hero saves the day, buying the coveted item as a surprise.

And last but not least, many wonderful stories feature the demimonde being dressed by their paramours and required to enter and depart via back doors to avoid meeting any of the "quality."

Is any of this true? Did Regency and Victorian ladies really shop like this?

The answer, of course, is yes they did!

Not only that, but you can, too, in some of the very same shops on your trip to London—no chaperone required. Prices at these grand dames of yore are high, but window-shopping remains as free today as it was back then. And if you're dressed appropriately—don't want to stand out too obviously next to the establishment's well-heeled clientele—and behave quietly, you'll be welcomed inside to browse like anyone else. I did and enjoyed every minute of it.

ROYAL WARRANTS: Most of these establishments hold them. This custom, which denotes royal patronage, began with Royal Charters to trade guilds—the first granted by Henry II in 1155—and by the 15th Century this practice had evolved to The Royal Warrants of Appointment. Today, they remain highly prized, demonstrating that the establishment sells to the current royals and that they offer the highest "service, quality, and excellence." There are currently about 800 warrant holders. Look for them displayed proudly on the wall.

NOW: The stores included in Ch. 8 all served the Regency and Victorian gentry, and visiting them is a real step back in time—if one overlooks such things as electronic cash registers and elevators. Unfortunately, however, they also come with modern prices. Stores are grouped by neighborhood under these headings: Ye Olde Department Stores, Inns of Justice, Piccadilly Shoppes, St. James's Shoppes.

◇❧──────────────•

ST. GEORGE'S, HANOVER SQUARE
1724–present

THEN: A favorite marriage venue of the beau monde, both real and fictional, this beautiful little gem of a church has been the religious home of the elite since 1724. Named after St. George, a Roman soldier turned Christian martyr and patron saint of England, this church was built when exclusive Mayfair was brand new. The block was named Hanover Square to honor the Hanoverian royalty then in charge.

John James, a pupil of famous architect Sir Christopher Wren, designed it. While the facade is a bit staid, with its square lines of gray stone, the interior of the small church is a warm mix of dark-wood pews, white walls with gold-leaf decoration, rich red carpet, and colorful stained glass windows. Very classical and bright. Be sure to look at the altarpiece painted by William Kent. Most surprising, the architect built it on a modest £10,000 budget (merely $2 million today). Among the early parishioners were King George II and George Frideric Handel.

The record year for St. George's weddings was 1816, with 1,063. One infamous nuptial was the Duke of Kingston (see Tattersalls listing) who married Elizabeth Chudleigh by special license, but it proved bigamous since she was already secretly married. Although convicted of bigamy, Elizabeth lived the rest of her life in exile as the wealthy Duchess of Kingston while legally she was always the Countess of Bristol. *Ah to have such troubles!*

Another seemingly innocuous marriage—recorded in 1793 in the registry between an Augutus Frederick and an Augusta Murray— proved equally infamous when it was discovered that the groom was really Prince Frederick, acting without the permission of his father, King George III, thereby violating the Royal Marriages Act of 1772. While the court annulled their marriage and their 2 children became illegitimate, the devoted hubby continued living with Lady Augusta against his dad's wishes. In the end, all it took to get Fred to separate from her was parliament granting him £12,000 and the King creating him Earl of Inverness, Baron Arklow, and a Knight of the Garter all in one day, November 27, 1801.

AMERICAN CONNECTION: In 1886, American Teddy Roosevelt married his future first lady at St. George's while a guest at Brown's Hotel. That made it fashionable to other Yanks, leading to the high society weddings of Lulu Pfizer (daughter to the founder of the large pharmaceutical fortune), Elizabeth Berlin (daughter of the famed songwriter), and more. Also, during WWII, US servicemen based nearby often worshipped there. While St. George's references pop up all over in romance novels, perhaps the most famous fictional nuptial there was that of Alfred Doolittle— remember the famous ditty "Get Me to the Church on Time" from *My Fair Lady.*

NOW: The Grade I structure recently underwent major refurbishment that, at £2.5 million, cost more than it did to build it. Our American Connection continues with the 2012 commissioning of a new pipe organ from a US manufacturer in Ooltewah, Tennessee. It's the first American-built organ ever installed in a London church. Today, St. George's remains a working church—guests may attend services or visit quietly at other times. The Sunday Eucharist features their renowned choir, and frequent public classical concerts are offered by church partners, London Handel Festival, the Royal College of Music, and Music in Mayfair.

How OLDE: 🧑🧑🧑🧑🧑
Price: visiting & attending services FREE | However donations toward the restoration are appreciated | Concerts vary from FREE to £10-£45 | **Hours**: Sun 8am–12noon; M-F 8am–4pm (Wed till 6pm) Closed Sat | **Tube**: Oxford Circus, Bond St, Piccadilly Circus, Green Park | **Map**: B | www.StGeorgesHanoverSquare.org verger@stgeorgeshanoversquare.org +44 20 7629 0874 | 2A Mill St, Mayfair

◇-℮✄-------------------------------------•

St. James's Palace
1536–present

This medieval palace was a surprise to me at first glance, sitting at the end of the short St. James's Street. It's utterly charming—like a mismatched fairytale castle plopped down in the middle of a modern city, two fluffy-hatted guards standing at attention on either side of the arched entrance. But what I hadn't expected from the pictures is how small it seems once one is actually standing in front of it. While smaller, the chambers are no less grand—the Throne Room "bedazzled" in gold leaf, crimson carpets and drapes, and sitting under a magnificent tasseled canopy on a dais is an impressive chair fit for a king...or queen. However, since tours aren't given, this I've seen only in photos.

Part of what makes this palace so quaint-looking, and fairly unique among London architecture, is the use of red bricks for construction, much of it original, in the Tudor architectural style. Not considered valuable today, in the 1500s it was extremely costly, modern, and luxurious.

King Henry VIII built it between 1531–1536 after demolishing the old Hospital of St. James. Dedicated to Saint James the Less, one of the original 12 apostles, it was a "Hospital for Leprous Women," maidens only, and he basically evicted them all so that he could make "a faire parke for his greater comoditie and pleasure."[59] Outside the walls of the original City of London, it served as his country lodge, the neighboring parkland his hunting grounds. It was also built to be his love nest with Anne Boleyn, and a fireplace within still bears the intertwined initials, H and A—although the other side of the hearth must have been finished after the head-chopping because it has only an H.

Notable events here include Henry's daughter, Queen Mary I, signing the treaty that surrendered Calais to the French in 1558. This French land, ruled by England for 150 years, was retaken in a week-long battle, Mary's forces reduced and delayed by a serious influenza epidemic in England. Its loss was to haunt her still on her deathbed; she's purported to have said, "Calais would be found engraved on her heart."[60] It was from here that Queen Elizabeth I set out in silver armor and white velvet upon a white horse to address her troops east of London, during the threat of Spanish invasion, her remarkable Amazonian presence emboldening the soldiers.

Notable life events at St. James's Palace include royal births: 4 monarchs and 1 pretender (James Francis Edward Stuart, son of the deposed James II). Notable deaths: Queen Mary I (her heart is buried inside the building, but did anyone look to see if Calais was inscribed?) and Henry VII's illegitimate son Henry Fitzroy.

Following the Palace of Whitehall's destruction by fire, all monarchs used St. James's as their residence for part of the year until Buckingham Palace was finished. Since then, no further monarchs lived here; however, Queen Victoria married Prince Albert in the Chapel Royal in 1840. It is still the home of the Court of Queen Elizabeth II, which doesn't mean these ladies live there, rather they hold events and perhaps have staff there. And most recently, in 2013, baby Prince George was christened within the royal family chapel.

NOW: It's worth a visit to admire the architecture from the outside. However, if that isn't enough, you can always live there. *Seriously, you can!* For the first time in history, the monarchy is renting out two flats in St. James's Palace, although the annual rent is a bit steep—£250,000 ($310,000) annually payable to the The Queen.[61] Of course, then you'll have to deal with the neighbors—Prince Charles and his wife, plus the Princesses Beatrice and Eugenie. *Yikes!*

For the rest of us, we normal folk can't set foot inside, as this is one of the few royal palaces that are not open to the public. You can, however, watch the opening part of the Changing of the Guard here. Arrive early to watch the Queen's Guard line up in formation before marching down The Mall to the gates of Buckingham Palace (see Ch. 7 for dates/times).

◇─❧──────────────────────●

TATTERSALLS
1766–present

THEN: Many a romance novel makes mention of Tattersalls, and some even have the heroine watching races there. But I never got much of a sense of what the place is like—was it rugged and rough or elegantly refined?

Richard Tattersall founded the auction house with the substantial savings he'd acquired over 20 years of service to the 2nd Duke of Kingston, most of it as his stud groom, where he learned the trade. Tattersalls original location was on Hyde Park Corner, then the outskirts of London. Besides having the Duke's patronage, Tattersalls straightforward honesty and businesslike conduct quickly established his reputation as a quality dealer of horseflesh. He also, shrewdly, reserved two rooms at his premises for the Jockey Club (an elite social club dedicated to horse racing) where soon "all betting upon the turf was regulated."[62]

He numbered among his clients and friends the Prince of Wales and prominent members of the Whig party, and handled sales and horse purchases for Prinny, his former employer Kingston, and even the King of France and the Dauphin. He also married well—the granddaughter of the 12th Baron Somerville—and is buried at St. George's, Hanover Square.

The original Tattersalls was located on land that is today the back of the Lanesborough Hotel, but when his 99-year lease on the property ended, his great-grandson moved the business to a much bigger, more impressive building in nearby Knightsbridge in 1865. With the death of the last descendant in 1942, the business passed to partners, and eventually was moved in 1965 to Newmarket, center of British thoroughbred racing.

NOW: Tattersalls claims to be the oldest bloodstock auctioneer in the world (more than 250 years in continuous operation), and today auctions 10,000 thoroughbred horses annually in just 15 sales at either the Newmarket headquarters 60 miles north of London or at Fairyhouse, outside Dublin. Buyers come from more than 50 countries, but only those with deep pockets need apply—think the royal families of Dubai and Qatar. The top "lot" in the most recent sale went for 500,000 guineas. *Yes, guineas.* By tradition, all sales are still conducted in this coin that was withdrawn in the Great Recoinage of 1816. The value attributed is

The original Tattersalls in 1842 . . .

1gn=£1.05, so 500,000gns equals £525,000—that's about $654,000 US for a horse. Also by tradition, the extra 5 pence per pound is the auctioneer's commission—in this case £25,000, or about $30,000. Not bad for a few minute's work. **Fun Fact** ∿ if you had an actual guinea coin in your possession, it would be worth about $300 due to the roughly 8.3grams of 22 carat gold in it.

In truth, most of the horses do not sell for this kind of money. Many "lots" can be had for as low as 800gns ($1,000), but like buying an old "pile" one must not forget about upkeep and maintenance. No small thing, unless you already happen to own a ranch. However, if one thinks about it in Regency terms, horseflesh was almost the only available means of transport (excepting boats), and certainly no car can be had for that price, even if you add in the cost of maintaining the animal for a year.

One can visit Tattersalls on sale days by pre-registering to buy. Or, behind-the-scenes tours can be had through Discover Newmarket that include several venues, lunch, and a tour of Tattersalls (£85pp, about 11 dates annually, www.DiscoverNewmarket.co.uk). Other tours for £36 are offered through the National Heritage Centre for Horseracing & Sporting Art, a museum (www.PalaceHouseNewmarket.co.uk). For more fun, go during Newmarket Open Weekend in September, and £30 gets you tours of many venues, including Tattersalls and the Jockey

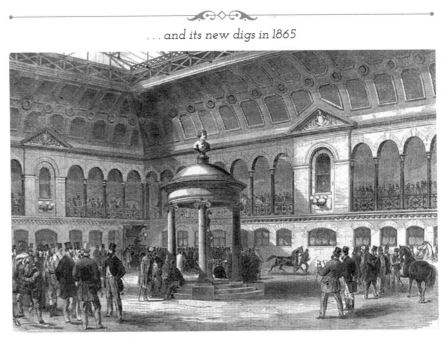

. . . and its new digs in 1865

Club, plus races, trainer talks, and a regional food festival. Even better, the £50,000 proceeds go to charity (www.NewmarketOpenWeekend. co.uk). If you do find your way there, look for the Palladium of Tattersalls in the yard. This famous rotunda (pictured on pages 96-97) was twice moved from its original location. Built by the founder to honor his friend George IV, it still has the original bust of the King on top and the fox underneath, signifying the hunt.

How OLDE: ♞♞♟♟♟
~ *the history's real but the place is 20th Century*
www.Tattersalls.com | +44 16 3866 5931
Terrace House, Newmarket, Suffolk CB89BT

◇-❧-⟋⟋------------------•

THEATERS ~ see list of period venues in Ch. 7

◇-❧-⟋⟋------------------•

TOWER OF LONDON
Circa 1100–present

This is a world-famous tourist sight and worthy of its own book— actually there are plenty, but I recommend *Experience the Tower of London*, the official guidebook published by Historic Royal Palaces and available used online or at the Tower gift shop. It makes a nice souvenir and includes everything you want to know, including the palace history and what you can see there. Because it's in every London tour book, this entry will focus more on love, tragedy, and death in the Tower (see visiting information in Ch. 7).

THEN: As sketched in the Arundel Castle and Domesday Book listings, William the Conqueror was determined to solidify his hold on his new country by building castles everywhere and reinforcing a feudal system under which every man owed military duty to their overlord and so ultimately to the King himself. While the City of London was independently chartered, William wanted to bring it to heel, so he built three fearsome fortresses immediately surrounding the city: Baynard's and Montfichet castles are long gone, but the Tower remains, virtually unchanged since it was completed.

The massive White Tower (so called because of the white Kentish rag-stone used) was a colossal reminder of who ruled the land. Sitting on the edge of the ancient city walls along the Thames, it could be seen for miles. He used Norman masons and imported some stone from his native Normandy, but the hard labor was all Anglo-Saxon. In those days, geld (a land tax collected from the nation's gentry and nobles to pay for defense) wasn't just money or goods, but also peasant man-work-hours provided by the various landowners—not quite slave labor, but close. It was finished by 1100 and protected by a com-bination of moats, ditches, old Roman walls, and timber walls, until stone curtain walls and nine towers were built by Henry III in 1238. More than 100 years had passed but rebel Londoners still chafed at their Norman overlords. Henry's son, King Edward I rebuilt more and bigger walls and moats resulting in the look we see today. Apparently the defenses were insufficient, because in 1381 in the Peasants' Revolt 10,000 rebels burnt and plundered the castle.

Besides intimidating Londoners and defending the city, the Tower has served a variety of functions: stronghold fortress, housing the royal mint, a menagerie (the animals were moved out in 1832 to start the London Zoo), and, notoriously, for incarceration and executions. Among the famous executions were Lady Jane Grey and of course Henry VIII's wives Anne Boleyn and Catherine Howard. Plus, possibly, Henry VI who died there in custody, and foul play is suspected.

While officially a royal residence for many years, it rarely served this purpose. More often, royals were installed there against their will on charges of treason (even Princess Elizabeth, who became Elizabeth I, was held there for a time). Kings also retreated into the strong-hold for safety (among them Henry III in 1238 and Edward II c.1310).

The Tower was lost only once. During the Civil War, Charles I forfeited it to the Parliamentarians and

King William's goal to display power was clearly successful.
Drawn by Spaniard Bernardino de Escalante on a visit to London, c.1550

he was executed. Then the original Crown Jewels were mostly destroyed, gems sold off and the precious gold and silver melted down. After the restoration of the monarchy, it was never again an official royal residence and less and less a prison. It was used mostly as military barracks, for storage of military equipment, and securing the new Crown Jewels. Eventually, interest in the historic importance of the citadel resulted in a renewal program (1812–1864) that saw the removal of unsightly offices, taverns, and the military barracks.

The Tower's treacherous convoluted history lends itself well to fiction. William Shakespeare set parts of Richard III there and many modern authors have also used it. Also set there is *The Yeomen of the Guard*, Gilbert and Sullivan's only operetta that isn't an "all's well that ends well" HEA. Also, the "Yeoman" of the title is the only character in all their works that's based on a real person, Sir Richard Cholmondeley (1460–1521). **Fun Fact** ~ his name is pronounced 'Chumley.' **Less Fun Fact** ~ one can see a tomb effigy of him in the Tower's St. Peter ad Vincula Chapel, and while there visit the graves of the three queens executed there. Watch for Anne Boleyn's ghost carrying her head under her arm.

The Tower saw blood and gore galore, but there was romance too! Albeit mostly tragic. Lady Jane Grey, England's Queen for just 9 days, was imprisoned by Queen Mary for plotting to steal the throne after Edward VI's death. Most likely, sixteen-year-old Jane was just a pawn, it being the work of her powerful father-in-law and her husband, young Guildford Dudley. While the father-in-law was permanently

Still impressive today

dispatched within three weeks, the couple was held separately in the fortress for seven months. On the eve of his execution, Guildford begged to see her again, perhaps to beg her forgiveness. Jane replied by letter that she forgave them both, but denied his request, feeling it would just increase their misery. They were executed on the same day in 1554, but he never got to see her again. Supposedly, she watched his death from her window, crying out upon its completion. Theirs was an arranged marriage of short duration, but he must have cared for her at least a little because in the wall of his cell in the Beauchamp Tower Guildford carved and scraped her name—"Jane"—where it survives to this day.

They were dispatched, but Bloody Mary's work had just begun. Having reinstated Roman Catholicism, she ordered 280 religious dissenters to be burned alive at the stake. Thankfully for Protestants, Mary's reign lasted only five years before she died of an illness in 1558, and Princess Elizabeth became Queen at age 25.

But back to the Tower and romantic tragedy in the doomed Grey family. As the story goes, Lady Catherine (sister to the deceased Jane) secretly married Edward Seymour, 1st Earl of Hertford, in 1560 without Queen Elizabeth's knowledge or permission. When Her Majesty found out, she was furious because, besides the lack of permission, Catherine was in the line of succession and birthing legitimate offspring could destabilize Elizabeth's weak hold on the crown. Unmarried and childless, the Queen didn't want any loose heirs running around. Lord and Lady Hertford were both separately imprisoned in the Tower, where she gave birth to a rarity, a healthy Tudor baby boy. Later, sympathetic jailers allowed secret visitation rights for the loving couple and the fertile lady became pregnant again. After that, an enraged Queen Elizabeth kept the two of them apart, but released each to separate house arrest outside of London due to the plague. Meanwhile, the church annulled their marriage, rendering the two

One of the revered Tower ravens

sons illegitimate and ineligible as successors. Five years later, Catherine died of consumption (tuberculosis), never having been reunited with her beloved. However heartbroken he might have been, Edward managed to overcome it to find favor with the Queen and to marry twice more—again in secret!

Then of course there's the unrealized love of Queen Elizabeth and Robert Dudley (Jane Grey's brother-in-law). They had connecting suites in the castles wherever Elizabeth lived, but he was married and she was The "Virgin" Queen who needed to retain her tenuous hold on the throne. The inner circle surely knew of her love for him. Later when his wife died by mysteriously falling down the stairs, Elizabeth must have realized that she could never marry him. Whether they ever consummated their love in the bedroom, if not in the church, will remain a secret, forever lost to the passage of time.

And yet one more Grey tragedy—it seems these folks just couldn't keep it in their pants. The dead Catherine's grandson, William Seymour, secretly married Arbella Stuart, cousin of then King James I in 1610. She was put under house arrest, but William got the Tower. With help, she arranged to have him smuggled out in a cart, but they missed their dockside rendezvous. Arbella set sail for the continent alone, but her ship was captured and she was interred in the Tower, while William managed to find his way to freedom in France. They never saw each other again. Arbella died of a broken heart in the Tower, compounded it seems by losing her mind and starving herself to death. Watch for her ghost haunting the Queen's House.

There is at least one HEA Tower tale. The love story of Lord and Lady Nithsdale. William Maxwell, 5th Earl of Nithsdale, met Lady Winifred Herbert at the court of Louis XIV in Versailles. They married some months later in Saint-Germain, France, in 1699, and settled in Scotland where they had five children. He was raised Catholic and joined the Jacobite rebellion, but was captured at the Battle of Preston and found guilty of treason. On the night before his execution on February 23, 1716, his enterprising and courageous Countess rescued him single-handedly. Winifred had planned meticulously. By her own accounts, she'd ingratiated herself with the guards on previous visits, tipping them for their kind care of her beloved. Accompanied by several ladies, Winifred visited him in his cell to bid him sad farewell. By exchanging cloaks and with the aid of makeup and fake hair, William was able to escape past the guards dressed as a woman—remember these were dark, poorly-lit times in prisons where visitors were routine. Although accounts vary, in the most credible version she/he was escorted out by the ladies, while the Countess remained in the cell talking as if he were still there. Quickly, they fled the city, and the country, ending up in Rome, where they lived happily ever after as members of the elegant coterie of exiles surrounding the Old Pretender (son of deposed King James II).

As for romance novels with the fortress as a setting, there's an 1840 romance novel that tells the Lady Jane Grey story. *The Tower of London* by William Harrison Ainsworth has been described as "an incongruous merging of historical romance and guide book."[63] More contemporary tastes will enjoy romantic tales by Philippa Gregory who offers first-person fictional retellings of the real royal ladies of the Plantagenet and Tudor houses, and Elizabeth Moss with her lust-filled novels featuring ladies in waiting at the Tudor Court.

NOW: As far back as the 1590s, there's been ad hoc tourism to see the Tower, where folks could pay to touch the Crown Jewels or see the Royal Menagerie. During the 19th Century it was formalized as a source of income to the Crown, and by 1900, more than 500,000 tourists were visiting each year. Today, the figure is over 2 million and the entrance fees substantially higher, but no romance history trip to London would be complete without visiting the White Tower. For details see Crown Jewels listing in Ch. 7. To see the chapel, one must take a complimentary Yeoman Warder Tour or go in the last hour of the day, usually 4:30pm.

Can't make it to London? There's a free online game, Beat the Gaoler— yes, *really*—where you play to free prisoners: http://www.hrp.org.uk/ tower-of-london/history-and-stories/palace-people/prisoners/play-our-game-beat-the-gaoler/#gs.UTYHoBk

How OLDE: ♛♛♛♛♛
See Ch. 7 Ceremony of the Keys for contact/visiting details.

◇❧───────────────●

VAUXHALL GARDENS
Circa 1661–1859

THEN: Vauxhall Gardens has been mentioned in fiction as far back as 1782 (Frances Burney's *Cecilia*), later by Dickens in 1836 (*Sketches by Boz*), and, of course, Regency romance author Georgette Heyer set pivotal scenes there.

Located on the south bank of the Thames, the land rented from the Prince of Wales as part of his Duchy of Cornwall estates, it was for years approached by rowboat,[64] which must have offered countless occasions for accidental amour.

"We're going to cross the river in boats?" she asked, eyeing the boat launch with alarm. Her grip tightened on his arm.

He nodded. "It's the only way to Vauxhall. Eventually there's to be a bridge, but it isn't complete." ...

Helping her into the boat was even more precarious than handing her into the carriage had been. Griff went first, wedging his boots fast against the floorboards and steadying his balance.

Pauline accepted his hand and took a cautious step onto a seat near the bow. But just then the waterman launched the boat. She stumbled. Griff had to catch her by both arms as she fell against his chest.

"Oh, bollocks." She struggled to correct herself, and the boat lurched.

His stomach nearly capsized. He had a vision—a brief, waking nightmare of a thought—in which she tumbled straight into the black water and all those heavy, embellished skirts dragged her straight to the depths.

"Don't move," he told her, tightening his grip. "Not yet."

He held her close and tight. For long moments they stood absolutely still—swaying in each other's arms while the boat regained its equilibrium.

"Are you well?" he whispered.

She nodded.

"Your heart is racing," he said.

"So is yours."

He smiled a little. "Fair enough."

Vauxhall Concert with a cast of Regency regulars: at lower left table Prinny is whispering in the left ear of Perdita (Mrs. Robinson) with Dr. Johnson seated at table facing out and eating.

So is mine, at least a little, from reading this short, heat-filled passage from Tessa Dare's *Any Duchess Will Do.*

A bridge was finally completed in 1816 that greatly eased access, but it seems a decidedly less romantic way to arrive at Vauxhall.

One feature made the gardens incredibly romantic—the illumination of thousands of oil-lamps, initially about 1,000 but eventually reaching numbers over 40,000. Can you imagine dark, pre-electrical London at night, and how fantastical it must have looked for them all to come on nearly simultaneously? Add to it sparkly, tinkling water fountains, orchestras playing original music by Handel and Arne, ballroom dancing under the stars, as well as exotic, beautifully painted Rococo pavilions, and even fireworks—and you had an adult playground unlike anything seen before. We rejoin Dare's heroine Pauline after they've disembarked and climbed a long set of stairs up the riverbank:

> "It's growing dark," she said. "Should we head toward the pavilion?"
>
> "Not yet," he said, catching her arm. He guided her off the main walk, into a darkening grove of trees. ...
>
> "It's starting," he said, turning her head. "Look."
>
> Pauline looked. She caught sight of a glowing orb. One single ball of light, hanging in the distance.
>
> She blinked, and there were two of them.
>
> And then ten.
>
> And then...thousands.
>
> A warm glow spread through the gardens like a wave of light, touching here a red lamp, there a blue or green. Breathless with delight, she tilted her head back. The trees above them were strung with lamps on every branch. The glow traveled from one to the other, and before long the entire grove was illuminated. The effect was similar to standing beneath a stained glass church window at the sunniest part of the day. Except this was night, and all the colors had a luminous richness. The lamps were like a thousand jewels, hanging from every tree and carved stone archway. ...
>
> She laughed and clapped a hand to her cheek. ...
>
> "It's magical," she said.
>
> "Yes," he said, softly. "I think it is, rather."
>
> She turned to the duke, giddy with the beauty of it. He wasn't looking around at the thousands of lit globes hanging from the trees.
>
> He was watching her.

Vauxhall Pleasure Gardens makes the perfect setting for a variety of romance plot twists—mistaken identities, clandestine rendezvous, ruined reputations that prompt elopements or shotgun weddings. Shame on the unwise fictional heroine who allows herself to be led to an outer walkway where darkness makes possible a stolen kiss, unless, of course, matrimonial-trapping was her secret goal all along.

Vauxhall began in 1661 as "New Spring Gardens"—a free park of several acres of trees and walkways, with the sale of food and drinks the moneymaking aspect of the venture. In 1785, it was renamed Vauxhall Pleasure Gardens and expanded to include abundant attractions such as music concerts, hot-air balloon ascents, circus-type acts (tightrope walkers, jugglers, lion tamers) all for the low price of one shilling admission (roughly $10 today).[65]

Like coffeehouses, the gardens were a place where all levels of society were allowed to enter once they paid admission. That didn't mean, however, that the masses mixed with the gentry. The rich would ensconce themselves in private supper boxes where they could dine and watch *hoi polloi*. These precursors to the modern amusement park became so popular there were many of them around the world, including Sydney Gardens near Bath, which was frequented by Jane Austen.

Ever wonder where the name "Vauxhall" originated? There are related but conflicting theories, but conclusive proof may be lost in the past. Here are three:

✦ A long-lost manor house was once situated in the area called Vauke's Hall, and the renowned diarist Samuel Pepys (a fan of the early garden) popularized this by calling it "Fox Hall" until, strangely, it changed to Vauxhall[66]

✦ Sir Falkes de Breauté acquired the land in marriage and renamed the existing manor Falkes Hall, (or sometimes Faulke's Hall) which changed over time to Fox Hall, and lastly, again strangely, to Vauxhall[67]

✦ Yet one more source reports that the estate (c.1615) was owned by vintners John and Jane Vaux.[68]

As an odd side note, the Russian word for railway stations "vokzal" derives from Vauxhall Pleasure Gardens, but how that happened is an equally conflicted story for another time.

The advent of train travel in the mid–1800s made excursions to the countryside or the sea suddenly very easy, which led to the decline of the various pleasure gardens. Vauxhall went bankrupt in 1840, and then changed hands several times until it finally, after nearly 200 years of operation, closed for good in 1859. Social housing was built there until finally slum-clearance demolition allowed for part of the park to be restored in the 1970s.

NOW: Thanks to the 20-year effort of The Friends of VPG, the park is thriving today. On any given summer day you can play sports, ride a horse, take in a Tea House Theatre poetry reading, enjoy a picnic, watch an outdoor movie, or even dance under the stars. For something approximating the more fanciful times of yore, plan your visit for April to coincide with the St. George's Festival (England's Patron Saint). Launched in 2013, this annual London Tournament features medieval combat, Punch and Judy shows, Falconry, Morris Dancers, and more. Granted the period reenacted is several centuries earlier, but it's still a rousing trip back in time.

For a 4D glimpse into what Vauxhall or Ranelagh were like, visit the Pleasure Gardens Hall at the Museum of London (Ch. 7) to walk among the costumed mannequins and hear the sounds of the night.

How OW OLDE: ⚜🏵🏵🏵🏵
~ *the park's very nice but not a pleasure garden*
Price: FREE   **Hours:** Daily 24/7 but perhaps keep it to daylight hours
Tube: Vauxhall | www.fovpg.com | 139 Vauxhall Walk, Lambeth

◇⟋⟍⟋⟍————————————————————•

WHITE'S
1693–present

THEN: The quintessential setting for a Regency hero—fictional or not. Sulking over the antics of his feisty heroine or hiding from the matchmaking clutches of a meddlesome mother. A private sanctuary steeped in tradition for the upper-crust gentleman. A gambling hell where fortunes were won and lost over the turn of a card or roll of a die.

In real life it was that and more, but it didn't start that way. Founded in Mayfair a half mile away, it was originally Mrs. White's Chocolate House on Chesterfield Street. Doesn't that sound charming! However, originally Mrs. White was really an enterprising Italian immigrant Francesco Bianco (who changed his name and his gender, not really) when he took up selling hot chocolate, coffee, and tea. He did marry, however, and after Francis died the Widow White became the shop's proprietress.

Coffee houses were all the rage at the time, although unlike the later private gentlemen's clubs, these were egalitarian establishments where mostly-male gentry mixed with regular folk over the, then, newfangled cocoa and coffee beverages, reading papers, discussing politics, and trading gossip. The considerable importance of these early cafes is described by Algernon Bourke, a proprietor of White's c.1888, in his 1892 *History of White's*:

> *In the reign of Charles II... they were the only means for the expression of public opinion. There was at that time nothing representing the modern newspaper in existence ; public meetings and platform oratory were unknown, and the coffee house was used for the discussion of news, and the propagation of political opinion. Much of which was, quite naturally, hostile to the Court...* [69]

Over the next 80 years, the establishment transformed into the private club we know today. In 1778, White's moved to its current location at 37–38 St. James's Street where it became the unofficial Tory party headquarters in opposition to the Whig party, based in Brook's down the street.

White's was redesigned many times, and in 1811 the now famous bow window was introduced. This spot inside was to become the seat of power for the club's most influential members, including the 1st Duke of Wellington. One of the most influential to reign there was a commoner, dandy Beau Brummell, who held court for many years, ridiculing or approving of the dress and manner of members inside and passersby outside. Wrote the Hon. E. Beresford Chancellor in his 1922 *Memorials of St James's Street*:

> *"It was the spot where questions of etiquette were settled; where reputations were made or marred; where the social life of London*

White's Club, on the left of St. James's Palace.
(*From a Drawing of the time of Queen Anne.*)

◇⋙

White's in the early 1700s
(at left)
and today (at right)

was placed under the microscope and studied; where characters were laid on the operating-table and dissected. Like Almack's, it became a tribunal as redoubtable as was ever erected under the Venetian Republic or the Inquisition of Spain."[70]

White's reputation as a den of iniquity was mostly  the result of truly outrageous gambling and the scandalous antics of its earlier members. White's "betting book" was not restricted to sports, but included just about anything that caught the coxcombs' fancy, whether is was Lord Alvanley's £3,000 bet (about $315,000 in today's dollars) on how fast two rain drops would run down the bow window (c.1816; strangely the winner was not recorded), to another member betting £1,500 that a man could live underwater for 12 hours (he lost his money and the poor sod he'd hired to do the deed lost his life; c.1774),[71] to the bedroom antics of salacious Queen Caroline. "Great sums of money have been won and lost on the queen's returns," said member Charles Greville.[72] Bets recorded were sometimes of "vague character" (such as one member betting "a certain gentleman a certain sum, that a certain event does not take place..."), while others were of "pleasing comprehensiveness." So, those wagers that are written into modern romance fiction about when or who someone will marry are true to life and far less outrageous than many of the real ones.

Besides gambling, other activities included drinking in a rather tiny barroom but one that holds the world record for never having closed (we're talking open 24/7 for more than 200 years), plus billiards and private dining, but perhaps its biggest draw was the quiet serenity and tradition found inside its Grade I listed Portland stone walls. In 1929, the establishment truly became a private club when the owner was forced to sell and the members raised money to buy it.[73]

Now: White's is still a private club—considered the oldest, grandest, and most exclusive in London—and it *still* requires a Y chromosome to enter. Royalty, aristocracy, and the powerful elite comprised its membership throughout its history, and that hasn't changed with a reported ten knights, seven barons, six viscount, eight earls, one marquess, two dukes, and two HRH's (Charles and William,) among the current crop. As an aside, there is reportedly only one member who ever gave up membership voluntarily (rather than being forced to shamefully resign, as sometimes happened), and that was former PM David Cameron who did so in 2008 to protest the no-women rule.[74] In truth, very few women have set foot inside the hallowed halls, but among the lucky were, possibly, the Raggett sisters who inherited the club from their brother in 1859 and then appointed a male manager.[75] Rosa Lewis, a renowned chef that oversaw the club's kitchens (c.1900) must surely have entered the club, although probably through a side door, and Queen Elizabeth was actually invited inside in 1991. So, while it's 100% authentic with my highest 5 Filigree rating, if you're a female out to see the famous romance sights, the most you can hope for is to stand outside and gaze at the firmly shut door. That said, I doubt the average Joe could make it past the front door either.

While women can't get in, that hasn't stopped many a fictional heroine from trying with varying success. In Victoria Alexander's *Yesterday and Forever*, a time-travelling 20th Century woman is desperate to locate her Regency hero before she must leave him to return to her own time.

> *"I have to talk to him. I have to make him listen, try to make him understand. If, of course, I can find him."*
>
> *"That's not at all difficult. I believe he is at his club, White's. It has become a second home."* [says the hero's sister Lydia]
>
> *"Great." Maggie leaned forward eagerly. "Where is this place?"*
>
> *"It's on St. James Street, of course."* ... *"Oh no, Maggie. You wouldn't. You couldn't. It's not permitted for a respectable woman to even be on that street, let alone go into a club. Your reputation will be ruined."* ...

[Undeterred, Maggie storms the male bastion with Lydia there for support.]

"*What do you think? Should we knock or just barge right in?*" *Maggie eyed the entry to Adam's club. Well aware of the startled male eyes peering at them from a nearby bow window, she and Lydia paused to consider their next step at the door of White's.*

"*Well,*" *Lydia said brightly,* "*I should think if we knock, it would allow them the opportunity to refuse us entry. I believe barging in may well be our wisest choice.*"

"*Good move.*" *Maggie squared her shoulders and took a deep breath. While the idea of intruding on a hallowed men's club, a sacred shrine to testosterone, held a lot of appeal, now that she was actually here, the reality of what she and Lydia were about to do sent a flurry of winged creatures fluttering in her stomach.* "*The best defense is a good offense,*" *she murmured.* "*Let's go.*"

Maggie gripped the door handle and shoved, nearly stumbling when the barrier to the masculine sanctuary opened smoothly. They stepped firmly across the threshold. Maggie barely registered a vague impression of dark wood and dim lighting before the apparent guardian of the male stronghold bore down on them, sputtering and spewing like a masculine avenging fury.

"*I beg your pardon, miss, but women are not permitted to enter. This is a men's facility and we do not—*"

No spoilers here—to learn what happens between Maggie and her hero Adam, you'll have to read the book, but as a sop to our wounded female pride at being denied entrance, I will share with you Lydia's thoughts as she left the club.

...taking in as many of the details of White's as she could. ... She peered around. It was all rather disappointing. She wasn't sure exactly what she had expected, but something...well...more. This was the epitome of the English men's club, the ultimate haven for the men of her world. A sanctuary where they pursued such manly pastimes as drinking and gaming. And it appeared dull and boring.

"*What a shame,*" *she murmured under her breath and swept through the hallowed portals of White's with a vaguely superior sense that even if men deemed it necessary to hide away from the world surrounded by their own kind, it was somehow pleasant to know the women who were forbidden entry weren't missing very much at all.*

Personally, I think I'd have loved the Regency version of White's where all manner of crazy happened, but today's aristocracy holed up inside must, indeed, be having a stodgy, quiet time. It's certainly worth a look from the outside as you imagine the heroes of the past carousing inside. You won't find any sign or even a street number identifying it, but the famous bow window is still there. Also, if using your smartphone to guide you, make sure you're not directed to Leman Street instead, where a lap-dancing strip club of the same name currently resides.

How Olde: ♞♞♞♞♞
Price: Darling, if you have to ask... | **Hours**: Street view open 24/7
Tube: Green Park | **Map**: C | No website (too exclusive for that)
+44 20 7493 6671 | 37 St. James's Street

WHITE'S COMPETITORS
1762–present

There were many rivals to White's—although none are true competitors to that most venerable of institutions. Sometimes the Y-chromosome-infused "Quality" held membership in multiple clubs. And there were a couple that even admitted women. *Oh my!* Considering their high social appeal and overall desirability, the cost of membership—today generally under £2–3,000 annually—is way too reasonable to provide a barrier to entry to *hoi palloi*…instead roadblocks continue in the old fashioned way, by requiring the sponsorship of a current member and the rest of the members voting.

For most clubs, strict discretion remains *de rigueur*. And thus we've stumbled upon the biggest appeal of these old clubs. With privacy dead in an era where no mishap escapes mobile-phone-recorded replay on social media, endlessly and forever, rare is the leaked photograph or video from inside one of these private bastions. *Heck!* That even appeals to me.

How Olde: ♞♞♞♞♞
~ *Some are older than others, but they're all authentic*
Price: They're all closed to the public, so priceless unless you are invited in—then it's FREE

Here briefly are other historic London gentlemen's clubs:

THE ARTS CLUB: (1863) Housed in an 18th Century Mayfair town house, it is not generally mentioned in romances but it should be with its fanciful interiors (an eclectic mix of Moderne and whimsical interpretations of other periods) and its stated purpose—to provide a haven for those involved in the arts, literature or sciences. Historically, the Royal Academy was influenced by the desires of the Arts Club's membership and machinations. Notables ∿ **Then**: Dickens, an original founder, plus Liszt, Rodin, and the American James Whistler. **Now**: HRH Prince Philip, American actress Gwyneth Paltrow, and Rolling Stone member Ronnie Wood.

Tube: Green Park | **Map**: B | www.TheArtsClub.co.uk
+44 20 7499 8581 | 40 Dover Street

THE ATHENAEUM: (1824) Founded as a writer's club for the intellectual elite; however, they were not as liberal minded as the Reform Club, given that women—even highly educated thinkers—were not admitted to membership until 2002, twenty plus years after the Reformers.

Designed by Decimus Burton—*great name for a romance hero or maybe a villain*—the building is gorgeous from the outside, Neoclassical with Parthenon-copied bas-relief frieze skirting the top and a fun gold statue of the Greek goddess of wisdom, Athena, crowning the front portico. There is an extensive library of 80,000 books and a restored Smoking Room (paradoxically smoking is no longer permitted there). In 1886, it became one of the earliest buildings in the world to be lit by electricity from its own generator, not surprising since club member Michael Faraday's laboratory research helped bring electricity to use with the discovery of electromagnetic induction. Notables ∿ **Then**: Charles Darwin, plus a veritable who's who of authors including Dickens, Hardy, Kipling, Stevenson, Tennyson, Charles Dodgson—also known as Lewis Carroll—and American Washington Irving of *Legend of Sleepy Hollow* fame. **Now**: Baroness Susan Greenfield, who's also the first female head of the Royal Institution, and, too numerous to name, more than 50 Nobel Prize winners, heavily weighted toward science and medicine, although every category is represented.

Tube: Charing Cross | **Map**: C | www.AthenaeumClub.co.uk
+44 20 7930 4843 | 107 Pall Mall

BOODLE'S: (1762) While founded by Lord Shelburne, a future PM, it was named after the first head waiter, a lowly mister Edward Boodle—distinguishing itself as perhaps the only club dedicated, in a way, to a someone in "service." After White's, it's the second oldest club in the world and women still aren't allowed membership. Notables ∽ **Then:** Churchill, Cavendish, and Ian Fleming, of the James Bond novels. **Now:** Julian, Baron Fellowes of *Downton Abbey* fame. Boodle's Orange Fool—a sort of trifle with orange flavoring—is still a specialty there today.

Tube: Green Park | **Map**: C | www.Boodles.org | +44 20 7930 7166
28 St. James's St

BROOK'S: (1762) Along with its close neighbors, Boodle's and White's, it's located on the toniest street in town, if you consider that at any given moment the highest echelons of power and nobility might be ensconced within any of these three ancient bastions. I've no idea how long one would need to loiter on this short street pretending great interest in one's mobile phone, but eventually a lord or MP is bound to exit—but, of course, you'd also have to recognize them because just like the clubs, they don't wear signs. Also like its neighbors, Brook's still doesn't allow women members, however, they are allowed inside as guests provided they enter from a side door. And use the loo in the rear!

Tube: Green Park | **Map**: C | www.brooksclub.org
+44 20 7493 4411 | 60 St. James's St

THE EAST INDIA CLUB: (1849) This was founded, as one would guess by employees of the East India Company, for its staff on leave from their posts around the world and for pensioners. With the disbanding of the company in 1874 and therefore no future members, it merged with other clubs serving sports and public schools to become a general-purpose men's club. It remains just for men today, although females abound in the form of waitresses. Oh, and women guests may enter to eat in one upstairs dining room, and we may buy a box of their "Linden *Lady* Mint Creams," available online for £8. Sponsorship is a must for membership. However, unique to the East India, public school graduates are almost guaranteed entry provided their former Headmaster proposes them.

Historically, the building is notable for being the place where the Prince Regent received news about the successful Battle of Waterloo, and inside they have an "American Bar" in gratitude to the American officers who stayed there during WWII. More recently, the club made the news in 2014 when its accounts manager was convicted of embezzling more than £500K. No biggie, however, given that this club is rumored to be among the richest, sitting on hefty cash reserves and a £100M plus building.[76] Notables ∾ **Then:** Prince Albert and Lord Mountbatten. **Now:** UK Independence Party head, Nigel Farage.

Tube: Piccadilly Circus, Charing Cross | **Map:** C
www.EastIndiaClub.co.uk | +44 20 7930 1000 | 16 St. James's Sq

THE REFORM: (1836) Housed in a rather drab square building (their website prefers imposing and palatial), it does have handsome interiors. Inspired by Italian Renaissance architecture, it just screams old-world-clubbiness. It also has a rare distinction among old gentlemen's clubs of having "reformed" itself to admit women members (1981). Its mission has also changed dramatically—initially all members were pledged to support the Great Reform Act of 1832 and it served as the Liberal Party headquarters. Today's mission is purely social, however, they pride themselves on their high quality speaking roster and library of more than 75,000 books (although I'd guess not a lot of romances to be found there). Most notably, they're renowned as the place where a famous bet was conceived about an incredible journey. Frenchman Jules Verne was not a member, in fact never set foot inside, but he made it world famous by starting and ending his novel, *Around the World in Eighty Days* (1872), inside the venerable institution. Notables ∾ **Then:** Churchill, Forster, Wells, James, Thackeray. **Now:** Prince Charles and Camilla, Duchess of Cornwall.

Here is another unique feature—it's possible for the average Joe to get inside! Sort-of. By prior arrangement, organized groups may arrange weekday morning tours (min 10 people)—so get organizing if you'd like to step inside the hallowed walls of an old-world London gentlemen's club. See website for details. Price: £10 pp donation to their Conservation Charitable Trust if you can wrangle an organized tour; dress code enforced. Sometimes one can gain entry during Open House London in September, although they don't participate every year (learn more in Ch. 7).

Hours: by prior arrangement as above | **Tube:** Charing Cross
Map: C | www.ReformClub.com | +44 20 7930 9374 | 104 Pal Mall

ROYAL AUTOMOBILE CLUB: (1897) This is the baby of these clubs. Founded to support all things horseless carriage, it sponsored the earliest motor races in the world (1900 & 1905). The 1911 building featured such innovations as electricity and an air filtration system for London's coal-sooty air. King Edward VII awarded it the "royal" moniker, and it oversaw UK motor sports until 1999. Sponsorship of motor events remains a strong focus, but activities make it primarily a social club today. They have admitted women since 1999, and they're unique in offering a children's junior membership (children must follow the same dress code).

I've yet to run across a romance novel that features the RAC, but I'm including it because it's the only one of these hallowed societies that this author can speak to from personal experience. I won an invitation inside through a friend of a friend. The member, an expat American, gave me a tour (the Italian marble swimming pool is gorgeous) and treated me to dinner. The truly sumptuous décor screams money, as did the Bugatti Veyron sports car on display in the lobby. It's still an automobile club at its heart and its 5,000-item archive covers all aspects of motoring memorabilia and publications. Paintings of cars are everywhere too. The food and drink was Britishly understated but delicious, and as I recall the guest menu did not display prices (one does not split the check here). The stunning dining room was mostly empty, giving it a subdued atmosphere and making me feel the need to talk in hushed tones. I could easily envision a 1920s romance novel set here—it would be all fancy roadsters, beautiful women in fringed dresses, handsome rich racecar drivers, and something suspenseful...there was definitely an air of intrigue too.

Hours: as with all these clubs, requires invitation by member
Tube: Charing Cross | **Map**: C | www.RoyalAutomobileClub.co.uk
+44 20 7930 2345 | 89 Pall Mall

WINDSOR CASTLE
1070–present

World famous and immense, this is one of the official residences of Her Majesty The Queen, and if her standard flies from the Round Tower then she's home. This is a working royal palace, used for living (particularly on weekends), and for ceremonial events and State Visits from other heads of state, such as the US president. St. George's Hall is so long it can host banquets with 160 people seated at the same table. St. George's Chapel is the spiritual home of the Order of the Garter. Founded by King Edward III in 1348, it's the oldest order of chivalry in the world.

Today's Order comprises The Queen, The Prince of Wales, and 24 Knight Companions, plus other Royal Knights. You may recall that when the errant Prince Augustus was brought to heel he was made a Knight of the Garter (see St. George's Hanover Square).

Like Arundel Castle, Windsor was established by William the Conqueror to solidify and guard his new-found power. It took 16 years to complete, and its easy  access to London and a good hunting forest made it immediately a favorite royal residence. Henry II converted the castle to a palace with royal apartments, and began to replace the original timber curtain wall with stone. The original keep was rebuilt into the Round Tower in 1170. From 1350–1370, Edward III transformed this military fortress into a gothic palace, spending £50,000 ($32 million today)—more than any king had spent on building to that point. Over the next three centuries, subsequent kings and queens expanded, repaired, and modernized Windsor. By 1683, Charles II had turned it into an opulent baroque palace. Under George III and IV, the exterior was transformed back to a gothic

Windsor Castle in 1658, by Wenceslas Hollar

castle, its appearance made more imposing with added height to the Round Tower and the creation of towers and battlements (1796–1830).

It's fascinating to realize that the facades of many of these incredibly old looking castles have been transformed repeatedly through the centuries, often modernized but then eventually returned to a grander, more imposing, version of their original medieval appearance.

George IV's work cost nearly £300,000 ($32 million today), and for the most part, this is the castle we see today. The caveat is that much of the interior is a modern reconstruction. In 1992, a fire erupted in Queen Victoria's former chapel, which destroyed many of the historic staterooms. An extensive, meticulous, five-year restoration rebuilt these spaces, but obviously they are reproductions of the originals.

Now for the human aspect. Henry I married his queen here, and subsequent monarchs either liked the place and visited often (all Henrys V-VII, and Elizabeths I-II) or didn't (Edward VI). Henry VIII enjoyed hosting extravagant feasts, while Edward VI's puritanical beliefs led him to discontinue fancy events. King Charles I enjoyed living at Windsor, but during the English Civil War (1642–51), it became his prison, along with captured royalist officers. After his execution at the Tower of London, his body was interred without ceremony in the vault beneath Windsor's St George's Chapel. This did not deter Charles II after the restoration of the monarchy—rather it made him determined to solidify his right to rule by making it his principal residence.

The monarch most closely associated with Windsor was George IV (Prinny). Besides building his oriental palace (see Brighton Pavilion), he furnished Windsor's State Apartments in the grandest style as well as expanding and redesigning the gardens to what we see today. After all

Windsor Castle today

his work, he was only able to enjoy the finished castle for a year and a half before he died in 1830 at age 67. More recently, King George VI and his Queen considered Windsor to be their home. All throughout WWII during the heavy bombardments they stayed at Buckingham Palace in support of the London citizens, but they joined their daughters—Princesses Elizabeth and Margaret—at Windsor for evenings and weekends. The princesses were raised at Windsor, and it remains The Queen's beloved home.

NOW: Visiting Windsor Castle is an easy day trip and can be combined with other sights and activities (Ch. 9). Make sure to check online for special closures and know that semi-state rooms are only open in winter. Your entrance fee includes the State Apartments, Queen Mary's Dolls' House, and St. George's Chapel with a self-guided multimedia tour, plus guided tours of the Precincts. Expect airport style security, and certain items—such as long umbrellas, backpacks—must be checked (complimentary). Purses are okay. Open drinks and food are not permitted, and there are no dining options there. The Castle is up a steep hill and there's a lot of walking, 2½–3 hours worth. Wheelchairs are permitted on the grounds but not within the State Apartments (they may be checked). See website for detailed information on disability access, including visitors with ASD; plus there are discounts and caregivers are free. The ticket lines are longest from 9:30–11:30am.

For any Royal Collection Trust property, tickets purchased directly from them can be converted at no cost into a 1-Year Pass. This could be useful if you are staying overnight, and wanted to return the next day. This must be done on the day of your visit, and there are some restrictions, particularly for sights with timed entrances. See www.RoyalCollection.org.uk/1-year-pass for details.

---

*𝓗*OW OLDE: ⚜⚜⚜⚜⚜
Price: £20.50 | When State Apartments closed £11.30
Hours: Mar-Oct 9:30am–5:30pm; Nov-Feb 9:45am–4:15pm
Closed Dec 25–26 | Check website for closures for state ceremonies/events | Semi-State Rooms only open Sept-Mar and never if State Apartments are closed | St. George's Chapel is closed to tourists on Sun; all worshippers are welcome to attend services
Getting There: see day trips Ch. 9
www.RoyalCollection.org.uk/visit/windsorcastle
+44 30 3123 7304 | Windsor, Berkshire, SL41NJ

$\mathscr{Y}$e Olde Maps

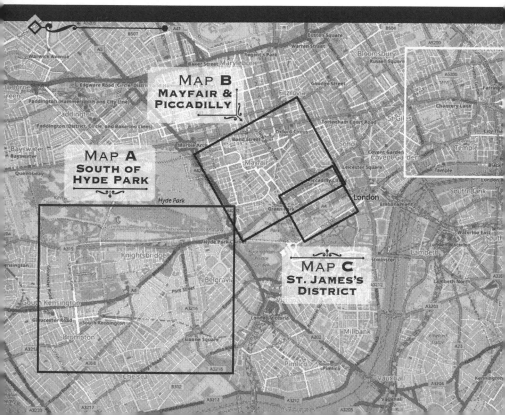

MAP **B**
MAYFAIR &
PICCADILLY

MAP **A**
SOUTH OF
HYDE PARK

MAP **C**
ST. JAMES'S
DISTRICT

CHAPTER 4

Hear ye, hear ye! Maps are coming your way
and a Museums Quick Guide too!

Goldilocks would approve. The maps that follow are not *too old*, like the one at left from 1624. Nor are they *too new* for a historical guide, like the one below (from 2017). They are, instead, *just right*...old but still somewhat useful. Think of them as records, rather than maps, which cover the areas marked here. These excerpts from Stanford's 1862 Library Map provide a snapshot into the past, showing us where places are that no longer exist and what's already there by Victorian times. Tube stations have been added, along with new street names where needed to locate a numbered sight, but...

TAKE HEED! There are streets that are long gone or whose names have changed, so consider these records informational and **not** a replacement for a good London map. Lastly, our Museums Quick Guide ends the chapter with all museum details in one place.

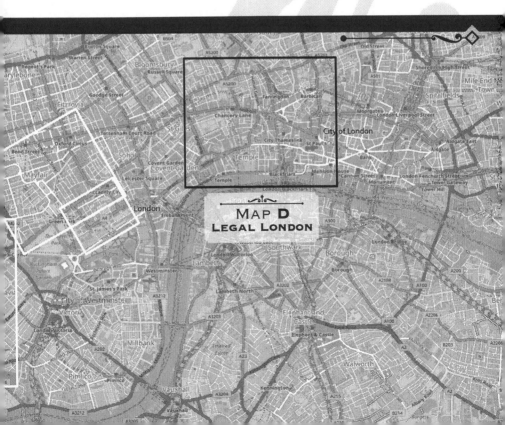

MAP **D**
LEGAL LONDON

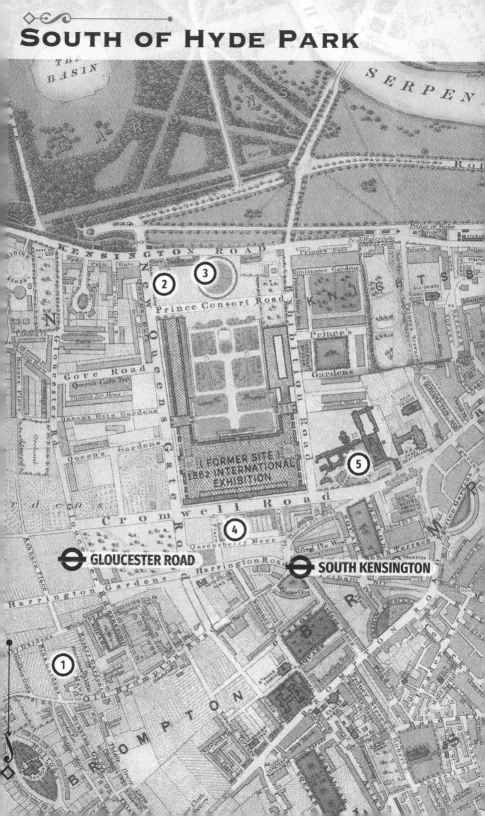

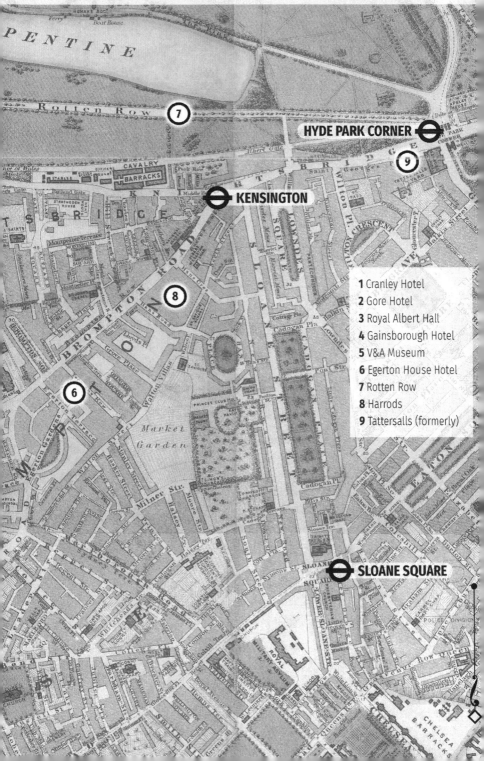

HYDE PARK CORNER

KENSINGTON

SLOANE SQUARE

1 Cranley Hotel
2 Gore Hotel
3 Royal Albert Hall
4 Gainsborough Hotel
5 V&A Museum
6 Egerton House Hotel
7 Rotten Row
8 Harrods
9 Tattersalls (formerly)

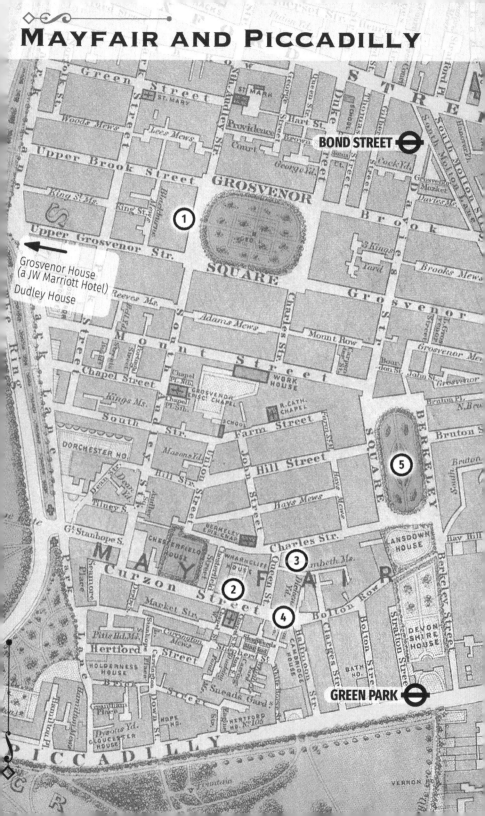

MAYFAIR AND PICCADILLY

Grosvenor House
(a JW Marriott Hotel)
Dudley House

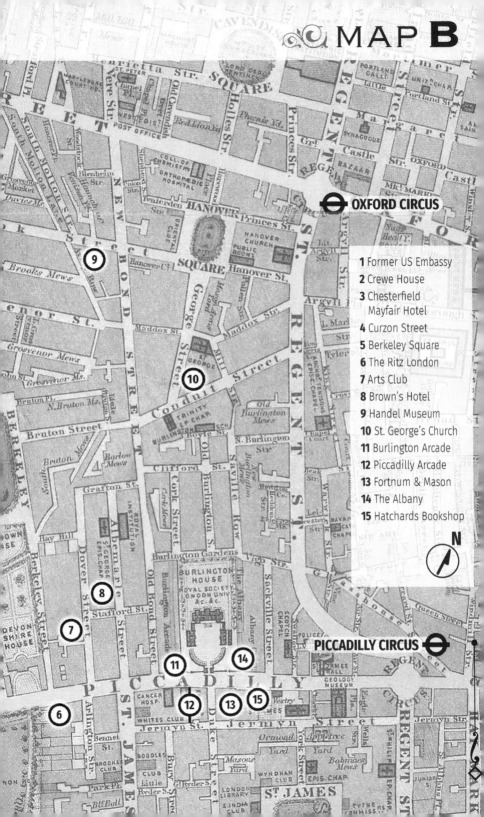

⊖ **OXFORD CIRCUS**

1 Former US Embassy
2 Crewe House
3 Chesterfield Mayfair Hotel
4 Curzon Street
5 Berkeley Square
6 The Ritz London
7 Arts Club
8 Brown's Hotel
9 Handel Museum
10 St. George's Church
11 Burlington Arcade
12 Piccadilly Arcade
13 Fortnum & Mason
14 The Albany
15 Hatchards Bookshop

N

PICCADILLY CIRCUS ⊖

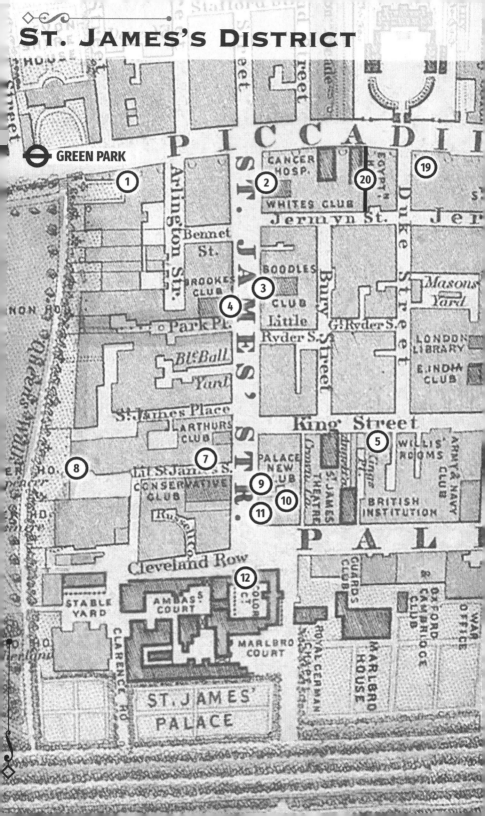

St. James's District

MAP C

PICCADILLY CIRCUS ⊖

1 The Ritz London
2 White's
3 Boodle's
4 Brook's
5 Almack's (former)
6 East India Club
7 Truefitt & Hill
8 Spencer House
9 Lock & Co.
10 Pickering Place
11 Berry Bros. & Rudd
12 St. James's Palace
13 Royal Auto. Club
14 Reform Club
15 Athenaeum Club
16 Floris
17 St. James Church
18 Hatchards Bookshop
19 Fortnum & Mason
20 Piccadilly Arcade

CHARING CROSS ⊖ →

N

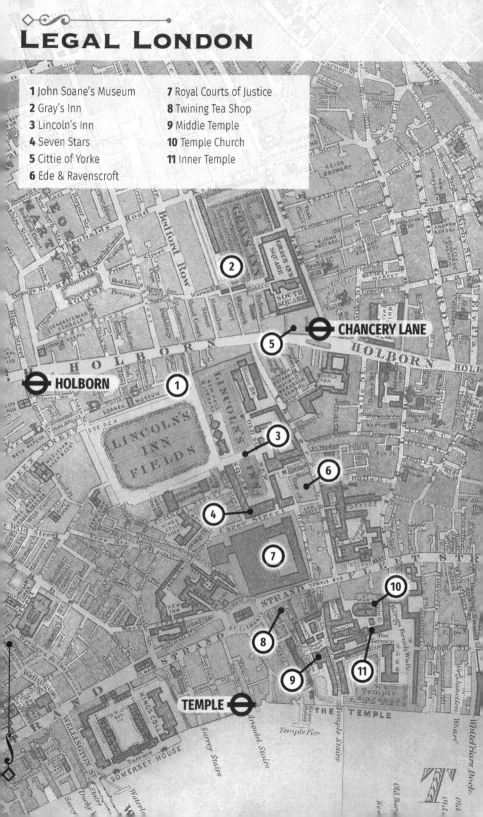

LEGAL LONDON

1 John Soane's Museum
2 Gray's Inn
3 Lincoln's Inn
4 Seven Stars
5 Cittie of Yorke
6 Ede & Ravenscroft
7 Royal Courts of Justice
8 Twining Tea Shop
9 Middle Temple
10 Temple Church
11 Inner Temple

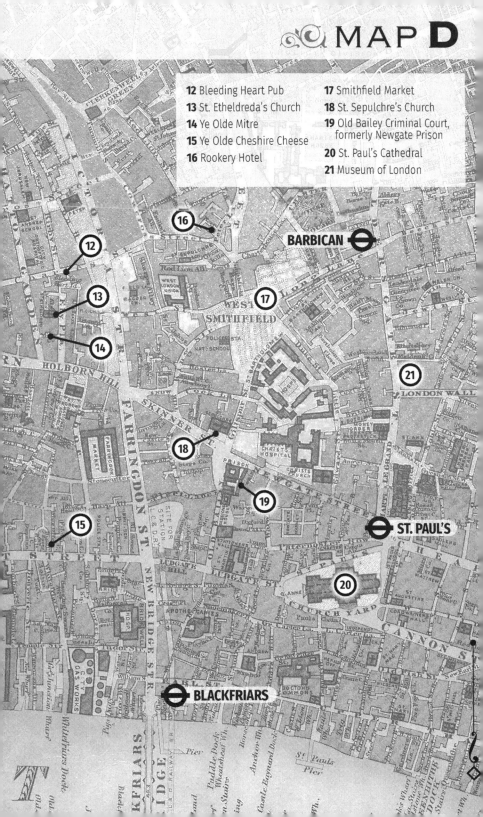

MAP D

12 Bleeding Heart Pub
13 St. Etheldreda's Church
14 Ye Olde Mitre
15 Ye Olde Cheshire Cheese
16 Rookery Hotel
17 Smithfield Market
18 St. Sepulchre's Church
19 Old Bailey Criminal Court,
   formerly Newgate Prison
20 St. Paul's Cathedral
21 Museum of London

MUSEUMS QUICK GUIDE

TAKE HEED! Check websites for unscheduled closures. Mobility access varies in these old structures; websites are good about providing details on access and special accommodations provided. Discounted admissions information and the "voluntary contribution" are described at the end.

Note: *These have full descriptions and histories in Ch. 3.

THE BRITISH MUSEUM ~ **Hours:** Daily 10am-5:30pm | Fri to 8:30pm | Closed Dec 24-26, Jan 1 | **Price:** FREE admission | **Tube:** Tottenham Court Rd (6 min walk), Holborn (8), Russell Sq (10) Goodge St (12) | www.britishmuseum.org | +44 20 7323 8299 | Greet Russell St

BUCKINGHAM PALACE (STATE ROOMS) ~ **Hours:** Summer (roughly mid July-Oct) 11am-3pm | Closed rest of year | Requires timed ticket; adv purchase strongly advised | **Price:** £23 for palace to £39 for combo ticket w/Mews & Gallery

The Royal Mews (fancy carriages, stables, and sometimes horses) ~ **Hours:** Feb-Mar & Nov Mon-Sat 10am-4pm | Apr-Oct Daily 10am-5pm | All times approx. | Closed Dec 1-Jan 31 | Allow 1 hr for visit | Closed during State Visits and other dates; check website | **Price:** £11

Queens Gallery (changing exhibits from her art collection) ~ **Hours:** Daily Apr-Oct 9:30am-6pm | Nov-Mar 9:30am-4:30pm | Last admission 1 hour before closing | Closed Dec 25-26, Jan 1 | Allow 1-1.5 hours | **Price:** £10 | **Tube:** Green Park (9 min walk), Hyde Park Corner (11), St. James's Park (11), Victoria (15) | www.royalcollection.org.uk | +44 30 3123 7300 | Official address: London

CHARLES DICKENS MUSEUM ~ **Hours:** Tue-Sun 10am-5pm | Last admission at 4pm | Open Bank Holiday Mon | Closed Dec 25-26, Jan 1, & 1 day in Nov for Christmas decorating | **Price:** £9 | **Tube:** Russell Sq (10 min walk), Chancery Lane (11), Holborn (14) | www.DickensMuseum.com | +44 20 7405 2127 | 48 Doughty St

FAN MUSEUM ~ **Hours:** Tue-Sat 11am-5pm | Sun 12-5pm | Closed Dec 25-26 & Jan 1 | 1 hour touring time | **Price:** £4 | Tues free for Sr/disabled | London Pass holders FREE | **Overground:** Greenwich Station (7 min walk) & Cutty Sark DLR (5) | www.TheFanMuseum.org.uk | info@thefanmuseum.org.uk | +44 20 8305 1441 | 12 Crooms Hill, Greenwich

THE GEFFRYE MUSEUM OF THE HOME ~ **Hours:** Tue-Sun 10am-5pm | Closed Mon | Open Bank Holiday Mon | Closed Dec 24-26, Jan 1, Good Friday | **Price:** FREE Admission | Almshouse Tour £4 pre-booking required | **Tube:** Old Street, Liverpool (20 min walk) | **Overground:** Hoxton Station (5) | www.Geffrye-Museum.org.uk | +44 20 7739 9893 | 136 Kingsland Rd, Hoxton

HANDEL & HENDRIX IN LONDON ~ **Hours:** Mon-Sat 11am-6pm | Last admission 5pm | Closed Dec 25-26 | **Price:** £10 | **Tube:** Bond St (4 min walk), Oxford Circus (8) | www.HandelHendrix.org | +44 20 7495 1685 | 23 & 25 Brook St

THE HOUSEHOLD CALVARY MUSEUM ~ Hours: Daily Apr-Oct 10am-6pm | Nov-Mar 10am-5pm | Last entrance 45 min prior | Closed Mar 25, Apr 24, Dec 24-26 plus for state needs; check website | **Price**: £7 | Free with London Pass | **Tube**: Westminster (6 min walk), Charing Cross (8), Embankment (10) | www.HouseholdCavalryMuseum.co.uk/index.php | museum@householdcavalry.co.uk | +44 20 7930 3070 | Horse Guards, on Whitehall Rd

IMPERIAL WAR MUSEUMS ~ Hours: IWM **London** (modern warfare from WWI on Bedlam) **Hours**: Daily 10am-6pm | Last admission 5:30pm | Closed Dec 24-26 | Allow 2-3 hours min | **Price**: FREE Admission | **Tube**: Lambeth North (5 min walk), Waterloo & Elephant/Castle (15) | +44 20 7416 5000 | Lambeth Rd

CHURCHILL WAR ROOMS ~ Hours: Daily 9:30am-6pm | Last admission 5pm | Closed Dec 24-26 | Allow 90 mins | **Price**: £17.25 | **Tube**: Charing Cross, St. James's Park (both 10 min walk) | +44 20 7930 6961 | Clive Steps, King Charles St

HMS BELFAST (a WWII ship) ~ **Hours**: Daily Mar-Oct 10am-6pm | Nov-Feb 10am-5pm | Last admission 1 hr prior closing | Open Bank Holidays | Closed Dec 24-26 | Allow 90 mins | **Price**: £14.50 | **Tube**: London Bridge (5 min walk), Tower Hill (20) | +44 20 7940 6300 | The Queens's Walk | **For all 3 museums: www.iwm.org.uk**

KENSINGTON PALACE ~ Hours: Daily Mar-Oct 10am-6pm | Nov-Feb 10am-4pm | Last admission 1 hr prior | Closed Dec 24-26 | **Prices**: £15.50 | **Tube**: Queensway (9 walk), High Street Kensington (10), Notting Hill Gate (10) | www.Hrp.org.uk/kensington-palace | +44 20 3166 6000 | Kensington Gardens

MUSEUM OF LONDON ~ Hours: Daily 10am-6pm | Galleries close at 5:40pm | Closed Dec 24-26 & Jan 1 | **Price**: FREE admission | **Tube**: Barbican (5 min walk) | www.MuseumOfLondon.org.uk | +44 20 7001 9844 | 150 London Wall

NATIONAL PORTRAIT GALLERY ~ Hours: Daily 10am-6pm | Thur-Fri to 9pm | Closed Dec 24-26 | **Price**: FREE | Fee for special exhibits | **Tube**: Charing Cross (2 min walk), Leicester Sq (3), Embankment (9) | www.npg.org.uk | +44 20 7306 0055 | St. Martin's Pl

THE SHERLOCK HOLMES MUSEUM ~ Hours: Daily 9:30am-6pm | Closed Dec 25 | **Price**: £15 | **Tube**: Baker Street (3 min walk) | www.Sherlock-Holmes.co.uk | curator@sherlock-holmes.co.uk | +44 20 7224 3688 | 221b Baker St

18 STAFFORD TERRACE/THE SAMBOURNE FAMILY HOME

18 Stafford Terrace ~ Hours: Daily 10am-5:30pm | Closed Tue | **Price**: £9 | Public tours Wed & Sun 3pm included with ticket | 12 Holland Park Rd

The Sambourne Family Home ~ Hours: Open Wed, Sat, Sun | Times vary; open access is limited; most times by tour | Some costumed tours | Twilight costumed tours 3rd Wed of the month | See website | **Price**: Open Access £7 | Tours £10 | 18 Stafford Terrace **Tube**: Kensington Olympia (5 min walk), High Street Kensington (10) | Neither museum is mobility accessible | www.Rbkc.Gov.uk/subsites/museums.aspx | +44 20 7602 3316

DENNIS SEVERS' HOUSE ~ Hours: Mon, Wed, Fri 5-9pm | Reservations recommended | Mon 12-2pm & Sun 12-4pm | **Price**: £15, day only £10 | **Tube**: Liverpool Street, Aldgate, Aldgate East (all 9-11 minute walk) | www.DennisSeversHouse.co.uk | info@dennissevershouse.co.uk | 18 Folgate St, Spitalfields | +44 20 7247 4013

SIR JOHN SOANE'S MUSEUM ~ Hours: Tue-Sat 10am-5pm | Closed Sun-Mon & Bank Hol | Closed Dec 24-26 & Jan 1 | **Price**: FREE but some tours have a nominal fee | **Tube**: Holborn (5 min walk), Temple (15) | www.Soane. org | +44 20 7405 2107 | 13 Lincoln's Inn Fields

TOWER OF LONDON* ~ Hours: Summer (Mar-Oct) 9am-5:30pm | Winter (Nov-Feb) 9am-4:30pm | Sun-Mon opens 10am | Crown Jewels close 1 hr earlier | Closed Dec 24-26 & Jan 1 | Min 3 hours touring time | **Price**: £21.50 includes Crown Jewels | **Tube**: Tower Hill (5 min walk) | www.Hrp.org.uk | +44 20 3166 6000

VICTORIA AND ALBERT MUSEUM ~ Hours: Daily 10am-5:45pm | Closed Dec 24-26 | Fri open to 10pm but some galleries close at 5:30pm | **Price**: FREE admission | **Tube**: South Kensington (4 min walk) | www.vam. ac.uk | contact@vam.ac.uk | +44 20 7942 2000 | Cromwell Rd

WALLACE COLLECTION ~ Hours: Daily 10am-5pm | Open most Public Hol | Closed Dec 24-26 | **Price**: FREE admission | **Tube**: Bond St (7 min walk), Baker St (11), Oxford Circus (13) | www.WallaceCollection.org | +44 20 7563 9500 | Manchester Sq

---

EXPLAINING ADMISSION FEES, VOLUNTARY DONATIONS, AND CONCESSIONS:

Entrance fees listed in this Guide are the lowest **adult rate purchased online excluding the 'voluntary donation.'** Often there are combination tickets for extras that might be a better deal; check websites for options. Because rates can change at any time, they might not be exactly as listed here.

Voluntary Donation: This complicated scheme (called Gift Aid) benefits UK nonprofit institutions but only applies to donations made by UK citizens. By adding on a voluntary donation of £1-3 the organization can claim the entire amount as a donation and also get an extra 25% back from the government in grant aid. From foreigners, there's **no** added benefit to the organization, except for the extra little donation you make. It's perfectly acceptable to pay the standard fee. Organizations have gotten tricky by sometimes placing the higher rate first or even burying the real admission fee in the fine print. Please feel free to request the rate without the 'voluntary donation.' If you have extra funds, then, of course, the museums will appreciate the gift, but you shouldn't feel obligated.

Concessions: This is the UK term for discounts, which are usually offered for children, seniors, students, and the disabled (and for a disabled person, if there is a required caregiver, that person is often free). Family rates for adults/children are usually a good deal.

Savings Tip: The Membership Program for the **Historical Royal Palaces** (Tower, Hampton, Banqueting House, Kensington, Kew, Hillsborough) is a good value if you plan to visit multiple palaces. A single one-year membership is £50 and a joint (2 named adults) is a bargain at £73. Do the math to be sure based on which palaces you want to see. In addition to skipping the long ticket-buying lines, you'll get FREE unlimited access to 6 Historic Royal Palaces, 10% off Kew Gardens admission, 10% discount in many HRP restaurants and shops (including Kensington's Orangery), a free copy of *The Private Life of Palaces* (est. $12 value), and invitations to member events (click on Member Events at the HRP Membership page to see if any correspond to your visit). You also have access to the private Member's Room at Hampton Palace—so bring your picnic lunch and dine inside a former "grace-and-favor" apartment (Ch. 3). Membership can be purchased at each palace (at the Tower go to the Welcome Centre or Group Tickets) but to save valuable time on your trip, purchase in advance online: www.HRP.org.uk.

Savings Tip 2: The **Royal Day Out** combines Buckingham Palace State Rooms, Queen's Gallery, and Royal Mews into one long day of royal-ness. At £39.50 it saves £3.80 over buying separately, but it must all be done in one day. Or you can get a Queens Gallery/Mews only ticket for £17.70 (£2.60 savings). **Tip:** 1-Year Pass conversion is FREE and allows you to go back on a second day to any of these three. It works too with Royal Day Out, but you'd still need to visit each site, but who says how long you have to stay? (Exception: Buckingham State Rooms which are a timed visit and probably won't be repeatable during busy seasons.) For the others, get your ticket stamped before leaving and you can come back another day on your trip. Learn more: www.RoyalCollection.org.uk/1-year-pass.

Printable Maps: If you'd like to take 8½ x11-inch versions of our Victorian-era maps with you on your grand adventure, you can download them from our website at www.RomanceReadersGuides.com/maps. Remember, these are not replacements for a high-quality, modern London map. You'll want one of those (or an app equivalent) too!

CHAPTER 5

Dining like an English lady or a bloke in a pub

To truly experience the life of our favorite romance heroine, we can't just walk in her footsteps. We need to eat and drink like her too. However, as any romance fan knows, aristocratic ladies rarely ate in public establishments—rather they dined privately at home or at a friend's home or, even better, at grand balls. Public consumption by the nobility was the exclusive purview of gents in coffee houses, brothels, or their private clubs.

One notable exception was at coaching inns, but only the truly desperate heroine would be caught eating in the taproom with the riffraff—instead, ladies and their heroes dined in private salons, served by the innkeeper or his wife. Today, a few of these ancient posting inns remain in London, converted entirely into pubs and featuring local ale and traditional English cuisine. Some have always operated as pubs, the majority of which are, not surprisingly, located in the oldest part of London. Commonly referred to as 'The City' or 'the Square Mile,' this area is roughly one square mile in the heart of London where legal and financial services began and still reign supreme.

Dining in public finally became acceptable for English ladies with the advent of Afternoon Tea. This was served first in fine homes where many a fictitious heroine—and real-life hostess too, I would guess—has felt her hand shake as she carefully poured a cup of tea for an especially important visitor, the illustrious grand dame or handsome young noble.

Today's Afternoon Tea experience is thankfully less stressful, except, perhaps, for the strain it puts on one's pocketbook. But a visit to London would not be complete without this quintessential Victorian experience. While places vie for customers with a range of offerings from traditional to avant-garde, I've strived to offer the most authentically Victorian teas at a variety of price ranges—and some fun ones too.

Besides tea, historical dining can be had mainly at ancient pubs and a few Victorian-era hotel restaurants. Historical liquid concoctions are even harder to find, but check out the St. Pancras (Ch. 6), which pours Victorian-inspired cocktails. Also in this section are a few novel dining experiences such as eating in an underground vault. As always, planning ahead will help ensure a more pleasant experience and—since there are millions of tourists and locals competing for spots at these special places—making a reservation is highly recommended. Lastly, besides my own experiences, I've averaged the star ratings of various review sites to get the most accurate score.

$\mathscr{A}$ Duchess's Delight ⁓ the invention of afternoon tea

There is nothing more English than afternoon tea, and this wonderful tradition is alive and well in modern England. From High to Cream to Champagne, there are many types, and almost every hotel offers something—but before I delve into the delicious, I'd like to offer the briefest of history lessons

While tea was consumed in England from the 1660s—and was a favorite of Charles II and his queen Catherine of Braganza—the Afternoon Tea ritual is a relatively recent invention of Anna Maria, 7th Duchess of Bedford (1783–1857), who was Lady of the Bedchamber to Queen Victoria. As we know from our novels, the upper crust ate a large morning meal of heavy English fare. It was displayed on a buffet in the Morning or Breakfast Room and one either served oneself or indicated to the footman what was desired. Luncheon wasn't a common meal then and, if served at all, was a very light snack, with dinner a late evening feast.

The Duchess reportedly complained of "having that sinking feeling" (otherwise known as low blood sugar), and one afternoon in the 1840s instructed her servants to bring a pot of tea and some little cakes to her boudoir in Woburn Abbey, the family seat. Soon she was inviting friends to join her, and it proved so popular that upon returning to London she brought her new custom to her city friends. *Voila!* The Afternoon Tea was born.

As an aside, Afternoon Tea is still served at Woburn Abbey in Bedfordshire, 50 miles north of London (£16, includes garden entry; reservations essential; www.WoburnAbbey.co.uk).

Back in 1840s London, other royals quickly copied Anna, and within just a few years 'taking tea' and tea parties in *ton* homes were all the rage. Besides keeping a delicate female's blood sugar from crashing, it provided yet another opportunity for the Victorian lady in her finest day dress to demonstrate her gracious hospitality while also showing off her fine china, embroidered linens, polished silver, and the skill of her cook.

Sometimes these tea parties were held outside. We've all read the scene where the gentry enjoy a "*simply lovely*" afternoon sipping tea, perhaps on a plateau with a beautiful view or near the ruins of an ancient castle—a particularly important trope allowing the heroine and hero the chance to conduct a more private conversation while strolling within sight of the chaperone. However, what about those poor servants lugging all that stuff up to the hilltop? Heavy wicker baskets, blankets, food and steaming pots, sometimes even tables and chairs. Did they get to eat too, one wonders? Even the leftovers?

For the less well-heeled, another option sprouted as industrious restaurateurs opened public tearooms. It is in those establishments that we, today, may dine like a Regency lady.

Here's a brief explanation of the various selections available to us.

TYPES OF TEAS 〜

AFTERNOON TEA: This version, dating from the 1840s, was served generally around 3pm and was associated with the English aristocracy. Today it still involves some degree of dressing up and the use of fine manners: avoid clinking cups, splashing tea—and absolutely no finger licking! As with all types, it always begins with quality tea and a teapot. The fanciest include white-glove service, fine bone china (often floral patterned), linen tablecloth and napkins, and a three-tiered tray of sweets and savories. Eating from the bottom up, the lowest platter holds crust-less finger sandwiches—usually of the roast-beef, ham, cucumber, egg mayonnaise with cress, and smoked-salmon varieties. The middle tray holds scones, ideally warm, with clotted Devonshire cream (a sort of less sweet but delicious thick whipped cream) and berry preserves. And finally the top features desserts of pretty little sweet cakes and pastries, the more inventive the swankier.

CREAM TEA: While the English are known to put milk in their tea (a rare habit for Americans), this type of repast simply means a car-bohydrates-only version of Afternoon Tea, usually only scones, clotted cream, preserves, and maybe a macaroon or two. And it costs less.

CHAMPAGNE TEA: No, this isn't some kind of fancy new tea infused with bubbles, rather it's just Afternoon Tea served with a glass of champagne—and a full teapot too. Next stop, the loo. The price will be increased by the cost of the bubbly. A lesser-known name for this, but more fancy, is Royal Tea.

HIGH TEA: Arriving circa 1893, served around 6pm, and associated with northern England—High Tea was also called Meat Tea and was essentially an early dinner at home for factory workers. It got the name because, rather than being served on a low table (we call them coffee tables), it was served on a "high" kitchen table. A hearty rustic meal with mugs rather than fine china, it included cold roast beef or cold Yorkshire pie (meat), fish, sausages, potatoes, plus coffee, ale, and the usual carbohydrate treats. Later, a light snack, such as a sandwich, followed as supper. As an aside, this custom, sometimes called just "tea," spread to Scotland, Australia, and New Zealand, but calling it "tea" occasionally caused confusion when guests arrived hours late for Afternoon Tea, thinking they would be getting a meaty meal.[1]

In the US we, too, have mixed up these terms, probably thinking it sounds fancier to say High Tea or English Tea or High Afternoon Tea, but whatever we call it, it still tastes just as good! That said, unless you want to stand out like an American sore thumb, you'll want to use the term 'Afternoon Tea' when making reservations. And while we're talking digits, don't stick your pinkie out either. *Simply not done, my dear.*

TAKE HEED! Modernizing the Afternoon Tea is all the thing these days, such as Tea-Tox at Brown's Hotel (a healthy version, but don't worry, they have traditional too) or Mad Hatter's Tea at The Sanderson (pink and green sandwiches). Many sound delicious, but definitely try the traditional version for your true Victorian heroine experience.

TIP: While they might not always offer, requesting seconds of a particular item is absolutely acceptable and should be accommodated, at least in the nicer establishments. At the same time, asking to take the leftovers home is like asking to pack up food at a buffet restaurant—sometimes it's okay, but most times your request will be politely declined. Also, every patron is entitled to their own little teapot and choice of tea—and if you sample your companion's flavor, that's your business. Prices listed here are for the traditional Afternoon Tea—champagne is extra.

*N*ow on to the places where you can indulge. The list is divided into sections for Afternoon Tea, Ancient Eats and Historic Pubs, and Period Dining in Hotel Restaurants.

Afternoon Teas
For a King's Ransom ∼ £50 and up

THE ENGLISH TEA ROOM
AT BROWN'S HOTEL

This *feels* like one of the most authentic tea experiences in London. Quiet, intimate, refined. It's the Grand Gentleman of tearooms. Queen Victoria and Winston Churchill visited regularly—not to stay in the hotel, but for this tea. The parlor has its original 145-year-old dark-wood paneling with Jacobean detailed plaster ceiling and working fireplaces. Seating at small tables for two with wingback chairs or on settees with coffee tables is like having tea in a friend's home—if your friend lived in a Georgian-era mansion and had a butler and staff! The waiters are friendly and deferential but not obsequious, rarely fail to offer seconds, and even bring the scones later so they're still warm after the sandwiches have been consumed. This is the place to meet an old friend and spend the afternoon catching up—no one will rush you. Or

Champagne Tea – Brown's

meet a little later and make it an early dinner—you'll leave pleasantly full and ready for an evening at the theatre. While unquestionably spendy, my experience and that of online reviewers say it's worth the splurge. Celebrate with a glass of French Ruinart Champagne for an additional £10.

FEATURES: Gluten-Free Afternoon Tea menu and vegetarian options. Live piano music sometimes. **TIP**: When reserving, request a window seat if you want to people-watch or by the fire if it's winter. Also, alert them if it's a special occasion (birthday, etc.) and they may bring out a special little cake.

STARS: 4 ～ Reports that leftover dessert can be taken home. Dress Code: smart casual with collared shirt for men; no sportswear, t-shirts, shorts, or sneakers. Trust me, you'll feel more at ease wearing your more polished look.

How Olde: ♔♔♔♔♔

Price: £55 | **Hours:** 12–6pm | Table is available for 2 hours but in practice, patrons are not rushed. | **Contact/Location:** see Ch. 6 Brown's or email: tea.browns@roccofortehotels.com

---

THE PALM COURT AT THE RITZ, LONDON

If Brown's is the place to while away a quiet afternoon in exclusive comfort and care, then The Palm Court is *the* place to go to celebrate! Festive, grand and gorgeous. It's the Grande Dame of tearooms with feminine décor in golds and pastels, clientele dressed to the nines, and waiters in tuxedos. It has earned a spot in history—it was one of the first places a single Victorian lady could go un-chaperoned. Just going to The Palm Court is an occasion, but even better, use it to commemorate a sweet sixteen's birthday. Honor a recent graduate. Romance a special anniversary. Or proclaim your undying love and propose.

The Palm Court is the showpiece of the Grand Gallery, the hotel's wide central walkway. Set back between two marble pillars and up three wide marble stairs, it is a glorious Belle Époque stage of gilt mirrors, glittering chandeliers, and, of course, giant green palms. Everyone up there feels special. Everyone down below wishes they were up there. But you can't walk in off the street and hope to be seated. First there's the dress code, which applies to the entire hotel (more on that later). Second, reservations need to be booked well in advance—4 weeks for Mon-Wed and as much as 5 months for Thur-Sun. For the holidays, do it earlier. If all else fails, call the hotel directly and ask about cancellations.

The Palm Court at the Ritz in Victorian times ∿ *and even lovelier today*

While undeniably a once-in-a-lifetime event, the service is swift—this is not the place to while away your afternoon. The waiters will take your order—*stat!*—and the food will appear so quickly it will seem like magic. This is because they need to be ready for the next seating time. Please know that you're allotted 1½ hours for your experience, and if you arrive late, you'll lose some time. Splurge with champagne for an additional £16. A Celebration Cake is an extra £11 (order 48 hours in advance).

FEATURES: Allergen menu available upon request. Resident pianist and harpist add musical ambiance. Silver teapots and delicate floral china. **TIP**: Arrive early for coat check and the loo; with all the guests seated at the same set times, you don't want to waste any of your 1½ hours in lines. You're entitled to your full time, so even if the bill is presented, you can enjoy your tea until the clock chimes (well, no clock will really chime; you'll need to check your watch). A 15% food discount is sometimes offered Mon-Thurs for the 11:30am and 5:30pm teatimes.

STARS: 4½ ∼ Several reports of swift service. The food will come quickly, but you don't have to eat it quickly. On the plus side, many report that the food is replenished often, to the point where you're so stuffed it'll feel like Thanksgiving Dinner. While some report that photography isn't allowed, the menu clarifies that photographs can be "taken discreetly"—but don't include other patrons. Dress Code: Jacket and tie required for gentlemen; appropriately festive for ladies; and nowhere in the hotel may sneakers or sportswear be worn.

*H*OW OLDE: ⚜ ⚜ ⚜ ⚜ ⚜
Price: £54, £30 for children | **Seatings**: 11:30am, 1:30pm, 3:30pm, 5:30pm, 7:30pm | Table available for 90 min, no more
Details: See Ch. 6 The Ritz or telephone +44 20 7300 2345

*F*or Landed Gentry ∼ £30-50

THE CHESTERFIELD MAYFAIR HOTEL

This Red Carnation branded hotel, in the former town house of the Earl of Chesterfield, has long won awards for its tea offerings with its gracious service and delicious menus. Recently, they upped the ante with

The Chesterfield Mayfair ～ like an English garden party, even when it rains

the "Charlie and the Chesterfield Afternoon Tea" (through 11/20/17). It's festive, colorful, charming. And, as you might imagine, there's a special focus on "chocolate"—not usually a plentiful ingredient in the afternoon repast. While the menu is not the most authentically Victorian one might find, don't worry, all the usual savories are served, and the sandwiches get particularly high marks. In addition, you'll get extra sweets, including a mini red-fizz soda, Willy Wonka bar, and chocolate scones! This is a good place to bring your little Oompa Loompas, and sometimes Willy Wonka even visits the tables to amuse the kids. For the adults, there's a live pianist. For Americans, he sometimes plays music from Disney movies. To top it off, guests are given an Everlasting Gobstopper and a "golden ticket" to open upon their next visit with prizes like free champagne.

Tea is served in the Butler Restaurant and the Conservatory, a pretty glass-roofed room full of greenery, a fountain, and Victorian country charm. You'll want the Conservatory—it feels like taking tea at a garden party. Described as a "hidden gem," it's also a good spot for special celebrations, but the atmosphere is more relaxed, quieter and intimate than larger venues. I met a friend here and we stuffed ourselves silly— and we both left with a cute Red Carnation box of leftovers complete with, what else, a red carnation bloom. Top it off with a glass of bubbly for just £7 more—a bargain!

FEATURES: Vegetarian and Gluten-Free options. They only use free-range eggs and are "committed to using sustainable fisheries." **TIP**: Call ahead to request seating in the conservatory. Try the flowering "Dancing Dragon" tea—it's fun to watch the little tea bouquet unfurl while it stews in a clear teapot. You're allowed to try more than one flavor of tea! Also tell them if it's a special occasion—they might surprise with a special cupcake or treat. They let you take leftovers!

STARS: 4½ ∼ A few reports of slow service or missing items (like the fizzy drink), so be sure to politely request anything you see others being served. Dress Code: None, but this is a festive place and a conservative luxury hotel.

*H*OW OLDE: 🎎🎎🎎🎎🎎
∼ *the most fun but not the most authentic*
Price: £39, child £20 | **Hours**: 1-5:30pm | **Details**: See Ch. 6
Chesterfield Mayfair, email meetch@rchmail.com, or telephone +44 20 7491 2622

THE EGERTON HOUSE HOTEL

Taking tea here is like visiting a friend's English country house—a hundred years ago. The small Victorian-era drawing room—with sparkling chandelier and cozy fire—will feel like you're stepping into a romance novel, and the small size lends an intimacy to the experience that can't be found elsewhere. As my only tea recommendation in the Knightsbridge area, if you're planning to tour the Victoria & Albert Museum or shop at Harrods, make a reservation to this quiet oasis for a pleasurable afternoon before venturing back out into the fray.

And then there are the martinis! Well-heeled locals know to stop in for that perfect drink at the perfect temperature. In fact, Egerton is sort of secretly famous as the place to go if you want a cozy rendezvous. The tiny little bar tucked in a corner is tended by a gentleman in white tails who'll treat you like an old acquaintance *and* the valuable customer that you are. After decades in service, the wonderful Antonio has retired, but Esley has stepped in to fill his friendly shoes and reports are he's doing a great job. He'll make all the classic and modern concoctions too, but I recommend their signature drink, simply named: The Martini. It's not shaken, nor stirred. Rather the glass is frozen and the gin is too, down to -22°C (-7.6°F). With a dash of vermouth and a single squeeze of lemon, *c'est parfait!*

~ *For the guys surprise!* If your partner is an amateur mixologist, treat him or her to a one-hour Martini Masterclass complete with canapés, and Esley will reveal the secrets to making a perfect martini (£45pp, reservations required).

The Egerton is a small luxury hotel with exquisite service, and don't worry that you're not a guest there. They welcome all for tea or cocktails. Tea reservations are advised, and request drawing room seating in advance as overflow is placed in the bar or dining room.

FEATURES: Gluten, Vegan, and Vegetarian tea menus. Children's Teddy Bear's Picnic with Edwin includes a coloring pack and mini Edwin bear to take home. If by some chance you travel with your pooch, this is the only Doggy Afternoon Tea out there, with meatloaf, biscuits, dog ice-cream, and a chew toy to take home. **TIP**: 25% discount through Booktable (from Egerton website, subject to availability). Unlimited tea and coffee too, plus they'll package the leftover foods.

STARS: 4.5 ~ Dress Code: business casual. Hours: tea 12-6pm, so you can make it lunch or a pre-theatre dinner. Cocktails into the evening.

How OLDE: ⚜⚜⚜⚜⚜ ~ *great place for a martini too!*
Price: £40, child £20, £15 for doggy tea | Hours: tea 12–6pm
Details: See Ch. 6 Egerton House, bookeg@rchmail.com, or
telephone +44 20 7589 2412

Esley, the Egerton's master mixologist at work

ANNA'S AFTERNOON TEA AT THE PARK ROOM

Grosvenor House, A JW Marriott Hotel

The hotel is not nearly old enough to deserve a place in this guide, but it's here because of the strong American and royal connections described in Ch. 6. Afternoon tea can be had in the Library (really a lobby area) or in the Park Room restaurant. The lobby is nice if you're in the mood for the relaxed atmosphere of sitting on a divan with the meal spread on a linen-covered coffee table—closest to how it was served in Victorian times.

However, most will find dining in the Park Room more celebratory with a pianist playing light, flirtatious music, some sounding quite Victorian-esque. The festive atmosphere is carried into a traditional tea presentation with white linen, white china accented in mint and gold, and wait staff in mint-green vests. The Executive Pastry Chef oversees a team of nine pastry bakers to create delicious and visually eye-catching treats. I found the finger sandwiches particularly good—shrimp with Marie Rose sauce and roast-beef with creamed horseradish—as well as the clotted cream with just a hint of sweet. Signature teas, from Scotland to India to China, and ∼ *for the guys* who want something a little stronger than tea or bubbly, they offer inventive signature cocktails, many featuring their Serpentine Gin, commissioned exclusively from Blackdown of Sussex. There's even a hard tea (called The Unusual Golden Tea) if you want your tea and your liquor all in one glass. Or add a glass of champagne for £10. Their children's tea comes pint-sized with a cuddly Grover to take home (the official Grosvenor stuffed bulldog in butler's black-tail).

Be warned, however, that the décor is contemporary with only a hint of old world in the classical lines and long drapes. The room is spacious and, adding to that luxurious feel, the tables are spaced well apart. They work to make up for their lack of Victorian atmosphere by featuring the 7th Duchess of Bedford's role in establishing this tradition. And they make the experience their own with understated elegance and a sort of relaxed formality—an oxymoron I know, but somehow still true. Check out the website (www.ParkRoom.co.uk) for their Afternoon Tea Etiquette where, among other things, you'll learn which direction to stir your tea and whether the clotted cream goes on top or beneath the jam on the scone. A weighty question, to be sure.

Try the Jasmine Pearl
flowering tea

That, notes an English friend, is "a very weighty question!! Connoisseurs and commoners alike—indeed rival counties—have almost come to blows over it!!!! (And obviously, the cream goes on top of the jam!)."†

FEATURES: Gluten-Free tea menu. **TIP**: Their extended tea hours mean you can make this a late lunch or an early pre-theatre dinner. For romance, ask for a table by the window with a view of Hyde Park, particularly pretty during the holidays when lights festoon the stately old trees. Prepaying through other websites can bring you unlimited champagne for 1½ hours (Bookatable). Too stuffed to finish, you can take the cake slice home in a fancy little box. Let them know about any celebrations and they might surprise your celebrant.

STARS: 4.5 ∼ Dress Code: None listed, but the primarily female diners dressed fashionably well. Upon my query, the waitress said that in the summer, there might be Americans in shorts, but that wouldn't be my recommendation, not unless they're darn nice shorts.

*H*OW OLDE: ⚜⚜⚜⚜⚜
 ∼ *a very classy but not old-world experience*
Price: £42.50, child £15 | **Hours**: Daily 12:30–6pm; pianist 2-6pm
Details: See Ch. 6 Grosvenor House or telephone +44 20 7399 8452

---

† *I'd love to know your thoughts on the great clotted cream and jam layering controversy at www.facebook.com/RomanceReadersTravelGuides.*

St. Ermin's Tea Lounge

The St. Ermin's is a mix of lux modern and period splendor, and they carry that eclecticism into their afternoon tea—with old world décor, Victorian-slash-ultrahip food presentation, and signature tea menus. Décor: their "Tea Lounge" is up a grand double staircase where you'll either be seated at a glass table looking over an ornate banister or inside the small period room with the traditional white tablecloth-covered tables. It made me wish I had dressed the part in a Victorian day-dress and enormous hat with feather plumes. Presentation: you'll dine on red- or blue-flowered English country china, but the serving tray has morphed into a sort-of bookshelf with a handle. The other three-tiered tray used sometimes is more to my taste, and I wanted to slip it into my shopping bag (*I didn't!*)—it was round like an upright hatbox, modern, and super cool. And, lastly, the food: They have the usual trappings—savories and sweets—but St. Ermin's likes to mix it up with seasonal signature creations that are distinctly foodie, incorporating ethnic seasonings and unusal flavorings. Most recently, it's Gin & Ginger, with these essences infused in their delecacies. A suggested mini-decanter of gin and unlimited tonic is advised to truly appreciate the experience. For me, that would only work if I were staying at the St. Ermin's and could head immediately upstairs to sleep it off, but it might be just the thing to entice your man to join you. Also, stress ∾ *for the guys* the master spy-history of the place (see Ch. 6).

The St. Ermin's takes the farm-to-table trend to a delectable extreme. They operate a rooftop plantation with a thriving colony of bees and a compact kitchen garden. Not only can you buy jars of their urban-farmed honey, but also they serve the honey, fruits, and vegetables in their restaurant and afternoon tea. Even their cocktails can get a hint of honey. Their adorable Buzzy Bees Tea for children (offered weekends and school holidays) features a yellow window box with bumblebee decoration, and even the cake icing looks like a beehive right out of *Winnie the Pooh*. Afterwards, head to the third floor and you can watch, from behind a glass window, the 350,000 Buckfast bees busily buzzing about making honey.

FEATURES: Each table has two mini-hourglass timers for making sure your tea is properly brewed—the green sand for green tea (3 mins) and the black for black (5 mins). Gluten-free menu. **TIP**: Bargain Bubbly—just £35 for afternoon tea and unlimited Prosecco for 1½ hours.

STARS: 4 ∾ Dress Code: Business casual. Tea Lounge is open weekends/holidays only; otherwise served in the modern library.

*H*ow Olde: 🌸🌸🌸🌸🌸
~ *the hotel is Victorian but the tea is Millennial*
Price: £29, child £15 **Hours**: 12-6pm **Details**: See Ch. 6 St. Ermin's Hotel or telephone +44 20 7222 7888

*F*or the Governess on Holiday ~ *under £10*

◇❧────────────────◆

THE ORANGERY AT THE FAN MUSEUM

Cream Tea without the fancy (and expensive) extras—a terrific bargain and a pleasant excursion to Greenwich! Simple, charming, delicious. Served in the museum's Orangery. It's super quaint—the inside painted like you're inside a Victorian gazebo and complemented by black & white tiled floor, white china, and bentwood chairs at round little tables—à la French bistro. The menu is a pot of tea or a cafetiere of coffee, and generous portions of Victoria Sponge, choice of lemon drizzle cake or salted caramel brownie, and a scone with clotted cream and

•────────────❦◇❧────────────•

The delightful Fan Museum Orangery!

jam. You'll be stuffed with sweets. This author surreptitiously wrapped the brownie in her paper napkin and tucked it in her purse for later.

As an aside, Victoria Sponge is an authentic English treat. The cake is first mentioned—called Bisket Bread—in a 1615 English housewifery book: *The English Huswife, Containing the Inward and Outward Virtues Which Ought to Be in a Complete Woman* by Gervase Markham (page 114[2]). The Victoria part—named after Queen Victoria—is raspberry jam and whipped cream sandwiched between two layers of sponge and dusted on top with caster sugar (called superfine in the US).

FEATURES: Anyone with allergies/food intolerances should contact the museum in advance. **TIP**: For added adventure, take a ferry on the Thames to Greenwich Pier (*see* excursion to Fan Museum, Ch. 7). Museum Admission *must* be purchased to take tea here, but admission is FREE for London Pass holders and on Tuesdays for seniors/disabled. Wheelchair accessible. Also an inexpensive venue for small afternoon parties of 32 or less, such as showers or birthdays.

STARS: 4 ∾ Almost universal praise. Dress Code: none.

How **OLDE**: ♟♟♟♟♟
Price: £8 plus £4 museum admission | **Seatings**: Tues & Sun 1:45pm, 2:15pm, 3:15, 3:45pm—Reservations Required | **Drop In Seatings**: Fri & Sat 12:30-4pm—Walk-Ins Only, seating not guaranteed | You have the table for 1 hr 15 min | **Details**: See Fan Museum, Ch. 7 & 9, for history/directions
Email for reservations: info@thefanmuseum.org.uk

Ancient Eats and Historic Pubs

The food in English public houses is pretty standard fare. Dishes such as fish & chips (fish & French fries), bangers & mash (sausages and mashed potatoes), meat pie, and the like, constitute 'pub grub' and are so common that one can expect a certain level of quality when ordering. When pubs offer fancier fare there's risk it might not meet your expectations. I note when it's best to stick to the basics.

ANCHOR BANKSIDE

Est. 1665

THEN: Today it's the sole survivor of the riverside inns that existed in Southwark during Shakespeare's time. Why mention the bard? This neighborhood was home to the Globe, Swan, and Rose theatres and was the genesis of great theatrical inspiration. It's almost certain that he imbibed ale here more than once after a late night of rehearsals or perhaps to celebrate a hit.

Official records for the Anchor only date back to 1822, but other sources make clear this place was around long before that. And prior to that, things were rather grisly. It was a Roman grave (400s). Later there were bear and bull baiting pits, which in turn were used as plague pits (1603)—and yes, plague pits mean just what you think. By 1665, things had recovered enough that Josiah Childs could open a pub here. Over the course of its long history, it has been a tavern, brothel, brewery, ship's chandler, perhaps even a place where pirate goods were stored. Its 18th Century nickname was Thrales of Deadman's Place. Ralph Thrale had purchased the Anchor Brewery in 1729,[3] and we can surmise why it was called Deadman's Place.

Sitting right on the Thames, the Anchor Bankside offers great views of central London, but for one ancient patron this was a horrific experience. After trying with no effect to rouse help to fight the Great Fire of 1666, Samuel Pepys (the famous diarist) and his wife ended up watching it consume London from the Anchor, writing that he took refuge in "a little alehouse on bankside and there watched the fire grow." Can you imagine hearing the roar of a fire so big it made its own wind, the rain of burning ash like a hellish snowstorm, the screams of animals and humans, and the destruction of some 13,000 buildings—four-fifths of London City was destroyed. That's 87% of the 80,000 citizen's homes. (for a good timeline, see www.Telegraph.co.uk/news/2016/09/05/how-the-great-fire-of-london-unfolded-350-years-ago-hour-by-hour.) Macabre Fun Fact: There are some theories that the Great Fire helped end the Plague, wiping out the dense area of infestation and replacing it with wider streets and cleaner homes.

While the fire even set boats ablaze in the Thames, it didn't succeed in jumping the river to get to the south side. However, the pub was burned to the ground a mere four years later, in a smaller south bank fire. So the current structure dates to 1775.

NOW: The Grade II listed Anchor Bankside looks scrumptiously "Merry Old England" both inside and out—there's even a cobblestone street in front. However, it's also a major tourist site, so unless one goes very early on a weekday, expect huge crowds, sometimes-surly service, and possibly dirty bathrooms. You'll need to be armed with determination, but the fish and chips is delish and the conversation fun. We managed to find seats by asking to join other tourists from Nice and Barcelona, which resulted in a delightful, good-natured, game of international telephone—Spanish-English-French translating because no one spoke all three. Fun! Nearby sights include the reconstructed Globe Theatre and the Clink Museum (see Prisons Ch. 3).

TIP: Sign up for Taylor Walker Email Club and get £5 off your meal. Check website for periodic specials. In summer, try to score a table on the roof terrace for great views of the river and the waterfront promenade crowds. Pre-book a table because it's super busy, and, bonus, you'll get table service, rather than having to queue at the bar.

STARS: 3 ～ Disinterested service drags ratings down, but the Anchor gets high marks for food. Try the steak & ale pie, and the usual F&C is reported to be fresh here. Dress Code: None...well shirt and shoes, *you know!*

𝓗OW OLDE: ♔♔♔♔♔
Price: mains £10–15 | **Hours**: food M–Sat 11am–10pm, Sun 12–9pm (drinks longer) | **Tube**: London Bridge | www.Taylor-walker.co.uk/ pub/anchor-bankside-southwark/p0977 | +44 20 7407 1577
34 Park St, Southwark

⸻◇❤✍◦————————————•

CITTIE OF YORKE
Est. 1430

THEN: A pub site since medieval times, the current incarnation is Victorian (although the building dates only to the 1920s, when it was once again rebuilt in the Victorian style). The front looks like a movie set, and I love the big, old square clock! The inside is all about ambiance—the dark wood interior, long wood bar, giant beer barrels, wood-beam ceiling, and a great iron fireplace in the center.

NOW: Expect it to be crowded with tourists and legal-eagles, even standing room only, and for a tired tourist with aching legs that might be just too much to bear. If you manage to snag one of the Victorian-style dark-wood cubicles you'll be lucky. Oft frequented by lawyers from Gray's Inn, next door. If you spot clean-cut young women in black, ghastly-unattractive business attire complete with black tights—they're not secretaries, but new barristers.

Owned by Samuel Smiths, the prices are a great value, but don't expect haute cuisine or hand crafted beers. Features: super cheap beer—a pint for £3.10—and good prices on pub grub. **TIP**: If you're not claustrophobic, check out the ancient Cellar Bar and you might find a seat there, plus you'll get faster service.

STARS: 4 ～ Reports are decent pub food at a good price. Thank you to reviewer Kristine for this yummy recommendation. I'll surely try next time I'm there: 2/3ʳᵈˢ chocolate beer and 1/3ʳᵈ cherry beer. **TAKE HEED!** As a Samuel Smith branded pub, its all their proprietary drinks with brew names that won't necessarily ring a bell—you'll have to ask if you want to know what you're getting. Dress Code: tired, sneaker-wearing tourist is just fine.

*H*OW OLDE: 🏵🏵🏵🏵🏵
～ *while the building is new-ish, the décor is ancient*
Prices: mains £7.50–13 | **Hours**: M-Sat 11:30am–11pm | Closed Sun
Tube: Chancery Lane, Holborn, Farringdon | **Map**: D | No website
+44 20 7242 7670 | 22 High Holborn (Legal London)

◇～〜───────────────────────●

THE GEORGE INN
Pre–1543

This is as authentic as they come—by far the oldest working pub and only surviving galleried inn building within London. However, today this Southwark (south of the Thames) establishment is such a tourist stop and frequently so filled with pub-crawling young people that it won't provide an authentic experience of dining in a posting inn. Certainly any Regency heroine would have banished herself to her upstairs chamber, rather than face the mobs below.

THEN: Originally called the "St. George Inn," due to its proximity to the nearby church, this was originally a medieval coaching inn across the river from "The City." As an aside, the famous Tabard Inn (demolished in 1873) where Chaucer began *The Canterbury Tales* was in the same neighborhood. Both were burned to the ground and rebuilt after the Great Fire of Southwark in 1676. The George was recreated in the "old plan," having open wooden galleries leading to the chambers on each side of the inn-yard," reports Mr. Timbs in his old book, *London and Westminster.*[4]

At the time, London Bridge was the only crossing to the city along Borough High Street, and The George was one of many inns offering lodging and food for visitors and merchants who either wanted to spend the night outside the city proper (less expensive) or arrived after the gates to the city had clanged shut for the night. Just like any of our romance novels, the patrons arriving by carriage would have their horses immediately seen to by servants in the stable yard, while the well heeled would be shown to private chambers and served meals. Those on a budget would eat in the public rooms alongside locals.

These Borough High Street inns were exceedingly profitable operations until the advent of the railway, which made it possible for people to visit London for their business and return home on the same day. Additionally, train travel being considerably less arduous than coach travel, the coaching aspect of these inns evaporated almost overnight when the London Bridge Station opened in 1836.

The Borough High Street inns quickly deteriorated, becoming everything from tenement housing to railway ticket offices, but in the end most were demolished. Serendipitously, The George was eventually sold to the Great Northern Railway, where it was used as a receiving house for goods shipped on the railway—roughly 100 tons were weighed every day. This kept the building useful for a while, but soon lorries replaced trains and again it faced destruction. Luckily, in 1937 The National Trust bought it, protecting it from demolition, although only the south wing remains.[5]

NOW: Greene King brewery operates the Grade I listed building as a pub and restaurant under lease from the National Trust. The ground floor is divided into a number of connected bars. Today's Parliament room used to be the waiting room, and the Middle Bar was formerly the coffee room. Charles Dickens was known to spend a lot of time there, and refers to The George in *Little Dorrit*. Much earlier, Shakespeare was also a guest here. The upstairs restaurant, where the bedrooms once were, will feel more authentic with exposed beams, tapestries, old maps, and drawings. On a nice day you can eat outside at picnic tables.

Food: Typical pub grub. Features: Free Wi-Fi.

TIP: Sometimes 12-5pm specials, such as Burger & Chips, and the Ale's on them (see website for current offerings).

STARS: 4 ∽ Reports of slow service. High marks for beer, but stick to traditional English fare here. Dress Code: none.

*H*ow Olde: 🍷🍷🍷🍷🍷 ~ *eat upstairs for period ambiance*
Prices: mains £12 and up | **Hours**: Daily 11am–11pm; Sun 12–10pm
Tube: London Bridge | www.George-Southwark.co.uk |
hello@george-southwark.co.uk | +44 20 7407 2056
75–77 Borough High St, Southwark

GORDON'S WINE BAR IN KIPLING HOUSE
Est. 1890 in a 17th Century cellar

This feels like an adventure. First you have to find the unassuming place and the narrow doorway. Then you climb down a steep set of rickety stairs, the darkness almost palpable. Finally, you arrive in an arched wine cellar. There's no 'decoration' per se, it's enough that it exists. Dark. Dusty. But definitely *not* dreary. Vintage bottles line the shelves. Yellowed newspapers adorn the walls. And it's old, so very old. It feels like all sorts of intrigue must have taken place here—smuggling perhaps, prisoners held captive, the writing of famous stories. And it's like nothing has changed—or been dusted—since it opened 125 years ago.

Thought to be the oldest wine bar in London, it's owned and operated by the Gordon family. Only wine is served along with "traditional well priced grub." The rustic stews are wonderful.

Take the stairs down, down, down...

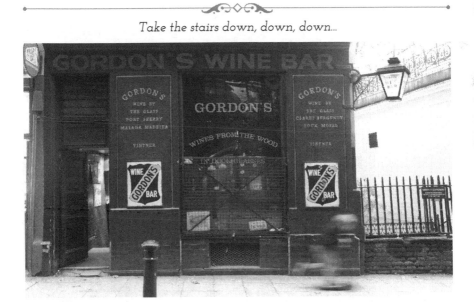

There's also outside seating for 80 along Watergate Walk, but the period atmosphere is downstairs in two vaulted rooms dating to the 1600s. The first has a high ceiling and houses the bar and food service (order here) plus a few old wooden tables. The other space is the truly atmospheric and claustrophobic section. It feels like a cave. Low ceiling, lit primarily by candles stuck in empty wine bottles, and seating for about 30 at 9 long tables. At the far end is the coveted spot, the oldest part—called "the cage" because it's set behind rusted iron bars and looks like a medieval prison. Dating perhaps to the 15th Century, it's reserved for bookings of 8–10 people. As an aside, I am claustrophobic, but I managed to enjoy myself just fine down there—while the ceiling is low, the space is fairly long.

THEN: The earliest reference to this Strand neighborhood was in 1237. Owned by the Bishops of Norwich, it was a large estate on the banks of the Thames. Following Henry VIII's dissolution of the monasteries, the Duke of Suffolk took control in 1536. Francis Bacon, the famous philosopher and onetime Lord Chancellor of England, was born here in 1561 when it was called York House. The Dukes of Buckingham owned it from 1622 to 1674. Heavily in debt, the 2nd Duke developed the land and built houses, including the first house on this exact site (c.1670). Rebuilt after a fire, it became home to the diarist Samuel Pepys (1688–1701).

Today, the bar resides in a third rebuilt building dating from 1792. However, for most of the building's history, the place stood on the banks of the Thames. It was even used as a seed warehouse from 1820–1864, but that ended when the river was embanked and pushed back 164 feet. Fun Fact: Next to Embankment Gardens, look for an ornate white stone York House watergate, a remnant of the earlier mansion, which shows where the Thames originally ended.

The building was then turned into accommodations in 1880, and the first of the three successive different Gordon families moved in, with Angus Gordon opening the cellar bar in 1890. The most illustrious tenant was Rudyard Kipling; he wrote *The Light That Failed* there (1889–1891). The building was renamed in his honor in 1950. Other authors that frequented the bar were Tennyson and Chesterton. Due to the fact that a playhouse once stood directly opposite, and because it's near Covent Garden, the bar has long been popular with actors, including Laurence Olivier and Vivien Leigh in the last century.

FUN FACT: The first Gordon Bar owner Angus Gordon was one of the few remaining 'free vintners' chartered to sell wines without a license due to a long ago pact. Back in 1364, Edward III granted 15 such charters, passed down through generations, because the King was unable to repay a loan vintners had made to him. Another quirk—the current bar is owned by 'Gordons' but they are totally unrelated to the original Angus. In 1975, Luis Gordon, chairman of Luis Gordon & Sons, sole importers of Domecq sherries to Britain for more than 200 years but not a chartered vintner as none exist anymore, came across this bar and took it over. Just a happy coincidence that he had the same name, and his family continues to run it today.

NOW: As recently as 1990, we almost lost this unique establishment. Then-owner Luis Gordon was a character and lovingly—luckily—refused to make any changes or improvements to the historic bar. He was also a fighter. He, like his predecessors, only leased the place, and in 1990 fought a 333% rent increase that would have bankrupted the bar—the property owners sought to kick all tenants out and build a new something. Using newspaper ads to get the word out, the family won the battle in 1995. With Kipling House apartments selling for more than £2 million today, the building isn't likely to be torn down anytime soon.

FEATURES: Go for the afternoon "plates"—they're a bargain and yummy. Award-winning wine list at reasonable prices. Sherries/ports served from the barrel. **TIP**: Seating is first-come, first-serve; no reservations, except for online booking of "the cage" for 8–10. Otherwise, to be assured of a table arrive around 4pm. Sharing tables at this popular place is *de rigueur*—just smile and ask to join. This place is described as "ludicrously crowded," but that's because it has unparalleled medieval atmosphere downstairs and great prices and delish food. Celebrate with a glass of sparkling Prosecco, only £7.25. A glass of red can be had for a bargain £5.50. Or try some "Fat Bastard Rosé"—'cause don't you just love the name! Also on offer are Vegan, Low Sulphite, and Biodynamic (organic) wines.

STARS: 4½ ∾ Nothing but positives, but tall people—watch your head! Dress Code: casual.

*H*ow OLDE: 🌿🌿🌿🌿🌿
Prices: mains £9–11 | **Hours**: M-Sat 11am–11pm; Sun 12–10pm | Real food 12:30–3pm; Tapas only 6–9pm | **Tube**: Embankment, Charing Cross | **Map**: D | www.GordonsWineBar.com
info@gordonswinebar.com | +44 20 7930 1408 | 47 Villiers St

LAMB & FLAG
Est. 1772

THEN: It's hard to say which pub is truly the oldest in London—and what does that mean anyway? Oldest building. Earliest site for a pub, because none have been run by the same owner for all these centuries and most of the buildings have been rebuilt at some point. Longest in continuous operation, perhaps. Certainly we're not looking for the oldest food or ancient-est soured ale. Regardless of all these considerations, the Lamb & Flag is one very, very, old public house. And it's thought to be one of the oldest, if not the oldest in London proper.

When your romantic suspense hero needs to meet his contact somewhere—*this* would be the place. And while no lady of quality would *ever* dine here, it's an ideal setting for the disguised princess to hide out or the barmaid to meet her prince. And there's darn good food too!

Founded as The Coopers Arms, the name changed to L&F in 1833. The name has ties to the Knights Templar, and the Holy Lamb bearing a golden streamer is a Templar theme and also representative of the Middle Temple (the legal version, see Inns of Court, Ch. 3). While the brick façade dates only to 1958, it's believed the frame is 18th Century,

which replaced the first one built in 1638, which was also believed to be a pub, but can't be proved. It was also nicknamed the Bucket of Blood, because of the bare-knuckle prize fighting that took place there early on.

The alleyway beside the pub is also the site of the famous Rose-Alley Ambuscade, an ambush that took place late at night in 1679 and is

◇❧
Can't get much more
Ye Olde than this!
Plus great pub grub.

something that could be right out of a romance novel. The English Poet Laureate, John Dryden, was beaten by thugs hired by John Wilmot, 2nd Earl of Rochester, angry over the poet's anonymous *Essay upon Satyr* that made mockery of him. Funny thing—John didn't write it, yet another John did. Well, John D. survived . . . barely. John W. was unencumbered by proof of connection to the dirty deed. But in the weird way of bullies, it was the elderly Dryden who was seen to have lost his honor.[6] Following the attack, he was often mocked and he never succeeded in finding out who was behind it.

NOW: Up a small alleyway off Garrick Street, this is a step back in time—the surroundings are super quaint, with hanging flower baskets and ye-olde-style lamps, and there's even a skinny cobblestone lane. It was my favorite pub and my DH remembers fondly the bangers and mash. The steak and ale pie also gets high marks. On summer days one can enjoy a pint outside standing on the street, but on the cold rainy day we were there, we lucked into two stools at the window ledge. Upstairs in the Grade II listed building there's more table seating, in what were most likely bedrooms in yonder days. Owned by the Fuller Smith Turner's chain, it serves standard pub food. Reservations can be made for table service. Features: Live Jazz Night on the first Sunday of the month (since 1993, from 8–10:15pm). **TIP**: Their Sunday roast is a delicious value.

STARS: 4 ∼ But some reports of rude service. Dress Code: casual.

How OLDE: 🏵🏵🏵🏵🏵
Prices: mains £10–18 | **Hours**: M-Sat 11am–10:30pm | **Tube**: Covent Garden, Leicester Square | www.LambAndFlagCoventGarden.co.uk lambandflag.manager@fullers.co.uk | +44 20 7497 9504
33 Rose St, Covent Garden

THE SEVEN STARS
Est. 1602

THEN: Originally named the Leg and Seven Stars to attract Dutch sailors, who hailed from the Seven United Provinces of the Netherlands. Back then the docks were closer with the River Fleet nearby (now underground) and the Thames had not yet been embanked. The building's age is not definite, but it is ancient, having managed to escape the Great Fire, which stopped just short of this area. Shakespeare's plays were performed at nearby Middle Temple, so it seems likely that the Bard may have had a pint or two here. It's also believed that Charles Dickens used the pub as a model for The Magpie & Stump in *Pickwick Papers*.[7]

NOW: Today, rather than Dutch sailors, you're more likely to find Lincoln's Inn barristers. Actually, it can be crowded full of 'em, and by Friday night many will have left their venerable intonation and court manners behind in chambers. That's not to say they are all there carousing, but on occasion...

This pub is a rare thing in the age of chains—independently owned and operated by Roxy Beaujolais (co-presenter on the BBC's "Full on Food" show and a pub-food cookbook author). With her history, the fare is "Gastronomic Pub Food"—it says so on the window. But, really, it was delicious. Butter bean soup for my DH, and for me lamb hash with hints of Indian seasoning. It's hearty, meaty fare, but with enough unusual flavorings to make a foodie happy. The menu changes daily, so you'll get whatever she's in the mood to serve, although there's usually a vegetarian option. There are even fresh salads with flavorful house dressing—in a *pub!* They've a broad selection of unusual bottled brews.

This is not a fancy place, it's décor more vintage garage sale than genuinely old world, but somehow it works and feels authentic. As their website amusingly notes, The Seven Stars is "not overburdened with space." Tiny and laid out differently than most pubs, there's space for about 20 to sit and eat and 20 more to stand and drink. We found seats in the purple room to the left—quirky but not as historic. Go right upon entering for oldie-ness.

For many years, Tom Paine was a famous resident at The Seven Stars, but sadly in 2011 this Elizabethan-ruffled-collar-wearing cat has passed on to chasing mice in ghost pubs. Look for his replacement, Peabody, and for those white legal wigs on display in the window. Features: Unlike many of the Legal London pubs, this one stays open all weekend and you're more likely to enjoy a quiet visit at this time. **TIP**: Close enough to Covent Garden for a pre-theatre dinner. **TAKE HEED**! This is a quirky old Elizabethan building, Grade II, and the bathrooms are up very steep stairs—described as life-threatening by some (I didn't use them, which I can't for the life of me think why, since that's something I always check).

STARS: 4 ∿ Some complain of too-small portions. Others report too large. But mine was "just right." This is not the kind of place where the landlady wants to make nice-nice; rather she rules her roost from her favorite seat and doesn't seem to want to be bothered by anyone but her buddies. But sometimes she and her staff can be quite friendly. For me, the level of friendliness was...just right. Dress Code: casual.

*H*ow Olde: ♟♟♟♟♟
Prices: mains £11–25 | **Hours**: M-Sat 11am–11pm; Sun 12–10:30pm
Tube: Temple, Chancery Lane | **Map**: D
www.TheSevenStars1602.co.uk | +44 20 7242 8521
53 Carey St, Holborn (Legal London)

◇-❧⁄◦————————————•

SHERLOCK HOLMES PUB

Est. 1880s ⁓ *for the guys*

THEN: Formerly, this pub was a small Victorian hotel called the Northumberland Arms, and the building dates to the 1880s. Prior, this was the house of the Duke of Northumberland.[8] It seems likely that this is the same hotel referenced in Sir Arthur Conan Doyle's 1901 *The Hound of the Baskervilles.*" For documentary proof, here Watson watches Holmes examine a letter:

> He laid an envelope upon the table, and we all bent over it. It was of common quality, greyish in colour. The address, "Sir Henry Baskerville, Northumberland Hotel", was printed in rough characters; the post-mark "Charing Cross", and the date of posting the preceding evening.

Charing Cross is the correct postal address for this pub, plus Holmes and Watson were known to frequent the Turkish baths located next door at 25 Northumberland (the women's Moorish style entrance can still be seen in Craven Passage which runs alongside the pub). Additionally, less than a block away is Great Scotland Yard, which formerly backed the original police commissioner's Whitehall office.

At some point the hotel began operations solely as a tavern, and in 1957, the owners came into an unusual windfall—the Holmes exhibit from the 1951 Festival of Britain. Curated by the Westminster Library, this was a carefully researched recreation of the "study" of Sherlock Holmes and his partner Dr. Watson, upon the detective's return to London in 1894. In this display, installed upstairs where table-service dining is located, you'll see some of his most famous accouterment—his pipe, violin, and snuff box with a giant amethyst, a gift from the King of Bohemia when Holmes solved the great Irene Adler Papers caper.[9] Sadly, Sherlock has stepped out for the moment—*he's always out*—so you'll miss him on your visit.

NOW: Owned by Greene King brewers, it's a popular spot with tourists. As with most taverns, stick to pub grub for reliable food, rather than trying any fancier offerings. While there are the ubiquitous dark wood interior, old bottles, and beer casks, this is more about quirky fun than an authentic period ambiance. Features: Beer garden, free WiFi, and Traditional Sunday Roast. Doubles as a sports bar.

STARS: 4 ∼ High marks for the fish & chips starter platter and house beer. Recently reports of slow, "meh" service or cold food. Dress Code: casual.

How Olde: 🏅🏅♟♟♟
∼ *for the Sherlock Holmes or Steampunk enthusiast*
Prices: mains £10–17 | **Hours**: Sun–Thurs 8am–11pm; Fri–Sat 8am–12midnight (food 8am–10pm) | **Tube**: Charing Cross
www.SherlockHolmes-stjames.co.uk
hello@sherlockholmes-stjames.co.uk | +44 20 7930 2644
10 Northumberland St, St. James's neighborhood

◇–∾∽∾––––––––––––––––––•

TWO CHAIRMEN PUBLIC HOUSE
Est. 1729

THEN: Thought to be one of the oldest pubs in Westminster, it sprang up opposite the Royal Cockpit, built here in the early 1700s for upper class men to watch and bet on cockfights (see Cockpit Stairs Ch. 3). The new pub served sturdy workingmen who waited for the call of "Chair Ho," and then *two chairmen* would spring into action to carry a nob away in a sedan chair. Hence the quirky name.

What's a sedan chair? It's a little box big enough to hold one person (like a tiny carriage) that was carried by two men. While women might occasionally be inside one, given the strictures requiring chaperoning, it was more likely a lady would be transported inside a horse-drawn carriage accompanied by her husband, friend, or lady's maid. And this convenience wasn't just for elderly men. If the destination was too close to bother with the carriage, the sedan chair protected the elegantly shod and silk-stocking wearing noble from the dirty, muddy, human-refuse-filled streets and even from attack by thieves, since he'd have the protection of two burly men.

NOW: Great little pub tucked away from the hustle and bustle, but sadly not open on weekends. Pretty hanging flowers decorate the outside, and inside is superbly Victorian with burgundy drapes, period chandeliers, and an ornate fireplace (try to grab a leather wingback chair). Unfortunately, too-loud music and a slot machine mar the old-world feel. This neighborhood is full of small alleys and pretty mews, and the blue plaques abound commemorating the influential that once lived here. Owned by Taylor Walker, but they carry other brands of brew as well.

FEATURES: AC and WiFi. **TIP**: Sign up for Taylor Walker Email Club for £5 off your next meal. Check website for periodic specials. Upstairs is quieter dining (rickety old-timey stairs too). **STARS**: 4 ~ Steak and ale pie gets high marks. Dress Code: none.

*H*ow Olde: 🏺🏺🏺🏺🏺
Prices: mains £9–15 | **Hours**: M–F 12–11pm (food till 9pm); recently experimenting with opening Sat 12–5pm | Closed Sunday
Tube: St. James's Park | www.Taylor-Walker.co.uk/pub/Two-Chairmen-Public-House-westminster/c0677 | +44 20 7222 8694
39 Dartmouth St, Westminster

YE OLDE CHESHIRE CHEESE
Est. 1538

THEN: The current building only dates from 1667—yawn—when the pub was rebuilt after the Great Fire. In the intervening 350 years, "the cheese," as it's called, has remained largely unchanged. It has a Fleet Street address, but the entrance can be found around the corner on a quaint Wine Office Court alley.

Human activity in this area is prehistoric, but it's known that Fleet Street is one of the oldest roads leading to the original Roman city and was a thoroughfare by 200 AD. It was named after the Fleet River, which is now subterranean. Hard to picture it today in modern London, but it still runs deep down under Farringdon Street to the Thames.

By the 13th Century, the neighborhood was built up on the south side by different ecclesiastical factions—Knights Templar, Carmelite White Friars, and Black Friars. These areas retain their religious names today. While many attribute the pub's vaulted cellars to the White Friars, a 1270 map shows only one row of buildings on Fleet's north side and the Carmelite Priory well south.[10] Above that is completely blank, suggesting maybe that it was a field at the time. The cellars could still be ancient, perhaps leftover from a Roman ruin, or the Carmelites built a guesthouse sometime before 1538.

The rest of the history is spotty, but it's believed that the place was also a brothel in the 1750s, because a number of sexually explicit erotic plaster tiles were found in an upper room. (They were donated to the Museum of London in 1962.) The dark wood paneling is mostly from the 19th Century, but some is older and may date to 1667. A very old sign near the entrance states, "Gentlemen Only Served in this Bar." Luckily for us ladies, that is no longer enforced.

What is known about Ye Olde Cheshire Cheese is that it was a favorite of writers. Charles Dickens' favorite seat is next to the coal fireplace in the main-floor Chop Room, and he alludes to the place in his *A Tale of Two Cities* (a brass plaque commemorates the spot). Also look for a sign for Samuel Johnson, writer of the first English dictionary. Others included the poet Alfred Lord Tennyson, Yeats, and Sir Arthur Conan Doyle. For our American connection: Mark Twain and even Teddy Roosevelt were said to dine here.

NOW: The Grade II listed pub is run by Samuel Smith brewery, and it's exactly how you would picture an English pub—dark wood beams, low ceilings, little natural light, and open fireplaces give it a nice gloomy charm. There are four stories of small rooms, each offering different menus from pub grub to white-tablecloth, but the most atmospheric place to hang out is definitely an alcove in the arched cellar. Stick to traditional English items for best results. It is mostly self-service for the food and beer, so head to the bars to place your orders. As for bartender friendliness—imagine the gruff innkeeper of yore and you won't be disappointed.

FEATURES: ancient pub about sums it up. **TIP**: Walk around to find the room that most appeals to you. **TAKE HEED!** Might be best to visit this place for a mug of ale, rather than to fill an empty stomach. No reservations. Not wheelchair accessible. And, like many London establishments, there appears to be almost no heat—had to wear my coat through lunch.

STARS: 4 ∿ Reports that the food can be cold and the beer warm; and the service too runs hot and cold. One report of surcharge for using credit card. Dress Code: casual.

How OLDE: 🍺🍺🍺🍺🍺
Prices: mains £11–20 | **Hours**: M-Sat 11am–11pm | Closed Sunday
Tube: Temple, Blackfriars, Mansion House, St. Paul's | **Map**: D
No website | +44 20 7353 6170 | 145 Fleet St (entrance around corner on Wine Office Court)

YE OLDE MITRE
Est. 1546

THEN: During Elizabeth I's reign, this pub was built for the servants of the Bishops of Ely—an ancient order that sounds like something out of King Arthur lore. They're not that old, but the area is full of history. Henry VIII and his soon-not-to-be wife Catherine of Aragon attended a five-day feast hosted by the bishops at St. Ethelreda's crypt next door. Built in 1280, it's the oldest Roman Catholic church in London and one of only two remaining buildings from King Edward I's reign. Henry's daughter, Queen Elizabeth I, is rumored to have danced around a cherry tree (during May Day festivities) just in front of the pub with one of her loves, Sir Christopher Hatton.

The pub was rebuilt around 1772, after the bishop's palace was torn down. Along with a stone mitre (bishop's hat) from the palace, the cherry tree was also built into the

new front wall. Rumors are that it continued to live for a couple centuries. The church is the only surviving part of the bishop's extensive complex. Shakespeare's Richard II and III use these ancient sites as settings.[11]

NOW: Hidden down a skinny alleyway, you'll come to a tiny court as cute as they come! Unlike medieval times, the pavement's clean, potted flowers abound and, best of all, no one is going to toss their refuse down on your head. For anyone who's ever read historical romance scenes in taverns, the small square room past the main bar is as close as I've seen to my vision of one, with worn

Well worth hunting for...

wooden chairs, benches, small tables, and a Tudor fireplace. I doubt the small square windowpanes are original, but they certainly look old—the glass having that pleasing mottled look. And like very old buildings, watch your head—folks were shorter then.

In truth, the interior was remodeled in the 1930s, but they did a good job of keeping it Elizabethan, and the trunk of the 400-year-old cherry tree can still be seen in the corner of the front bar. Without TV's, gaming machines, or piped music, this is an authentic experience.

Ye Olde Mitre is too quaint to be real! But it is—I promise.

Today, Fuller's owns the Grade II listed pub and has received many awards for good ale and service over the years. They offer tapas, but their own English take on them, which means you can share a number of mini-sized traditional English dishes—lamb and mint pasties, steak & ale pie, Scotch eggs, and butchers pork scratchings. This is great for smaller appetites, like mine, since it's not often that one can try these in small portions. Summer months will find patrons enjoying standing-room-only in the alleyway, wooden casks serving as tables. Sometimes their chalkboard sign proclaims "Football Free Zone"—sounds great to me, given it's soccer—not football—and, anyway, I'm on vacation!

But it's not easy to find, hidden down an alley off the dead-end Ely Place (look for it between numbers 8 and 9). Better yet, continue to the end to visit gorgeous gothic St. Ethelreda's to view the stunning stained glass windows and magnificent arched wood ceiling. Want to drink your way through London—there's another passageway at lane's end, which leads to the Bleeding Heart Tavern. By the way, worship of King Midas is big here too. The neighboring road, Hatton Garden, which has a second alley entrance to Olde Mitre (again between 8 and 9), is the diamond trading capital of England with many fancy jewelry shops.

FEATURES: Free WiFi and garden seating. Planning a small event for 8–10? Reserve the super cute "Ye Closet," and have a little room all to yourself (a "snug" in British vernacular). **TIP**: Sign up for Fuller's "Join the Family" and you'll get a free pint or glass of wine. Their Beer Festivals (held 3x annually) are a great chance to sample beers from all over the world.

STARS: 4½ ～ In the winter, try Mulled Apple Cider with Sipsmith gin for £6.50—should warm you right up! Dress Code: none.

How OW OLDE: ♔♔♔♔♔ ～ *and the church too!*
Prices: small plates £1–4 | **Hours**: M-F 11am–11pm (food 11:30am–9:30pm) | Closed Sat–Sun | **Tube**: Chancery Lane, Farringdon
Map: D | www.YeOldeMitreHolborn.co.uk | 1 Ely Court, Ely Place
yeoldemitre@fullers.co.uk | +44 20 7405 4751

ST. ETHELDREDA'S
1250-Present

There's an interesting history of the church, the Reformation, and more, from the POV of the Catholic Church at their website. American Connection: ∼ *for the guys*: West Point Military Academy's Catholic Chapel is modeled on this church, and during WWII American servicemen on their way to the front lines would attend services here. Because of WWII devastation, the stained glass windows all date to 1952. One can see how old it is—the church sits lower than street level. Visiting the church is, of course, free, but donations for the ongoing restoration are greatly appreciated.

ℋOW OLDE: ⚜⚜⚜⚜⚜
Hours: M–Sat 8am–5pm | Sun only open for worship | **Masses:** M–F 1pm; Sun 9am, 11am (11am sung in Latin) | www.StEtheldreda.com | +44 20 7405 1061 | 14 Ely Place

𝒫eriod Dining in Hotels ∼ see Ch. 6 hotels for details

THE RITZ RESTAURANT:
Michelin-starred dining on English specialties in Louis XVI splendor. Pricey.

THE GILBERT SCOTT RESTAURANT:
St. Pancras Hotel offers classic English dishes in Victorian ambiance, plus a 3-course set menu that's a bargain.

QUEEN'S ROOM:
Amberley Castle's Queen's Room is gourmet cuisine in a 12th Century hall. Also pricey.

CHAPTER 6

Sleeping like a Princess or a Governess on Holiday

The *haut ton* families of London rarely took public lodgings while in town for the season, but today, alas, not many of us can afford to rent a house complete with staff. What we can afford with some saving and planning is to stay in a Mayfair town house turned boutique hotel, and if we're lucky even sleep in a cool antique four-poster bed. Staying in one of these bedrooms is a trip to the past, and it's easy to envision a Regency heroine, dressed for a ball, peering down at the street from her boudoir as she waits for her beau to arrive in a carriage. Or think of the fictional upstairs maid tending the rooms who later marries the owner and finds herself living there as its mistress. As noted in Ch. 3, things like this really did happen, albeit rarely.

Sleep like a princess in an antique gilded or four-poster bed!
Here at the Gore and at many other London hotels

And many fictional heroines are princesses-in-disguise or they marry-up the social ladder (such as Austen's Elizabeth Bennet), eventually finding themselves mistress of a glorious country estate or drafty medieval castle. Spending even one night in a castle hotel, easily accessible to London, can be a once-in-a-lifetime chance to feel like a princess, while walking the English gardens, dining in the great hall, or checking out the dungeon. And you can make it part of an easy overnight excursion to see other sights in the English countryside (Ch. 9).

But first, London, which offers a variety of historic lodging options ranging in price from bargain B&Bs even a governess could afford to five-star hotels costing a king's ransom. Each of the unique accommodations included here have some special connection to history, to romance, and often to America as well. And ∽ **for the guys** there are spies plus WWII ties, and for us, princesses, and ghosts, and other real-life delights.

TAKE HEED! In each listing we'll say what to watch out for, but in general staying in old and Grade listed buildings bring with it certain considerations. First, the rooms will probably be small and weirdly shaped. This is a top American complaint about European hotels, so go expecting a closet and hopefully you'll be pleasantly surprised. Second, the buildings may lack some modern conveniences, such as air conditioning or elevators (called lifts in UK), due to legal restrictions on changing these historic structures.

Unless specifically noted, **All** listings here offer these modern conveniences: lifts, en-suite bathrooms, television, hairdryer, credit card payment, air-conditioning (although in oddly shaped old buildings the cooling or heating may not be uniform). Is there a bathtub or only a shower?—this can vary from room to room within a hotel, so if this is important you'll want to confirm when making reservations. Any other amenities will be listed. TripAdvisor, Booking.com, and other UK review sites have been read extensively to find as many issues/quirks as possible about the properties listed here, since no one person—me—can stay in all the different rooms. The stars listed are an average of these sites. Still, it is not possible to warranty the standards of each listing because things, such as pricing or hotel services, can change overnight—so this Guide does not assume any responsibility for errors and urges readers to please contact the hotel if you have a specific need or concern.

Regarding smoking: it's illegal in all public areas in the UK (bars, restaurants, lobbies, Tube trains and stations, any public transport, etc.), however a few hotels offer smoking guest rooms. Because most listings here enforce a "Non-Smoking Policy" throughout their hotel, assume no smoking in the building at all, unless noted.

Lastly, the high cost of meals, cocktails, spa, etc., will be shocking to many. I found it by far the most expensive city that I've ever visited—think NYC-prices on steroids and you'll get the idea. Bargains can be had in London, but generally not for food/services in hotels. Breakfast is particularly expensive, so getting it included as part of the rate is ideal.

PRICE SCALES: each £ symbol equals $100 US

RATE CONSIDERATIONS: Many properties have a mix of room décor from modern (usually the least expensive) to period (sometimes with a four-poster bed and costing more). The Guide's price rating is based on summer website prices (a more expensive time) for the lowest-rate, basic double room. Four-poster beds and fancy suites will be noted, but they'll cost more, sometimes considerably more. Although, there are some bargains.

Listings are divided into Historical Lodging in London and Stay Like a Princess (outside the city). London is subdivided into: For a King's Ransom, Landed Gentry Would Feel Right at Home, and Governess on Holiday. While even the lowest category hardly seems priced for a governess's means, in London these rates equate to a three-star hotel. Therefore, one can expect any of the following might be true: it will be older rather than historic (as in, might need refurbishment), offer fewer services, and be in a less posh neighborhood (although safe). Conversely, such cheaper establishments are more likely to offer complimentary continental breakfast or other freebies.

ℋistorical Lodging in London
For a King's Ransom ∽ $400 and up

BROWN'S HOTEL, A ROCCO FORTE HOTEL
Est. 1837 ∽ £££££½

Coming in through the back door as I did, off skinny Dover Street, Brown's was at first unimpressive. It turns out that it isn't really the backside, just the Dover Street entrance, but it presents about as subtle a hotel entrance as can be. For that matter, the main Albemarle entrance is equally unimposing. One doorman, two small doors, three flags, and not much more. But that is what Brown's is all about—understatement, privacy, and in their words, "tradition and modernity."

Still, to the uninitiated on a first trip to London, it wasn't what I expected. After nodding graciously to the doorman and stepping confidently through the portal, I found myself in a hallway and no reception desk. It felt like a warren of little hallways with low ceilings, but I walked stoically onward with a show of belonging. It's definitely upper crust and old, but not showy or Victorian. The grandness of this place is more in the knowledge of all that has gone on within these walls, rather than in the décor, which is a fluid mix of eclectic styles and periods.

So why does Brown's rank first in this Guide? Especially at these prices? Because it is reputed to be one of the oldest full-service hotels in London. Because world changing events have taken place here. And because its history is chock-a-block full of princesses, important personages, and connections to America.

◇⟋⟍──────────────────────●

Brown's looks pretty much the same today.
No horses, though.

●

THEN: Brown's Hotel opened its doors at 23 Dover Street in four town houses in 1837, the year of Queen Victoria's accession. In the heart of Mayfair, surrounded by members of the peerage and nobility, the founder James Brown—previously a gentleman's gentleman—knew exactly how to make the upper crust feel at home. He was aided in that effort by his wife Sarah, a former ladies maid to Lady Byron, widow of the great poet. Sarah had a knack for managing the details that would make Brown's stand out as a place of superior service and refinement. It also helped that Lady Byron's recommendation brought the hotel to the notice of the right sort of people. All this made Brown's quickly successful, leading to the acquisition of neighboring houses—starting with the St. George's Hotel in 1889 that stood at its back along Albemarle (now the main entrance)—until eventually Brown's comprised 11 Georgian buildings all linked together inside (hence the many skinny hallways).

Just like in our historical novels, guests did not eat in public but took their meals in a private en-suite parlor, a staff butler handling all the details. These suites came complete with a servant's room. Smoking was not permitted in the rooms, and it was not until the late 1880s when a public smoking room was created to enable the gentlemen to smoke inside. Prior to that they smoked in a garden shed or the outhouse—that's right, indoor plumbing was not yet the thing either. But I was talking about the new public smoking lounge that brought gentlemen out of their private rooms. They understandably enjoyed their new retreat. This was followed quickly with another popular addition, the hotel's first public dining room—the first in a London hotel. And lastly, the addition of the English Tea Room, which is still in operation today.

Brown's English Tea Room has hardly changed since it opened more than 100 years ago.

Brown's was a leader in providing the most modern amenities. Between 1882 and 1885 lifts were installed, as were electric lights, and indoor plumbing for bathrooms in 1885.

Is there a princess in the house? If there were you would never know it. The hotel is renowned for its discretion. And the happenstance accumulation of new floors and buildings that created the warren-like layout also makes it conducive to slipping in and out unobtrusively. However, I'd guess nobility still stay there at times, because royals sure made Brown's their home away from home in the past. Among them were Queen Emma, Regent of Holland, and her 14-year-old daughter, Queen Wilhelmina. They attempted an incognito visit to London, but Queen Victoria decided they should have a grand ceremonial parade when they departed on May 9, 1895.

Queen Wilhelmina came back with her own daughter some 25 years later. The young Princess Juliana felt like a prisoner with all the protocol and security, and so Henry Ford (then the Brown's owner and no relation to the US Fords), arranged for the girl to exit Dover Street and run around the building to enter again on Albemarle. She was thrilled with her adventure and completely unaware that staff had been placed unobtrusively around the entire two-block route to ensure her safety.[1]

Fleeing war or going into exile brought many royals to Brown's: Napoleon III and Empress Eugenie (Franco-Prussian War, 1870–71); Queen Elizabeth of the Belgians and King Albert (briefly WWI); in exile,

The Queen Regent and Queen Wilhelmina of Holland. Incognito no more.

Emperor Haile Selassie of Ethiopia (1936); King Zog of Albania (1939); and King George II of Hellenes, who stayed there the longest, from 1924 to 1935, even making it the temporary official court of the Greek royal family.

As for intrigue, there were two "pretenders" who stayed there during the 1880s: Don Carlos who claimed the Spanish throne and the Comte de Paris, who claimed the French one. Imagine keeping their royal feathers unruffled when, at times, members of the opposition were also housed there. You can begin to see why the hotel's layout is a plus rather than a detraction.

As for US connections, there are many. Americans also brought this Guide's theme to Brown's: romance and love. Most notably, Theodore Roosevelt (then a 28-year-old widower) stayed here in 1886 and on December 2nd walked to the nearby St. George's Church, Hanover Square, to marry Edith Kermit Carow. Not yet president, he listed his occupation on the marriage certificate simply as "ranchman."

The next generation in this titular family brought more romance, when the newly married Mr. and Mrs. Franklin Delano Roosevelt stayed at Brown's for their honeymoon in 1905. The bride wrote later that she was "horrified to find that in some way we had been identified with Uncle Ted and were given the royal suite ... we had to explain that our pocketbook was not equal to so such grandeur, but that made no difference. We lived in it for those first few days in London."[2] Ah, to have such troubles, but still I can imagine that it was embarrassing for them, at the time.

Lastly, we come to world changing connections. Alexander Graham Bell made the first-ever telephone call in England from Brown's in 1876. While born in Scotland, Bell had made Boston his home. After inventing the telephone, he travelled back to England to interest the British government in his device. He discovered, after checking into Brown's, that there was a private telegraph line newly installed between the hotel to the Ravenscourt Park, home of then Brown's owners, the J.J. Ford family, some four miles away. Bell's equipment was attached at either end, but the first attempt failed—only crackling and taps—due to others using the line for telegraphing. However, a second attempt, well after midnight when the line was free, was successful. I cannot verify but assume Bell was also successful in finding English funding for his venture, because Sir William Thomas (later Lord Kelvin) and even Queen Victoria wanted personal demonstrations of the contraption.

Another lasting technological and American connection for which we all still benefit came in the form a meeting held there in June 1890—the International Niagara Commission which included scientists from the UK (Lord Kelvin), Canada, France, Switzerland, and the US. Under discussion was how best to use the power of Niagara Falls. While choosing no winner in the competition it sponsored, the representatives did move the "war of the currents" one step closer toward using "electrical methods" for harnessing Niagara Falls' power. This ultimately led to selecting the alternating-current system that was adopted throughout the world and still in use today.[3]

As for Brown's contribution to fiction, author Rudyard Kipling was a regular patron from 1892–1936 and wrote much of his work there, including *The Jungle Book*. More recently, Agatha Christie's *At Bertram's Hotel* (1965) was inspired by Brown's and Stephen King wrote the beginning of *Misery* (1987) seated at Kipling's desk, which still resides in the Dover Suite.

NOW: Brown's is the winner of many awards for excellence and receives extremely high reviewer scores. If you can pay the price, you'll have a prestigious five-star lodging in the center of Mayfair. The high cost puts it out of reach for many (your author included), however, for a more manageable fee one can visit The English Tea Room, where one can while away the afternoon soaking up the incredible history in the only space in the hotel that still feels distinctly Victorian (highly recommended; see Ch. 5).

HISTORICAL OFFERINGS: The aforementioned English Tea Room. Features: There are no four-poster beds here. The very British décor is a combination of contemporary/traditional with some period features and original artwork; each room is individually decorated. Their goals are personalized service (greeting guests by name), individual bespoke service as needed, and special programs for all ages of children, including providing whatever a parent needs (seriously, you could arrive with your babe and not need to bring a thing, not even nappies).

DETAILS: 84 rooms/31 suites. Check-in: 2pm/Checkout: 12pm. **ROOM:** Free WiFi, "Handy Mobile Device" (unlimited internet and complimentary calls to UK, other European countries, US, and more), iPod docking, minibar, bathrobe/slippers, twice daily room cleaning, safe. **FOOD:** HIX Mayfair restaurant, The English Tea Room, Donovan Bar (cozy, creative cocktail menu), 6 private dining rooms, 24-hour room service. **HOTEL:** Concierge, spa, 24-hr fitness center, luggage storage, bellman, lots of other niceties, and even more for suites. **STARS:** 4½

TAKE HEED! Be advised that the cheapest rooms can come with fire-escape views. The place feels more like entering a large private home than a grand hotel.

INSIDER TIP: HIX Mayfair offers a prix-fixe dinner at a great price. Special nicety: prices are listed on their menus—super helpful for anyone who wants to have an idea of the cost before making a reservation. Book room on their website to get free *high-speed* WiFi, free seasonal food/beverage offer, early arrival/late checkout (if available).

How OLDE: ♔♔♔♕♕ ～ *historic but doesn't look it inside*
Tube: Green Park | **Map:** B | www.BrownsHotel.com
+44 20 7493 6020 | Albemarle St, Mayfair

◇❧————————————————●

THE EGERTON HOUSE HOTEL

Est. 1890s in 1820s building ～ £££½

The Egerton is a small luxury hotel with exquisite service that gets unparalleled high marks. Walking inside will feel like you're entering a home, quaint but posh, and you'll be treated like family. If you want a quiet lodging in the Knightsbridge area, something intimate and personalized, you could hardly go wrong with the double-A rated, five-star Egerton.

THEN: The two adjoining red brick town houses were built in the early 1800s. No. 17 dates to at least 1824 when a gentleman of private means occupied it, followed in 1832 by a Queens Counsel barrister. From there it passed through several middle-class businessmen and jewelers. In 1888, Countess Berchtold moved in. Wife to the Austro-Hungarian politician Count Berchtold, who made his mark on history by delivering an ultimatum to Serbia following the Archduke Franz Ferdinand's assassination while visiting Sarajevo in 1914, which ultimately led to the First World War. The adjoining No. 19 was home to Benjamin Jutsham, the librarian at Carlton House in 1824. A lifelong friend of Prinny, later King George IV, his job was a sinecure since the Prince was not known for a love of reading. There followed a line of small businessmen, tutors, and such, until the late 1890s, when a hotel was founded in these buildings, although from 1943 to the mid 1980s it was operated as a low cost youth hostel.

The Egerton House's pretty red brick entrance

NOW: The privately-held Red Carnation Hotel Collection purchased the property in 2005 and undertook a lavish refurbishment to reopen it in their signature style. Each guest room is individually designed with antique or unusual pieces acquired by the founder and president Mrs. Beatrice Tollman. She also displays her eclectic art collection in her hotels, and at Egerton you might see lithographs by Toulouse-Lautrec, Picasso, and Matisse. Supposedly the pretty lady in the painting in the drawing room was the secret lover of the house's owner in Victorian times.[4] The Egerton receives high praise for its careful service, attention to detail, and luxurious décor. It was voted No. 7 for Luxury Hotels in the UK by TripAdvisor in 2017 and No. 4 in Top London Hotels by Condé Nast in 2016.

Is there a princess in the house? In the past, no—this neighborhood was high-level tradesmen, barristers, and such. While Jutsham might have hung out with Prinny, it seems unlikely the prince ever made it to his librarian's humble abode. Today, extreme discretion is their *modus operandi*, so you'll never hear it from them if a member of the peerage were to check in. However, it's more likely you might find yourself next to royals of the celebrity kind—they like both the privacy and the pampering. Only one US connection that I could find: look for the original *Snoopy* print by Charles M. Schulz on the barroom wall.

HISTORICAL OFFERINGS: Afternoon Tea in the Victorian drawing room or enjoy chess or read a book there. Highly personalized service just like the kind all hotels used to provide in olden times. Some rooms with princess canopies, half-testers, four-poster beds, and a suite with canopy bed.

Features: Two staff to every guest! Personalized service to a level unheard of elsewhere. For example, one guest posted about staying over the holidays with her daughters and discovering two wrapped gifts under the lobby tree for the girls with a personalized card on Christmas morning. The holiday decorations and unique amenities make it extra special. Or, if you're celebrating a romantic event, they can do it up nice with a romantic turndown. There is no public restaurant, but a full menu is offered in the Lounge for guests. They use only free-range eggs, are committed to sustainable fisheries, and have vegetarian/gluten-free options. They've a "We Care" team to implement local charity support and green initiatives such as natural resource conservation (solar panels, water), recycling, serving Belu water (100% carbon neutral company that donates profits to Water Aid), and more.

DETAILS: 23 rooms/5 suites. Check-in 2pm/Checkout: 12pm. **ROOM:** Free WiFi, US/Euro electrical sockets, welcome drink at arrival, fresh fruit and flowers in room, free still/sparkling mineral water, minibar, original works of art, bathrobe/slippers (children's sized too), Penhaligon toiletries, marble bathrooms with TV, Belgian linens, Bose music system, hotpot with coffee/tea, valet service, twice daily maid service, turndown, safe, DVD player upon request. Old fashioned metal keys, but high-tech security throughout hotel. Also, free "You forget it, we've got it," toiletries on hand (shaving kits, manicure kits, bandages, etc., even socks). **FOOD:** Lounge dining with full menu and 24-hour Breakfast, Afternoon Tea, The Bar, 24-hr room service.

You can take tea in The Egerton House drawing room

HOTEL: free self-serve covered candy dishes with nuts/candies in lounge, free newspaper, concierge, Red Carnation Hotel chauffeured transfers or can call taxis, free day-pass to Aquilla Health Club (swimming pool, Jacuzzi, steam room, sauna, fitness equipment, massages), Hyde Park jogging trail map, 20%-off Paul Edmonds salon services, massage/beauty/fitness services en-suite upon request, licensed babysitting/nanny service, free children's entertainment packs (coloring, Edwin teddy bear, London activity book), free crib and baby intercoms upon request, luggage storage. If that's not enough, pets are welcome at no cost and provided some free pampering too, or a full Pet Spa Service (fee) can be arranged for your pooch. **STARS:** 5

Few complaints, except the standard for European hotels—very tiny rooms, some oddly shaped, and surfaces cluttered with brochures/magazines.

TIP: Book direct for discounts (recently £50 dining credit), and check "Offers" page for good deals, including up to 30% off for booking early/prepaying, and over age 60 discounts. Contact them directly to request the type of décor you'd prefer as some rooms are more romantic or feminine than others (some Classics have princess canopy, some Deluxe Queens have half-tester or four-poster bed, one Studio Suite has canopied bed). Save money on breakfast at a nearby coffee shop or, better, head to the V&A Café's Gamble Room to dine in Victorian splendor for half the cost (museum is free; opens at 10am; breakfast options limited, so check out menu: www.vam.ac.uk/info/va-cafe).

*H*OW OLDE: ⚜⚜⚜⚜⚜
~ *make sure to request period décor guest room*
Tube: Knightsbridge | **Map:** A | www.EgertonHouseHotel.com
bookeg@rchmail.com | +44 20 7589 2412 | 17–19 Egerton Terrace

LONDON MARRIOTT HOTEL COUNTY HALL
Est. 1988 in 1922 building ~ ££££

It's a Southbank hotel in a massively big building, and a little awkward to find your way there. But on the plus side, it's convenient to transportation and has the most amazing views across the River Thames from many of the public spaces and from guest rooms for a premium. The décor is mostly contemporary—it feels like what it was, an old-style office building—but it's included here because of the American branding and the wonderful Library Lounge.

THEN: Started in 1911, this gigantor wasn't fully completed until 1933. It was designed by British architect Ralph Knott in the "Edwardian Baroque" style and faced with Portland stone. King George V opened the building for use by the London County Council in 1922. At its height some 2,000 London city employees worked here. It functioned thus for 64 years but not entirely without strife. Facing parliament, when the local government opposed the British government in the 1980s, the London Council would hang large banners with opposition slogans. This did not go over well with Prime Minister Margaret Thatcher. She abolished the council in 1986, and County Hall lost its purpose. It found other government uses for a period, before being sold to private Japanese investors.

NOW: Besides the six-story Marriott, the colossal Grade II* listed County Hall today houses a number of attractions, including London Sea Life Aquarium, London Dungeon, and Namco Station arcade. The giant Ferris wheel London Eye is next door. If it turns out you like the location but not the price, a budget Premier Inn is located within County Hall too (see below). And no one will stop you from enjoying Afternoon Tea or a nightcap in the Marriott's lovely facilities.

The Marriott opened as a five-star luxury hotel in 1998 and underwent major refurb in 2016. They've done a good job of retaining the historic character of the place, with photos from its construction in the lobby, early 20th Century artwork, and retaining wood-paneling and marble fireplaces. The guest rooms are all modern, but the views from the public spaces and some rooms are iconic—the River Thames, Big Ben, and the Houses of Parliament. Americans will find the lodging comfortingly familiar, and for once the biggest complaint will not be about tiny rooms. In general, they are the biggest in London in all price categories. Your ears will think you're back in the states, with 70% of the guests being fellow Yanks. Politicians from around the world stay here, including US Senators and Congressmen, and US Olympic teams too.

HISTORICAL OFFERINGS: Afternoon Tea in the Library Lounge. The space is charming with fireplaces, original oak bookcases, iconic views, and quiet alcoves. Seatings are 1.5 hours; £39 with unlimited sparkling wine that's topped up constantly. Features: Junior Suites with waterfront balconies, and depending on where the room is located, you might wake up to the chimes of Big Ben. All areas and guest rooms accessible.

DETAILS: 192 rooms/14 suites. Check-in: 3pm/Checkout: 12pm. **ROOM:** WiFi (£15 fee), dual voltage outlets/adaptors, robes/slippers, evening turndown service, pillow-top beds, hotpot with coffee/tea, minibar (the kind where one can't move any items or be charged), iron/board, trouser press, safe, newspaper upon request. **FOOD:** Library Lounge (Afternoon Tea, great views), Noes Lobby Champagne Bar (nice mix of old world and contemp), Gillray's Steakhouse & Bar (English; great views; bargain 3-course set menu w/Prosecco, £27), 24-hr room service. **HOTEL:** Free lobby WiFi, concierge, currency exchange, Free use of London County Hall Club and Spa (top two floors, views, fitness equipment, biggest-in-London indoor swimming pool, sauna, free classes, relaxation lounge), business center, babysitting (fee). **STARS:** 4

TAKE HEED! This is a big building—if mobility is an issue, request room near elevator and reconfirm a few days prior to arrival. River-facing rooms can be loud with the sound of wind. **TIP:** The opposite of other hotels in the Guide, this Marriott is aimed at the corporate market, which means bargains can be had for weekend stays. Experiment, but booking a Friday arrival will most likely yield the best savings, especially if you pay in advance (as much as £200 less).

MARRIOTT BRAND TIP: It's Category 9. You can use points for all or part of the cost, and both United and Amex rewards points can be used as well. If not a Marriot Member, join (no cost) and get free standard WiFi when booking directly, points sharing among members ($10 fee); Gold members get lounge access and free breakfast for 2. Also, Marriott has special rates for military, seniors, AAA.

𝓗OW OLDE COUNTY HALL: ♣♣♧♧♧
~ *not old but bigger rooms*
Tube: Waterloo, Westminster | www.marriott.com (search County Hall) | +44 20 7928 5200 | Westminster Bridge Rd

𝓗OW OLDE PREMIER INN: ♧♧♧♧♧
~ *not at all, but cheap*
Also inside London County Hall | Thoroughly modern, bare-bones hotel without bells and whistles | **Stars**: 4½ | **Price**: £½
www.PremierInn.com | I was not able to visit, so check online reviews carefully.

THE RITZ, LONDON

1906 ~ ££££

   Walking past the grand front along Piccadilly, it feels like you're going to the side entrance, but that is the main portal today. You'll enter an unassuming lobby housing the hotel registration and coatroom. Security is tight, with doormen and security personnel ensuring that visiting heads of state, royals, or celebs will feel safe and secure. Then you pass through another set of inside doors to enter The Long Gallery and... *Wow!*

   This hotel is as different from Brown's as one can get. High lofty ceilings, wide-open spaces, gold filigree, and sparkling chandeliers. Magnificent elegance on a grand scale. It's like you're walking into a palace. *Remember to hold that head high.* You've as much right as anyone to enter and enjoy a drink in the fab bar or a snack in the Gallery—provided, of course, you're dressed conservatively and appropriately (more on that later). There's another difference too. While Brown's has a

---

The Ritz, London, shortly after it opened in 1906.
Note Kent House to the right side, finally acquired in 2005.

distinctly masculine feel, with muted tones and dark paneling, The Ritz is all frothy femininity—pinks, golds, and gloriously sunny. It's a place made for romance and celebration.

THEN: Opening in 1906, The Ritz barely qualifies for a *historical* guide in a city that dates to 43 AD, not to mention the fact that its décor is French. But this Belle Époque masterpiece with a colorful past is a must-see for the romance fan. Conceived by Swiss hotelier César Ritz, who'd already opened the Ritz Paris to great acclaim, it was built to make a statement. The hotel was highly innovative with bathrooms for every guest room, double-glazing on the windows for heat and sound insulation, a sophisticated ventilation system, and brass rather than wooden beds (thought more hygienic). No modern invention was spared that might make a guest more comfortable. Designed in a French château style with large copper lions on the roof and Louis XVI furnishings, it represented grand high society and luxury. It was also the first major steel-framed building in London, but the boxy, imposing white-stoned structure did not sit well among its Georgian neighbors, having been compared to an "abandoned railroad station, forlorn and alone."[5] Its value was forever settled when it received a Grade II* listing.

The Ritz weathered two World Wars, and while a German bomb landed in nearby Green Park, no damage occurred to the hotel, except for lost revenue. During WWII, summit meetings were held with Winston Churchill, Charles de Gaulle (the head of the French government in exile), and Dwight D. Eisenhower.

And between the two wars, it was the place to go, filled with socialites and aristocracy, actors and actresses, anyone with means—all there to mingle and dine, see and be seen. American heiresses adorned in jewels were known to parade down The Long Gallery awaiting their guests, sometimes impoverished noblemen ready to bestow titles in exchange for funds to fix-up their country estates.

While Brown's Hotel was the place for matters of consequence, the Ritz was the happening joint. Said Sir Michael Duff remembering fondly the flamboyant 1930s period, "It had a special atmosphere about it...The Ritz was more like a club than an hotel; you were bound to see your friends there." While it no longer has such a club atmosphere, Jennie Reekie notes in her *The London Ritz Book of Etiquette* that among the movers and shakers of show-business, high finance, and the aristocracy this spirit of camaraderie lived on at least until the 1990s.[6] Which leads to…

Is there a princess in the house? Of course. And often, at least in the hotel's first fifty years. It's rumored there was even a special bell in the entryway so doormen could notify staff of the arrival of royalty.[7]

King Edward VII's early patronage helped make the restaurant popular. Through the 1930s these additional monarchs enjoyed dining there or dancing in the basement ballroom: George V of England, Marie of Romania, Amelie of Portugal, and Boris of Bulgaria. Reportedly, it was the first place that the Queen Mother (George VI's consort) ever ordered from a restaurant menu. And that Her Majesty Queen Elizabeth II, then a princess, celebrated WWII's VE Day by slipping out of Buckingham Palace to join the party at The Ritz, even taking part in a conga line dance down The Long Gallery and through the revolving doors.[8]

While the hotel is discreet about who has lived within its walls, it's believed that at one point four reigning monarchs all stayed simultaneously: King Boris of Bulgaria, King Farouk of Egypt, King Alfonso of Spain, and Queen Wilhelmina of Holland.[9] Others have included the Aga Khan III, who kept a suite for 40 years, and King Zog of Albania (great name), who arrived with suitcases stuffed full of gold bullion to pay his expenses. More recently, it was the first place that HRH The Prince of Wales appeared in public with Camilla Parker-Bowles, now The Duchess of Cornwall (1999). Then in 2002, he awarded The Ritz a Royal Warrant for Banqueting and Catering, the first and only hotel to receive this honor. With small affairs for her Golden Jubilee (2002) and 80th birthday (2006), Queen Elizabeth II continued the tradition of hosting royal parties at The Ritz.

Other notables included Charlie Chaplin, who visited in 1921 and required 40 policemen to escort him past the huge crowd of fans. In the 1930s there was the Russian Prima Ballerina Anna Pavlova, who actually danced at a party in the hotel after popping out of a giant basket of roses. Among Americans were Hollywood star Douglas Fairbanks and stage actress Tallulah Bankhead, who famously drank champagne from her slipper while at a Ritz press conference celebrating her arrival in London in 1951.

For the romance fan, there is the infamous love story of King Edward VIII and Wallis Simpson, an American divorcée who began an affair with him, then Prince of Wales, while still in her second marriage (c.1934). Needless to say, Edward's father, King George V, was less than pleased, but the Prince continued the liaison, showering Wallis with jewels, money, yachting vacations, and later, getting her presented at court (a no-no for divorcées back then). The Ritz played a small part in their illicit love affair—Edward and Wallis couldn't sit together in public (she was still married), so they held court at separate nearby tables in the Ritz's restaurant, both near the door for making quick exits. Edward was so in love with her that he abdicated the throne in 1936 after less than a year as king, marrying her six months later. So the woman who began a somewhat humble life as Bessie Wallis Warfield, born in a hotel cottage and dependent on wealthy relatives, became Her Grace, Wallis, Duchess of Windsor.

For the erotic romance fan, it might be speculated that there was more going on here: Edward was reported to be "slavishly" devoted and dependent" on her, a woman that didn't bow and scrape to him, nor moderate her domineering manner and abrasive irreverence.[10] *Hmmm.* Now there's an intriguing plot idea for an erotic romance novel.

Fiction connections are thin, however romance novelist Barbara Cartland enjoyed taking tea at The Palm Court in the 1930s, noting, "One could meet men without chaperones for lunch and tea. So you had lunch with the men you were keen on and tea with the rest."[11][12] However, her novel *Love at the Ritz* (1993) is not set there but in the Paris hotel of the same name. As an aside, wealthy South African, John Bailey, was in love with the young novelist and society beauty in 1932, but Barbara spurned him, so he turned around and married Winston Churchill's daughter Diana instead. The doomed couple divorced three years later but they spent their wedding night…where else but The Ritz, London.[13]

NOW: In 2005, The Ritz acquired the building that adjoins it. Formerly known as Wimborne House and dating to the 1740s, it has been meticulously restored to its Italian Renaissance splendor—truly stunning if you're lucky enough to get a tour—and the various private rooms are available for events. César Ritz tried to buy it from the beginning, but Lord Wimborne stubbornly refused. Today No. 22 Arlington Street is known as William Kent House after the original architect. César would be pleased to know this historic Grade II* mansion is now part of the family.

Today, the five-star Ritz London's many awards and high marks are a testament to the fine hospitality, luxury, and security on offer. Each room is individually decorated. The lavish Ritz Restaurant, serving three meals daily, was awarded a Michelin Star in 2016. The Rivoli Bar is an intimate gem—an Art Deco masterpiece of onyx marble, mirrored panels in silver and gold leaf, bamboo floors, and Lalique glass adornments (originally made for the Orient Express). If that isn't enough, the cocktail menu features more than 80 libations. The former basement ballroom is now the opulent Ritz Club, a private members-only casino. Unlike the hustle and bustle upstairs, this exclusive haven looks and feels like the grandeur of old Monte Carlo—with prices to match of course. But here's the best part: Ritz guests get complimentary membership during their stay.

HISTORICAL OFFERINGS: French period décor and antique furniture in the public spaces and guest rooms (although no four-poster beds). If you like romantic glitz, you'll be in Belle Époque heaven. Afternoon Tea (book well in advance; see Ch. 5) and The Ritz Club. And, Christmas! The entire hotel is transformed into a festive Edwardian wonderland—truly stunning and right out of a holiday romance novel. Features: Butler Service (they're in tails!) free with suites or £360 per day. Roll-Royce Phantom chauffeured limousine. Special programs for your little prince or princess. Periodic, black-tie Opera Champagne Dinners in Kent House where you can play princess for a night. High staff/guest ratio—360 employees for 134 rooms. They're committed to protecting the environment and have the goal of reducing energy use by 3% annually for the foreseeable future.

DETAILS: 112 rooms/24 suites. Check-in: 2pm/Checkout: 12pm.
ROOM: Free WiFi, iPod docking, fine toiletries, bathrobe/slippers, nightly turndown service, minibar, free newspaper, free local calls, safe.
FOOD: The Ritz restaurant, The Palm Court, The Rivoli Bar, six private dining rooms, 24-hour room service. **HOTEL:** Concierge, currency exchange, luggage storage, bellman service, business center, salon/spa, fitness center, children's club and babysitting, Ritz Fine Jewelry store.
STARS: 4½

TAKE HEED! By US standards, basic rooms may feel small. Dress Code: Reflecting the elegant nature of the hotel's architecture, The Ritz, London has a dress code as follows: Gentlemen are required to wear a jacket and tie (jeans and sportswear are not permitted for either ladies or gentlemen) for afternoon tea in The Palm Court and for lunch and dinner in The Ritz Restaurant and Terrace. In all other public areas in the hotel and The Ritz Club, smart casual attire is suitable. Please note that sneakers and sportswear are not permitted in any of the hotel's restaurants or bars. This is strictly enforced. While some might find this a nuisance, for many "Puttin' on the Ritz" is part of the excitement of going to The Ritz.

TIP: 15% off for booking 30 days in advance. Staying here gets you into The Ritz Club. Come in December—the lavish decorations and carolers add to the romance. As with Brown's, the excitement of visiting this historic hotel may be had for the price of afternoon tea, by no means a bargain but a worthy investment for a special celebration (see Ch. 5).

𝓗OW OLDE: ♕ ♕ ♕ ♕ ♕
Tube: Green Park, Piccadilly Circus | **Maps:** B & C
www.TheRitzLondon.com | +44 20 7493 8181 or toll free from US 1 877 748 9536 | enquire@theritzlondon.com | 150 Piccadilly

$\mathscr{L}$anded Gentry Would Feel Right at Home
$\sim$ *$200 to $400*

THE CHESTERFIELD MAYFAIR HOTEL
Est. 1973 in 1740s building $\sim$ £££½

The unassuming façade of this four-star hotel is a nondescript brown that belies the actual age of these three conjoined town houses. You'll know you're in the right place thanks to the signature red awnings, with even the top-hatted doorman sporting a red waistcoat and red carnation boutonnière. He'll smile and open the door, and then any sense of being underwhelmed evaporates as you step inside. The formal square entrance hall is all European elegance, from the white and black tiled marble floor to the rich wood paneling, tall Corinthian columns, red drapes, and large Victorian crystal chandelier. Dropping your eyes to the center table, you spot a round ball of red, which upon closer inspection is made entirely of fresh carnations. Apropos, as this is a Red Carnation Hotel. And the busy London streets suddenly feel very far away—you've found what feels like a private, old-world British club and you're a valued member, at least for a few days.

THEN: The exact erection date for the three houses that today make up the Chesterfield is unknown, but by 1749 the Misses Davenport were ensconced in No. 34 Charles Street (named after Charles, Lord Falmouth, who was Lord Berkeley's brother, of nearby Berkeley Sq. fame). No. 35 housed the Earls of Egemont, and No. 36 was soon the home of the Regency dandy, Lord Petersham (whose name today is synonymous with a silk ribbon and a style of overcoat). For two hundred years, these houses were run in the grand manner, with a full staff of butler, footman, upstairs and downstairs maids, and cook, at a minimum.

Charming, fun, and quirky!

Although the romance fan might wonder if the spinsters Davenport, or the ones who came after, were in reduced circumstances (since the spinster trope usually involves poverty). Perhaps inside No. 34 they spent time mending and turning their dresses to last another season. That is, until one of them met their hero—super wealthy, of course—and their situation improved.

The three buildings changed hands regularly but generally were home to aristocrats, members of parliament, and military leaders—the houses of Charles Street being renowned as "the abode of rank and fashion."[14]

While there are no records of any princesses staying here, there are some interesting American connections. In 1864, the sisters Ladies Louisa and Elizabeth Cornwallis (ages 65 and 59) moved into No. 36.—it was their grandfather Charles, 1st Marquis Cornwallis, who surrendered along with 7,000 British soldiers to General George Washington at Yorktown, Virginia in 1781. Regardless of his defeat, his status did not diminish—he later was knighted. We'll never know why the ladies remained spinsters, but it makes me wonder, given that the other three granddaughters married well. There's a second US connection: during WWII, Clementine Churchill, the Prime Minister's wife, opened No. 34 as a club for visiting American forces, a sort of early USO.

As for other interesting connections, by 1895 No. 36 was the home of Elizabeth, Dowager Countess of Carnarvon; she was stepmother to the 5th Earl, George Herbert who together with Howard Carter discovered the tomb of King Tutankhamen in 1922. If the name Carnarvon sounds at all familiar, it's because their family seat is Highclere Castle, the setting for the popular TV show *Downton Abbey*.

NOW: The three houses were combined into one hotel that opened in 1973, but it really took off in 1984 when Beatrice and Stanley Tollman bought it to start the Red Carnation brand (which also includes the Egerton). Over the years, the brand's attention to detail and customer focus has earned them high marks. Most recently, the Chestefield Mayfair was awarded the Number 21 spot in "Top Hotels in the UK" by TripAdvisor 2017 Traveller's Choice Awards and the Number 6 spot in "Best Hotel" in London *Travel + Leisure* 'World's Best' 2016 Awards.

Part of this success is due to the exacting attention to detail that is a focus of Red Carnation Hotels. For example, I was surprised to see the guest room's television remote sealed inside a plastic bag, a sticker indicating it had been sanitized. (Fun Fact: Remotes are among the dirtiest things in hotel rooms because usually they never get cleaned. Bring antibacterial wipes for switches/phones/remotes.) Another example, a few years ago all 1,800 staff members were required to watch a training video *just* on how to greet guests.[15] A second reason for the chain's success is how employees are valued. The company's been ranked in the top 10 of *The Sunday Times'* "100 Best Companies to Work For" at least three times in recent years, and it shows with staff turnover at no more than 27%[16] (low for the industry).[17] This job happiness translates into customer care with employees embracing the Red Carnation philosophy "no request is too large, no detail is too small."

The hotel is located in the heart of exclusive Mayfair and within easy walking distance to Buckingham Palace and Selfridges. As with other Red Carnation hotels, each room is individually decorated with the owner's finds from auctions and estate sales. Some rooms are more masculine and some more feminine, and it's absolutely alright to contact the hotel and let them know what mood "takes your fancy: bold, whimsical, exotic, elegant, or cosy." At the basic level some rooms have half tester or princess canopies, and beginning at the junior suite level there are some four-poster beds (sometimes metal frames, none canopied). This might be a good choice for two women. With cute twin-bedded rooms, some with half-testers, you can both be princesses.

The public spaces are gratifyingly period—with an amorphous sort-of old-world club or Victorian feel. I particularly like the dark-wood-paneled, old-leather-wingback-chaired, stag room (*I call it that because of the solitary mounted horns on the wall*). I could sit there with a cup of tea (or better still, one of their delish martinis) and happily read my romance novel till morning. Or till I fall asleep, at which point, hopefully a discreet employee would gently wake me and send me on to bed.

HISTORICAL OFFERINGS: Afternoon Tea in the pretty Conservatory and aforementioned four-poster and half-tester beds. Features: They also participate in Red Carnation's conservation Green Team program, the highlight of which is The Chesterfield Bees. Their rooftop hive houses 120,000 bees and they're out pollinating gardens in

Each room is different at The Chesterfield Mayfair

The Chesterfield Mayfair Library, a masculine room
straight out of a romance novel

a 3-mile radius. Their goal is to produce 160 pounds of honey each year, which is used in their restaurant. For Americans, they have an annual Thanksgiving Day feast on that holiday. ～ **For the guys** surprises: Bar Experiences (gin or whisky, £30). For couples, there's the Rediscover Romance package, which besides breakfast and 2 romantic cocktails, includes romantic turndown with rose petals, house champagne, chocolate dipped strawberries, a single red rose, and a heart shaped bath bomb. (*Me want!*)

DETAILS: 94 rooms/13 suites. Check-in 2pm/Checkout: 12pm. **ROOM:** Free WiFi, free still/sparkling mineral water, bathrobe/slippers (children's sized too), Fragonard Italian toiletries, hotpot with coffee/ tea, turndown service with nightly treats, iron/board, safe, umbrellas. **FOOD:** Butlers Restaurant (English cuisine, 3-course set £32), The Terrace Bar (trendy drinks, try the Eton Mess which comes with a hammer; pianist from 6:30pm Mon-Sat), and Afternoon Tea (see Ch. 5). **HOTEL:** free newspaper, concierge, currency exchange, Red Carnation chauffeured transfers (fee), luggage storage, massage/beauty en-suite, free yoga mat and DVD, licensed babysitting/nanny service (fee), free children's entertainment packs (coloring book, etc.), free crib. If that's not enough, pets are welcome at no cost and provided some free pampering too, or a full Pet Spa Service (fee) can be arranged for your pooch. **STARS:** 5

TAKE HEED! the usual American complaint—small rooms. **TIP:** Look for dining specials (currently 3-course lunch with champagne for £30 M-F and daily for dinner). Tell them if you're celebrating, they might surprise with free champagne or dessert. Book direct for discounts (recently £50 dining credit), and check "Offers" page for good deals, including up to 20% off for booking early/prepaying, and over age 60 discounts.

How OLDE: ♟♟♟♟♟

~ *just be sure to request room with period décor*

Tube: Green Park | **Map:** B | www.ChesterfieldMayfair.com/offers

bookch@rchmail.com | +44 20 7491 2622 | 35 Charles St, Mayfair

◇๛๛

THE GORE

Est. 1892 ~ £££

The simple façade of this white stucco town house decorated by a British flag could be the entrance to countless homes throughout the desirable neighborhood of Kensington. "The Gore" spelled out in bronze letters above the portico tells you this is the place. Stepping through the single front door into a skinny foyer feels more like you're entering the home of your dear old aunt Ada, an ancient lady who hasn't changed a thing—ever—in her Victorian-era home. The walls are replete with antique drawings, paintings, and old photographs. A crystal chandelier sparkles from the very high ceiling. Only the clerk standing behind a slender reception desk confirms this is a small hotel. That, and the uniformed bellman, who could just as easily be Aunt Ada's footman or butler.

The hotel is named after the Gore House estate that existed here prior to the area being developed as a housing

Very English Terrace town house just outside Hyde Park

tract in Victorian times. However, "gore" isn't the name of the original landowner, rather it just means a narrow, triangular plot of land between larger estates. Among the residents of Gore House (built in the 1750s) on this three-acre plot was William Wilberforce, renowned political reformer (1808–1821). Later the Countess of Blessington and her son-in-law Count D'Orsay lived there until debt forced them to sell off all their possessions and flee to Paris in 1849. The original building was torn down in the late 1860s and the current terraced houses were built.

Then, in 1892, the sisters, Miss Ada Cook and Miss Fanny Cook (descendants of Captain James Cook) opened The Gore hotel. Its proximity to the Royal Albert Hall, built and opened by Queen Victoria in 1871, made it immediately popular with patrons, either for staying overnight when in town for a performance or for pre-theater dining. Not much is known about this period, except it is rumored that Queen Victoria stayed here and that she even brought her own bed, leaving it behind to pay part of her board.[18] Wouldn't it be fun to sleep in Queen Victoria's bed—although it doesn't seem that anyone knows which one of the antique beds is hers.

The hotel has changed owners several times since it was founded, but luckily none of the new management sought to eradicate the quirky Victorian character of the place. Rather they have added to it. The Tudor Room—the most amazing suite in the hotel—is what remains of a restaurant started within the hotel by English restaurateur Robin Howard, who owned the hotel in the 1950s. He created The Elizabethan Room, a themed restaurant with actors playing wenches and bards, and traditional food served off wooden platters, such as artichoke pie and suckling pig. It proved very popular with Americans.[19] US connection: Robin Howard loved modern dance, using his wealth to sponsor America's Martha Graham Dance Company and later funding the start of an English one too. Supposedly, The Gore's walls were at one time adorned with many valuable paintings belonging to Howard that were sold off piece by piece to support his love of dance. If only these walls could talk, I think there'd be many an interesting tale to tell.

NOW: The Gore hotel is owned by the Italian Starhotels Collezione, but it retains its distinctive British appeal. I know it has gone through changes over the years…some, but it doesn't feel like it. The hotel feels timeless, like it has always been here and always will be. There are those that might call it stodgy, but that would be missing the point. The Gore is resolutely, happily, comfortable in its skin. It knows what it is and wants you to share in the fun of this bygone era.

The locals know this too, flocking to its Bar 190 after taking in a performance at the nearby concert hall (the hotel is an official partner of this landmark Victorian venue). This has been a trendy place for people in the know for most of its history. In 1968, the Rolling Stones held their "Beggars Banquet" album launch party there. In 1983, Beatles stars Paul, George, and Ringo hung out in the bar,[20] and more recently Ann Hathaway did a photo shoot here. Myself, I had the naughty pleasure of attending one of their private parties in Bar 190, an homage to *Fifty Shades* and no more need be said…well, okay, it was fun, and packed, and we danced for hours in the basement room. They have lots of signature cocktails, and if you're lucky, Cinderella's Carriage will be free for your enjoyment—this VIP corner holds a velvet-curtained, canopied four-poster day-bed setup, which can be pre-booked for private parties of six or less.

The Gore Library

For more sedate fun, have your own personal Victorian "at home" afternoon in The Library, a period Drawing Room, where you can read a chapter from your favorite romance novel while partaking of the complimentary self-serve tea. It's simple fare, just hot or iced tea and some biscuits, but the setting will bring to life any scene where the heroine is at home receiving callers. Perhaps it's the afternoon where she gets that long-awaited proposal.

Besides the Royal Albert Hall, the hotel is a stone's throw from Hyde Park and fairly close to Kensington Palace, the Victoria and Albert Museum, and Harrods.

HISTORICAL OFFERINGS: The hotel itself! The Gore has been described as a Victorian museum chock-a-block full of antiques. Many rooms have high ceilings and windows draped with sumptuous velvet curtains. The aforementioned Library room, available exclusively for hotel guests, is great for hanging out with friends. But that's not all…

Yes! We've found four-poster beds!! Each of the individually decorated rooms has period décor and antique furniture, artwork, and some have truly sumptuous, ornate, hundreds-of-years-old bedsteads—although I promise the mattresses aren't ancient. Here's your chance to sleep like a princess. Although, as anywhere these special rooms cost more, but in comparison to some four-poster period stays, these are a London bargain.

The five Junior Suites are distinctive and surprisingly within reach, pricewise. I was lucky enough to stay in The Miss Ada, named after the founder, which came with antique furniture, the coveted, canopied, mahogany four-poster bed, and tall, crimson-velvet draped windows overlooking the street. Peering out I could easily imagine myself a Victorian lady awaiting her beau. However, the surprised shout from my real-life beau upon encountering the bathroom led me to hurry over and peer inside—to find rich mahogany paneling, deep marble tub, and this utterly unexpected wooden throne. Fun! A second suite, named for her sister, Miss Fanny, is nearly identical but features plum velvet. It also comes with a throne.

Then there's The Lady Marguerite Blessington—named after the legendary Victorian authoress that lived in the original Gore House where she entertained her friends Dickens, Thackeray, and Hans Christian Anderson. It has a gold-mirrored bed and black-marble bathroom with claw-foot cast-iron tub.

The Dame Nellie suite—named after Nellie Melba, the prima donna opera star from Melbourne who performed at the Royal Albert—has theatrical décor with the bed set inside a tasseled, gold satin and silk tent, faux leopard-skin armchairs, French chaise lounges, and a mirrored gilt bathroom complete with large reproduction statues of Michelangelo's David and Antonio Canova's Venus Italica,[21] there to watch over you while you bathe.

And for our American connection, The Judy Garland. This legendary star loved The Gore and stayed here so often she was called a "resident." Here the color ruby is the star with red velvet in the curtains and elegantly draped over the bed, plus picked up in the chairs, rug, and pretty stained glass windows. This 'bringing your own bed thing' seems to be common here, and the bed in this room is reported to be Garland's own. It fits because this almost absurdly ornate, gold bedstead looks like something out of the Emerald City of Oz.

The Gore has something else unique in the city—the chance to sleep like an Elizabethan princess in The Tudor Room. The hotel's most expensive suite, it is set in the aforementioned, converted 1950s restaurant. It features dark medieval décor, a massive four-poster bed with carved wood canopy, an arched wood-beamed Tudor ceiling, and a large Portland-stone fireplace flanked by wingback chairs (book during winter to enjoy the cozy fire). There's a stained glass window portrait of Queen Elizabeth I, and even a 15th Century Minstrel's Gallery—for when you want a mandolin-playing quartet to serenade you while you sleep. Strange but beautiful!

The Tudor Room suite at The Gore

DETAILS: 50 individually decorated rooms. Check-in: 2pm/ Checkout: 11am. **ROOM:** Free limited-bandwidth WiFi, Frette Linens, robes/slippers, Penhaligon toiletries, minibar, iron/board, safe. **FOOD:** 190 Queens Gate (headed by a Michelin starred chef), Bar 190, 24-hour room service. **HOTEL:** Les Clefs d'Or concierge, luggage storage. **STARS:** 4½

TAKE HEED! Most rooms are very European-sized, but the biggest complaint was lack of coffee/tea-making facilities in the room. Most reports are generally very good—just remember you'll be lodging in an authentic Victorian-age property that, thankfully, has not received a massive rebuild into generic contemporary.

And, this hotel has some funky features. Personally I found the throne loo a hoot, but some might find royal constitutionals not to their liking. There are hand-carved beds in almost every room and bed sizes were not standardized in ancient times, so reports are that sometimes the modern mattress doesn't fit exactly. Other things for which you should prep your patience include the plumbing taking a while to get hot water and the A/C working too much or too little.

Don't hesitate to voice your needs when making a reservation and they will try to meet them. Ditto for the beds—if sleeping like a Victorian lady is your goal make sure you make your four-poster bed request when booking. Lastly, you might find it quicker to take the wide staircase rather than wait for the one slow, tiny lift. And, it doesn't reach the 5th floor—if mobility is an issue, make sure you request a room below the fifth. Ditto for the tubs—I adored the fancy old-world tub, but for some it might be difficult to climb into it.

TIP: The Junior Suites with wonderful period décor are *the* London bargain if booked and paid well in advance. For two ladies travelling together, book the Superior Twin and you'll each sleep in your own period tester bed. All rooms at the Deluxe level and above have a carved oak four-poster or half-tester beds. Some of the four-poster canopy beds are positively yummy—take a look on their website. And don't forget the rooms with a "throne."

*H*ow OLDE: 🪑🪑🪑🪑🪑
~ *can't get any more authentic than this*
Tube: High Street Kensington, Gloucester Road | **Map:** A
www.GoreHotel.com
thegore@starhotels.com
+44 20 7584 6601 | US 888 757 5587 | 190 Queens Gate, Kensington

◇⟨⟩~

Giving a new meaning to a constitutional monarchy

Grosvenor House,
A JW Marriott Hotel

Est. 1929 ～ £££½

It was with some excitement that I hurried to Grosvenor House along Park Lane from the tube station. This isn't a Victorian-era property, but I knew that this grand dame with a prime Hyde Park frontage had a history intertwined with royalty and America. I was eager to meet the hotel's historian, and he did not disappoint.

THEN: In 1665, Baby Mary Davies, age one, inherited the land in this area—swampy meads, at the time—when her dad died in the Plague. Reared by an aunt, in 1677 the heiress was paraded through London streets in "a carriage drawn by six horses in search of a husband."²² The 12-year-old commoner and heiress was married to Sir Thomas Grosvenor,

Three Grosvenor Houses – c.1763, 1882, and 1929

3rd Baronet, a descendant of William the Conqueror. They had 8 children, of whom 6 lived to adulthood. It was this union that led to the development of the Grosvenor estates that became Mayfair, Park Lane, and Belgravia. Thanks to her inherited property, the family became the richest private urban landlords in the country. And that's the reason the road became Grosvenor Street long before Grosvenor House was built by her great-grandson Thomas.

Gloucester House ∼ The first house on this site was built by Viscount Chetwynd in 1732. This initial squarish house was added onto by the subsequent owner, the Duke of Beaufort. In 1763, the entire estate, including the furnishings, a 15-room house (approx.), 2 porter's cottages, stable, and formal gardens was sold for £15,865 ($3 million today) to HRH, the Duke of Cumberland (for *Outlander* fans: he was the British commander at the doomed battle of Culloden). He didn't get long to enjoy it, dying of a hemorrhage in 1766. Then his nephew moved in—William Henry, Duke of Gloucester and brother to King George III—and he lived there until his death in 1805.[23]

Grosvenor House ∼ Robert Belgrave, 2nd Earl Grosvenor, had already been shopping for a house in Mayfair, his current one being located in a neighborhood that was going downhill fast because a National Penitentiary was planned nearby (later built as Millbank Prison). The Earl had already declared to the neighborhood board that the family was "decidedly in favour of Gloucester House." Thus when the owner passed in 1805, the Belgraves were able to snatch it up for £20,000 ($2 mill today). The house required extensive refurbishment, being reported to be "very dirty" and "so gloomy, that it appeared to defy all endeavours to render it light," noted *The Times*. By 1808 is was deemed suitable for living, and *The Times* now raved, "magnificence, elegance, and convenience." *The Morning Post* spoke of "truly magnificent" chandeliers and the grand staircase, and the house "adorned with the most rare specimens in the art of sculpture." Not all agreed—"Most expensively furnished, but in bad taste," noted Lord Lonsdale. It's estimated that the remodel and furnishings cost more than £80,000 ($7 more mill).[24]

The house passed down through generations until reaching Hugh Grosvenor, 3rd Earl Grosvenor, later 1st Duke of Westminster. (He was the same Hugh who bought Cliveden, listed later in this chapter.) In 1882, he added the palatial "loggia" to the front with its Roman columns and swags. It was here the house took on the look in the 1882 drawing. His son Hugh, 2nd Duke of Westminster, retained the house until WWI when the he put it and his country seat Eaton Hall at the disposal of the war effort from 1916–1920. By the end of the war, it was becoming clear that maintaining these big houses was becoming unsustainable, so the Duke decided to sell the house in 1925, and as a result, Old Grosvenor was torn down in 1927.

Were there princesses in the house? One would presume so given the brother of the king lived there for many years, but I've found no record of visits. However, in its new incarnation the answer is a resounding yes, as well as many American connections too.

The Grosvenor House Hotel opened in 1929 with 472 rooms. The building at first glance is modern, with no relationship to the illustrious past for which it's named, but upon closer inspection you can spot architectural allusions such as archways capping each corner of the roof and a faux curved loggia along the front.

Designed specifically for the American market, the builder first visited the US to study our hotel methods and facilities. Upon opening, Grosvenor House promised the best of everything and delivered—it was the first hotel to have a bathroom for *every* bedroom. They created refuse chutes to send garbage to the basement. And in a cosmopolitan city offering every possible type of cuisine, they added one that had been lacking—American fare. Later, there was an in-house big band performing nightly along with the Grosvenor House Girls (chorus line of dancers). And all the latest amenities, like electricity and lifts.

An office was even opened on New York's Fifth Avenue to take bookings, promising wealthy Americans that their servants would be accommodated for free in the inclusive rate of 18 shillings per night. These transatlantic reservations by telegraph required special codes to reduce the time and expense of booking. For example, ordering a "Caesar" meant reserving a sitting room, two double bedrooms, and a bath.

In the hotel's basement was another big feature—the "Great Room," a gigantic space built to be an ice rink. It had state-of-the-art refrigeration technology, and The Park Lane Ice Club was an instant hit, with big ice-skating parties and famous skaters performing. In a two-degrees-of-separation moment (three if you count the 85-year time span), I realized while standing in the Great Room that it was the closest I would ever came to the person for whom my mother named me—Norwegian ice-skater Sonja Henie, a three-time Olympic Champion who was known to practice here in the early 1930s.

In 1929, the Prince of Wales attended a Hallowe'en Ice Festival and Dance. Thus began a long connection between English royals and the Grosvenor House Hotel. It was also here that two young sisters, Elizabeth and Margaret, learned to ice skate. A few years later the innovative hotel built a wood floor that could be rolled out to convert the space into a ballroom, accommodating 2,000 guests. In 1934, the first Grosvenor

House Art & Antiques Fair was held, and soon after Queen Mary lent the annual event her patronage, followed by the Queen Mother, and lately HRH Princess Alexandria. There was also the Queen Charlotte's Ball, a tradition that dates to 1780 when King George III held a ball for his wife's birthday and the aristocratic daughters of "marriageable age" were formally presented at court, thereby launching them into the "marriage mart." The hotel took up this debutante tradition, and through 1958 young 'Ladies of Quality' were introduced to Queen Elizabeth II before attending the giant ball at the hotel, always gowned in virginal white, of course. Another big charity ball was the Royal Caledonian, which continues today and anyone can attend (see Ch. 7).

By the way, the ice rink was discontinued by the end of the 1930s, in favor of the more profitable ballroom, and a permanent floor was built—however, some of the refrigeration machinery still remains underneath.

American Connections: The most important was during WWII, starting with the Officers' Sunday Club Entertainment that provided an evening's respite from the war for some 300,000 Allied Forces over six years. Then it served briefly as an annex to the US Embassy's Immigration Section, issuing emergency visas to British mothers and children for travelling to America to escape the war. In 1943, the Great Room became the largest US Officers' mess in the world, ever. American staffed, it served more than 5.5 million meals in the two years of 1943–45.

～ *for the guys* As for statistics: during WWII more than five miles of blackout fabric covered the hotel's thousands of windows, 20,000 sandbags and 8,000 feet of timber protected against nearby bomb blasts, and fire fighting squads of employees successfully extinguished the many incendiary bombs that fell on the hotel. It was run like a small military operation—whenever an alert sounded, whatever time of day, employee squads of roof spotters, fire fighters, and demolition crews ran to their posts, all connected to a central control office by special telephone lines and pageboys (for many years the hotel employed young boys as messengers, something we'd frown on

◇❧────────────•

Up to 14,000 meals per day served to US Officers in the Grosvenor House Great Room turned mess hall in WWII

•────────────•

Grosvenor House in WWII ∼ It never closed even once during the war!

today but back then it was a doorway to upward mobility where one could even progress to leadership positions or concierge).[25]

Also for the war effort, in 1941, the Grosvenor staff provided a 38-strong platoon to the 1st County of London Battalion Home Guard; they often drilled on the roof. For a period, the basement Great Room also served as an Air Raid Patrol dormitory with staff sleeping on the floor, hotel visitors on beds in the ballroom balconies, and because everyone was jammed together there was even a woman attendant employed to gently waken snorers who might disturb others.

The Grosvenor hosted many Allied leaders, including General Charles de Gaulle, US Generals Patton, Marshal, and Eisenhower. The hotel is still proud that: "Grosvenor House in Battledress, sandbagged and walled about in concrete, with shuttered windows and austerity menus, never closed its doors for one hour, day or night, during the 2,074 days of World War II. The four great towers still stand and gaze across the deserted gun sites in the Park, the doors swing open to friends from the four corners of the world, the flags still fly."[26] The war in Europe ended on May 8, 1945, and in November, 3,000 Londoners and American GI's celebrated together, dancing to music played by the United States Navy Band in the Great Room.[27]

Grosvenor pageboy puts away the "All Clear" sign for the last time, on VE Day, 1945

American connections continued through the decades with such guests as Eleanor Roosevelt, Douglas Fairbanks Jr, Orson Welles, Jacqueline Kennedy Onassis, Henry Kissinger, Sammy Davis Jr, Muhammed Ali, and Secretary of State Madeleine Albright.

NOW: In 2004, Marriott took over management of this "Grande Dame of Park Lane," and after a four-year, multi-million-pound refurbishment launched it as a JW Marriott Hotel in 2008. The décor is classic contemporary in muted colors. For Americans, you'll find all the comforts of home in this large hotel and a great location overlooking Hyde Park. There is history here in this hotel, but all of it less than 100 years old and not apparent as you walk the halls.

HISTORICAL OFFERINGS: Daily Afternoon Tea in the Park Lane and, as above, once a year there is a grand Scottish charity ball that everyone is welcome to attend for the price of a ticket. Features: The Great Hall ballroom at 20,454 square feet. Family rooms with 1 king, 2 twin beds. Mobility accessible rooms and public spaces.

DETAILS: 420 rooms/76 suites. Check-in: 3pm/Checkout: 12pm. **ROOM:** WiFi (£10–15 fee), US voltage adaptors, hotpot with coffee/tea, free bottled water, bathrobes/slippers, evening turndown service, luxury linens, choice of feather/foam pillows, marble bathrooms, lighted makeup mirror, scale, minibar, iron/board, free crib, umbrella, safe, newspaper upon request. **FOOD:** JW Steakhouse, The Park Room (Afternoon Tea), Red Bar, The Bourbon Bar, Corrigan's Mayfair, Park Lane Market (coffee, pastries to go), 24-hr room service. **HOTEL:** Free WiFi public areas, ATM, currency exchange, coffee/newspapers in lobby, concierge, fitness center, babysitting (fee), SanRizz Salon, florist, onsite laundry, limo service (fee), staffed 24-hour business center (printer). **STARS:** 4½

TAKE HEED! No four-posters or period rooms. Food/cocktails here are all on the pricey side. Dress code casual, but I saw ladies dressed nicely for tea in Park Lane.

TIP: Executive and above rooms come with Concierge Lounge access (free breakfast, afternoon tea, hors d'oeuvres, dessert, free wine, sparkling wine, and soft drinks); do the math as this might be a better deal than buying these meals separately. Try for a park-view room or at least outside view. Corrigan's has a set lunch Mon-Fri that is a good price. Otherwise, save money by dining elsewhere. It's a Marriott Category 9: see Marriott County Hall for more brand savings tips.

How OLDE: ⚜⚜⚜☖☖ ∼ *contemporary décor and recent historical importance* **Tube:** Marble Arch | www.Marriott.com (search by London) | +44 20 7499 6363 | 86-90 Park Lane, Mayfair

THE ROOKERY HOTEL

Est. 1998 in 1764 building ∼ £££

∼ with sibling hotels Hazlitt's (1718) and Batty Langley's (1724)

First, I got completely turned around after popping out of the underground. The streets are not on a grid and quaint alleys abound—it's a place where you'll need a good map or GPS. After making a mental note not to forget the map again, I rechecked the local one back down in the station. This is an ancient district just outside the "square mile" financial district, a neighborhood that was also outside the law in the 1700s, and some of that character remains today. That's the second thing I noted, it's uber quaint, with many restaurants and pubs in some old period buildings.

THEN: From the Medieval times, Smithfield Market has anchored this area. When the house that would eventually become the hotel was built 350 years ago, cattle were herded en masse through the narrow streets on their way to slaughter and sale. This created a great deal of menial labor, and a community arose to house, clothe, and feed the unskilled laborers. Inside the City walls, just to the south, it was all law and order, but here anything went. In short, it wasn't a safe neighborhood—cut-throats, you know—and it certainly wasn't a place for young ladies of quality, night or day. It's the kind of neighborhood where Fagin, Charles Dickens' infamous exploiter of orphans, would have thrived, and real life versions probably did. It was a noisy, crowded, densely-packed slum of narrow streets and alleys, and citizens were packed into rickety hovels like too many baby crows in a dirty nest.

It's that similarity that gave the neighborhood its nickname, The Rookery. The nobs thought it similar to the local crows' nesting habits crowded onto treetops, so some believe. Others credit the term coming from old slang—"to rook" is to cheat or thieve. The crows were renowned for stealing food…as were the locals for plucking valuables from pockets. London abounded with rookeries, and they were so outside the law, so dangerous to enter no matter the time of day, that when Charles Dickens wanted to visit them for research, he was escorted by Inspector Field, chief detective at Scotland Yard, and a party of four, probably armed, guards.[28]

Not much is known about the house or its inhabitants—it wasn't the kind of place where record keeping was of high import. It probably housed a prosperous tradesman and his family, not yet ready for a Mayfair address, but certainly hoping to raise up his family, perhaps marry his daughter higher up the social strata. Which did happen to one lucky young lass. The Mary Lane (a charming attic suite in the hotel) recognizes a local servant girl who made good, marrying a diamond merchant and one presumes moving out of the rookery. You can see her portrait in her suite.

NOW: "The footpads and cutpurses have gone now," notes the Rookery's brochure, however, Smithfield Market remains—today the largest meat market in the UK. Because of its working-class history, there are no royal or US connections, nor notable happenings in its past. But there is charm a-plenty in this area. And, even better—perhaps due to the close proximity to fresh meat—this south Clerkenwell neighborhood is a foodie heaven. The inn may not have a restaurant, but there are delicious eats to be had all around—I suggest trying Coach & Horses or Hix Oyster & Chop House. It's now the kind of trendy district that attracts both Hollywood A-listers and high-society types wanting a little "slumming." Not! While the food is less expensive than elsewhere, this is no slum, not anymore. Then there is the hotel itself… and the reason it's listed here.

Tucked away on a quaint and quiet alley, the Grade II listed Rookery is situated in the only remaining Georgian houses on Peter's Lane. The inside is a Victorian fantasy of antiques, bygone features, stone flagged floors, and polished wood paneling. Unlike some places that save the period fun for the expensive suites, *every* room here has personality, and it will feel like you're living the life of a romance heroine—especially ones that are down on their luck, living on their last shilling in a rented room. If the décor isn't inspiration enough for the novelist, read the signs on the doors—each room is named after a real person from the Rookery's past—tradesmen, criminals, even prostitutes.

But to clarify, while the neighborhood might have once housed heroines on their last shilling, the guest rooms of The Rookery are all luxurious. You'll sleep on magnificent carved beds—many of them four-poster. Your bath might be in an actual Victorian-era claw foot tub, carefully restored to its former glory with polished brass fittings. Your toilet could be period too—not a throne, but unique. Some rooms have exposed wood-beam ceilings. Others feature fireplaces, and all have antiques, original old paintings, or other artwork. And for as long as you stay, you're not a guest but a resident, with your own key to the front door and anytime access to a fully stocked honor bar in the Conservatory, a room where you can choose from a book to read or entertain friends. It's supposed to feel like your home away from home. Expect Lady Grey, the resident cat, to inspect you while you relax before the roaring fire in winter or in the small garden in summer. And even though the building is an ancient, there is air conditioning in every room.

The Rookery doesn't stint on service either. Their hallmarks: old-fashioned hospitality and friendly efficient service—including concierge services for shows and restaurants or help meeting whatever special desires guests have. Lastly, while the hotel is all about the old, they've got most of the modern gadgets: televisions tucked in cabinets, music, and air conditioning (but no lifts).

HISTORICAL OFFERINGS: *Four-poster beds!* And, even the lowest priced Club Double has either 17th Century carved oak bedsteads or four-posters. The two Junior Suites have canopied 18th Century four-poster beds, separate sitting rooms, plus fancy bathrooms. The Rook's Nest is a two–story penthouse suite with views of St. Paul's and Old Bailey from its 40–foot spire. Contact the hotel directly, if you've got your heart set on a four-poster bed or claw-foot tub. Although no restaurant onsite, they do bring a breakfast tray to your room for a fee, complete with a fresh flower—just like the married women of *Downton Abbey.* Served from 7–10am, it includes: pastries, cereal, porridge, and bacon sandwiches. Features: 2 ground floor rooms adapted for disabled guests. **STARS:** 4½

TAKE HEED! There are no lifts in this three-story hotel or the sister hotels. Request ground floor rooms, if needed. Antique beds are smaller, usually double sized. Some rooms with claw-foot tubs have only hand-held showers. The rooms are small, some tiny. These are very old buildings, so at times the plumbing and room temperatures can be wonky. And, again, no elevators.

TIP: The hotel has single rooms—no four-posters but still a £159 bargain of Victorian elegance for the solitary traveler. All three hotels are quite popular with good reviews, so book early.

DETAILS: 30 rooms/3 suites. Check-in: 2pm/Checkout: 11am. **ROOM:** Free WiFi, hotpot and coffee/tea with real milk, trendy REN toiletries, towel warmers, minibar, safe, iron upon request. **FOOD:** 24-hr room service from a limited menu of British-y items. **HOTEL:** Concierge, arranging airport transfers, same-day dry cleaning/laundry, well-stocked honor bar, free cribs/cots.

A word on Hazlitt's and Batty Langley's ～ these sister hotels in Covent Garden and Spitalfields, respectively, offer the same features: period décor in a Georgian-era building, good service, and breakfast in bed for a fee. Both have four-poster beds at all price categories, except single twin-bed rooms (but even those are ornately carved antiques). Beautiful canopied and half-testers start at the Superior rate. Hazlitt's (30 rms) is known to attract a literary clientele because it's set in the former home of English writer William Hazlitt—you'll find autographed books in their library left by authors who've stayed here. Hotel is *not* mobility accessible. If you do stay at Hazlitt's be sure to read his biography—he led a tragic artist's existence and died poor, his brilliance nearly forgotten. Batty Langley's (29 rms) is the newest and is already on Condè Nast's 2017 Gold List as one of London's six best hotels. There is no close Tube but the over ground is nearby.

How Olde: ⚜⚜⚜⚜⚜
~ *every room is a fantasy of a bygone era*
Rookery ~ **Tube:** Barbican | **Map:** D | www.RookeryHotel.com
Reservations@rookery.co.uk | +44 20 7336 0931 | 12 Peters Lane, Cowcross
Batty Langleys ~ **Overground Station:** Liverpool, Shoreditch High St | www.BattyLangleys.com | Reservations@battylangleys.co.uk
+44 20 7377 4390 | 12 Folgate St, Spitalfields
Hazlitts ~ **Tube:** Tottenham Court Rd | www.HazlittsHotel.com
Reservations@hazlitts.co.uk | +44 20 7434 1771
6 Frith St, Soho Square

◇〜∘────────────────────────────●

ST. ERMIN'S HOTEL, MARRIOTT'S AUTOGRAPH COLLECTION

Est. 1899 in 1889 building ~ £££

Pass under the ornate Victorian iron gateway to stroll up a tree-lined lane and you leave the hustle of modern London behind. Walk through the front door and you've stepped back 100 years in time. Wow! Best Victorian lobby ever! Instantly, I wished I were here to attend a period costume ball just so I could descend the grand baroque staircase in a flowing gown on the arm of my dearest in top hat and tails. The paparazzi had better be on hand to snatch a photo.

THEN: But who is St. Ermin? And what is this hotel all about with its Parliament Bell and rumors of an underground spy tunnel? Saint Ermin was a 6th Century Welsh prince (most likely, son of King Hoel I Mawr). He fled the yellow plague in Wales, became a monk, and founded a monastery in Brittany. He's renowned for having slayed a dragon and saving the townspeople. He accomplished this by binding his vestment to the beast and ordering the dragon to drown itself in the river Sèche. Certainly the stuff of legends, and in this case saints. By the by, it started as the cult of St. Arthmael, but the name changed over time to—Armell, Armen, Armet, Ermyne, and finally Ermin.[29]

*A charming step back into Victorian splendor at the St. Ermin's,
c.1900 and today*

Jump forward 1,000 years and you get King Henry VII (also partly of Welsh descent), who was nearly shipwrecked off the French coastline, but his ship was saved during a terrible storm in 1483. He'd already visited the monastery and prayed to St. Armell, and was convinced it was due to the intercession of the Saint that he and his small armada survived.[30] Back in London, he built a chapel in his honor in 1496, and the area became known as St. Ermyne's Hill. Pilgrims would go there to be cured of gout, ague, and other fevers. There are even those that believe Armell might have been King Arthur himself.[31] Armell was a real man, but the mythical aspects seem like the plot of a clever fantasy romance. By the way, if you're feeling a little traveler's indigestion and it's August, St. Ermin's day is the 16th.

Today, statues of the saint can be seen in Henry's Westminster Abbey Chapel. There are other depictions around, but the most fascinating was discovered in 1813. A 16th Century "reredos" (a decorative altarpiece, in this case painted wood) was found at Romsey Abbey; it had been sealed behind an arch for centuries. The reredos now adorns St. Laurence Chapel at Romsey, and Armell is the top right figure with a small dragon at his feet wrapped in vestment. If you happen to find yourself in Hampshire along the coast, 83 miles from London, there are many other interesting relics, including the beautiful tomb of a small girl who died of scarlet fever in 1843.[32]

But back to St. Ermin's Hill in late 1800s. On the land where the chapel once stood is the St. Ermin's Mansions, high-status serviced apartments in redbrick Queen Anne architecture. The large block was converted to a hotel in 1899 by the famous theater designer J.P. Briggs, which accounts for the imaginative public rooms and magnificent two-story lobby with its undulating balcony and fanciful plasterwork (watch

---

Writing home from London to Lone Rock, Wisconsin, in 1907
(back of the postcard on previous page)

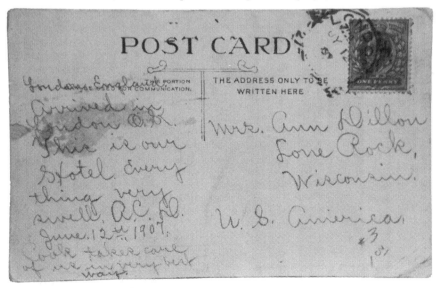

for elephants and tigers). There's an even prettier ballroom for events. The new hotel quickly became popular both for travellers (particularly Americans) and for locals stopping in for drinks, especially politicians, which brings us to the large bell mounted on the wall. Due to its proximity to the Houses of Parliament, a "Division Bell" was installed, one of about six in nearby buildings, and when it was rung it signaled a division was occurring and members of the House of Lords or Commons had 8 minutes to get there to cast their vote.

Is there a princess in the house? Nope, but ➴ **for the guys** there's something even better: Spies! Because of its location, near Parliament, the police, and other more secret bureaus, it became a hot-bed of intrigue starting in the 1930s. The hotel was used by the Secret Intelligence Service (now referred to as MI6), and because Section D headquarters were located at nearby 54 Broadway there were many spies around. Among the British agents who worked there at some point were Ian Fleming, Guy Burgess, and Kim Philby. And, in the run-up to WWII, the hotel was used for guerilla warfare classes, run partly by MI6. Among the trainees were playwright Noel Coward, and Anthony Blunt, who became a double-agent in the Cambridge Five spy ring.

In 1940, Sir Winston Churchill, known to enjoy a glass of champagne in the hotel's Caxton Bar, invited some high-level operatives to the St. Ermin's where he instructed them to "set Europe ablaze." They became the SOE (Special Operations Executive, today the SAS) in charge of covert operations during WWII. At first, they ran their operation by taking over an entire floor of the hotel. Throughout the war nearly all nearby buildings (sometimes even the basements of apartment blocks) held various secret agencies, including MI8, MI9, and the Government Communications Headquarters. As a central spot, the Caxton Bar was often used by these agencies and Naval Intelligence for everything from meeting field agents to interviewing prospective employees to just hanging out for a moment's respite. It was, in short, spy central, and this continued through the Cold War with the Soviet Union, where it was sometimes used as an MI5 safe house (seems oddly "unsafe" given it was well known that counter-intelligence activities were happening there).

And that's not all—there's rumored to be a secret passageway leading from underneath the grand staircase all the way to the Palace of Westminster, and further whispered that this is all somehow connected to the mysterious Q-Whitehall network. Supposedly the tunnel was ordered blocked up after 9/11, but it's a well-known secret that there are many tunnels under the streets in this area.

St. Ermin's Hotel, c.1900 and restored

Working again at the St. Ermin's Hotel, after years of disuse

The most infamous spy story happened in the early 1950s when British agent Guy Burgess frequently met his Russian counterpart at the hotel's Caxton Bar. But he was not just working for England. A part of the Cambridge Five Spy Ring, founded at that University, and an admirer of Marxism, Guy handed over thousands of documents, many top-secret, to the KGB and would meet his "handler" Yuri Modin in the bar. He was based for a time in the British Embassy in Washington, DC. He defected to the Soviet Union in 1951 to escape prosecution, as did fellow Cambridge spies Kim Philby and Donald Maclean. Burgess never took to Soviet life but he must have liked the Russian vodka, because he died from liver failure at age 52. Another member, the aforementioned Anthony Blunt, initially escaped persecution for his crimes, was even knighted for his service in 1956, but was finally outed as a member of the Cambridge Five and stripped of his knighthood in 1964.

For more spy stories and the hotel's involvement read *A Spy's Guide to London* by Roy Berkeley and *An Insider's Travel Guide to London Espionage* by Mark Birdsall—either would make a great ∾ **for the guys** surprise for the transatlantic flight. Or, while in London, take a London Walks spy tour (www.Walks.com, currently Saturdays at 2:30pm; £10pp, 2 hrs).

NOW: A 2016 *Condé Nast Traveller* People's Choice Award winner, the St. Ermin's completed a £30 million renovation of the Grade II listed building in 2012, restoring the public spaces to their previous glory and adding trendy, adventurous décor that plays on the plasterwork's animal themes. The guest rooms have clean classic lines but no period features. After decades of silence, the Parliament Bell is working once again—so if you hear it rung don't worry about a fire, but be sure to watch anyone running out the door. It could be a Lord on his way to vote. Also, be sure to check out the glass case with historical mementos and postcards. You can't visit the secret passageway, sadly, but there is something behind the center door between the stairs. I saw it and no more need be said...

HISTORICAL OFFERINGS: Afternoon Tea and the Victorian public spaces. Features: Family rooms with 2 double beds and 2 bathrooms! (Sleeps 5, if fifth is small child.). 8 fully accessible rooms. Private exclusive tours through Touriocity, such as City of Spies (£57), plus Regal London and Covent Garden. Rooftop bees and vegetable garden. Beekeeping workshops on summer Saturdays, complete with honey cocktail (2½ hrs, £35pp, select dates, book early). And ∾ for *the little guys and gals* a free St. Ermin's Spy Pack with puzzles, secret agent mission, and non-alcoholic cocktail—*shaken, not stirred.*

DETAILS: 290 rooms/41 suites. Check-in: 3pm/Checkout: 11am. **ROOM:** Free basic WiFi, multi-national electrical sockets, White Company toiletries, bathrobes/slippers, evening turndown service, marble baths, Nespresso & tea making, free bottled water, Bose sound, iPod docking, lighted makeup mirror, minibar, iron/board, safe. **FOOD:** Afternoon Tea Lounge and library (Ch. 5), Caxton Grill (modern European), Caxton Bar (combo bar & fireside lounge), Caxton Terrace (quaint outdoor space in summers with limited menu), 24-hr room service. **HOTEL:** Concierge, currency exchange, Touriocity exclusive tours, luggage storage, laundry/valet service, business center, 24-hr gym. **STARS:** 4½ Reports of "above and beyond service" with a smile, such as staff tracking down the taxi after a guest left her phone or *really* calling to let you know the room is ready, which is oft promised but oft forgot.

TAKE HEED! This is an old building with the usual tiny rooms and creaking wood floors. Some reports of noise issues. **TIP:** Substantial discounts for Advance Purchase (as much as £100). It's a Marriott, Category 8: see Marriott County Hall for more brand savings tips.

*H*OW OLDE: ⚜ ⚜ ⚜ ⚜ ⚜
 ∾ *public spaces are wonderfully period, but the rooms are not*
Tube: St. James Park | www.StErminsHotel.co.uk | Reservations@ sterminshotel.co.uk | +44 20 7222 7888 | 2 Caxton St

St. Pancras Renaissance© Hotel London

Est. and built 1873 ~ £££

The lobby is all big open spaces. Quiet bustle. Modern, but not. This doesn't feel like the destination, rather more a way station on your travels. And well it should, because the hotel was once the showpiece of a grand train station—St. Pancras—and today it's still connected by train and the underground to London, the rest of England, and even the continent (it's the London terminal for the cross-Channel Eurostar). For our purposes, this remarkable hotel is a convenient and comfortable home base, under the Marriott brand, for our exploration of historic London.

THEN: To really get this hotel, you need to put yourself into the historic mindset of the times. Mid–1800s London was exploding with prosperous activity. Hustle and innovation everywhere. Railway tracks crisscrossing the landscape suddenly brought everywhere within reach of everyone, and railway stations were the portals to this new world. The thriving Midland Railway Company wanted a station that would eclipse all the others, and Sir George Gilbert Scott, a prominent ecclesiastical architect, was ambitious enough to take on the challenge. After the station was completed in 1868, his grand vision and daring choices in the face of much criticism resulted in what came to be known as the "cathedral of railways."

Seeking inspiration from the nearly completed Gothic Revival Palace of Westminster (the Houses of Parliament), Scott sought to create something new that was as ornate as a palace but "softer, more colourful," as might be found in the Venetian Gothic style.[33] Adorned with spires and steeples, crowned with a massive clock tower, the ornate "palace" was dressed in a rather modest material—simple red brick—but his signature choice gave the structure vibrant color, a distinct contrast to the blander white Portland or sand-colored Aston stones popular at the time. That these bricks just happened to be manufactured in the Midlands region, bringing prosperity and recognition to the industrial heartlands where the railway was based, was certainly an added plus. It was magnificent and costly and beautiful and impressive.

The next task was building a grand hotel to go with it. Again, Scott was up to the challenge. It took an army of builders, stonemasons, artists, and tradesman five years to complete The Midland Grand. The magnificent exterior was recreated inside so lavishly that one might think a wizard out of *Harry Potter* had made a mistake and mixed up

The Midland Grand in c.1880 and the St. Pancras today

a gothic cathedral with a pasha's harem with a Venetian palace. Fun Fact: scenes from *Chamber of Secrets* and *The Deathly Hallows* were actually filmed here.

The extravagance cannot be overstated: arched doorways, large neo-classical murals, elaborately painted ceilings, marble pillars topped with intricate carving, wall-to-wall Axminster carpets, massive carved marble fireplaces, gold leaf, colorful flamboyant wallpaper, and furnishings of the finest quality. So fine was the finished hotel, that Scott remarked that it was "almost too good for its purpose."[34]

The hotel's great showpiece was the three-story Grand Staircase, a "masterpiece of High Victorian, neo-Gothic decoration and extravagance... reaching an extraordinary vaulted ceiling, painted with a celestial scene of stars and the Eight Virtues against a viridian sky."[35] One can imagine the impact ascending these stairs must have had on the newly arrived Victorian-era traveler, having just completed their long train trip to enter this over-the-top fairyland. It was surely a sign that these budding industrialists or merchants had arrived in a city like no other and in a hotel fit for nothing less than a king. It would tell them...they'd *arrived!* They were *someone!* They were the new lords and ladies of the modern times.

But that wasn't all. The Midland Grand was a marvel of the latest 1873 innovations. It had the precursor to an elevator—a pair of 'hydraulic

The St. Pancras's restored Grand Staircase

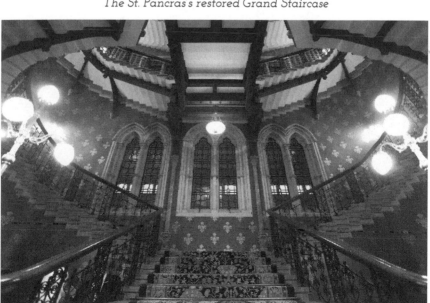

ascending chambers' to ferry guests up the four flights. It must have seemed like magic. It had the first revolving door in Britain, plus a novel electric bell service calling system for each guest room, and best of all, flush toilets with hot and cold running water in communal bathrooms, while other hotels still used chamber pots. Lastly, they had 22-inch thick concrete-slab fireproof floors, reassuring guests of their safety following the horrific 1834 fire that destroyed some of the Palace of Westminster. All this luxury and innovative comfort made it extremely popular, allowing the railway to charge the second highest rates in town—3 ½ shillings to several pounds per night. The total price tag for the hotel was also tops—£438,000 or $40 million in today's dollars. But this extravagance was worth it—The Midland Grand hotel was a huge success.

For just over 30 years.

The very things that had made the hotel so groundbreaking combined to drag it down. By the 1920s, the hotel was well behind the times. Remember The Ritz hotel with its en-suite bathrooms? It had already been open for 15 years, and every other hotelier was upgrading too. But guests at The Midland Grand still had to share just 5 bathrooms and 9 bathtubs among 300 rooms. The 22-inch-thick fireproof concrete floors that had been a pioneering safety feature in 1873, now made it impossible to upgrade the plumbing system. (You'll be glad to know that today's high-powered tools easily addressed this issue and every room now has its own flush toilet.) As the St. Pancras notes, "the very innovation that was designed to save the hotel helped finish it off."[36]

They really tried, though. A Moroccan coffee house was added plus an in-house orchestra, but multi-year operating losses forced the railway to close the hotel in 1935. For a while, parts of it were used for railway offices, but to cover up the decaying outmoded décor the interiors were "refurbished" with whitewash and the boarding up of pillars.

She survived bombings in two World Wars, but the greatest threat was still to come. In the 1960s, city planners were rapidly sweeping away the old to erect new city blocks, and the Grand Midland was in their sights. By then, even the railway station was mostly abandoned, with two newer stations receiving the bulk of rail traffic. If not for the concerted effort of the founders of the Victorian Society organizing a popular campaign to stop demolition and earning the hotel Grade 1 status in 1967, this Victorian masterpiece would now be sixties-era block apartments.

Before continuing this story, we must ask, is there a princess in the house? Not so much, although it did appeal to the industrious American spirit—guests included Cornelius Vanderbilt (one of the richest Americans at the time) and George Pullman (creator of the Pullman sleeping train car).

The Railway Booking Office, c.1880,
and today's Booking Office Bar at the St. Pancras

NOW: This Victorian lady, its finery painted over or gone, was finally abandoned in 1985 and she sat empty for 20 years awaiting an unknown fate. Then finally, the St. Pancras train station was chosen to be the terminus for the cross-Channel Eurostar service. This provided the impetus for tackling the derelict hotel, and after some fits and starts, the project finally got underway. Using original plans and decorating schemes, hundreds of conservation experts, specialist craftsmen, and painters began a painstaking restoration that took a full decade to return the hotel to its past grandeur.

While the furnishings are modern, Victorian features have been carefully preserved in the public spaces. Such as in the current Booking Office Bar, named after its previous purpose as a rail-ticket office. While taking a break here to enjoy a martini after a busy London day, I could almost feel the ghosts of travelers past—Victorian ladies, busy merchants, wide-eyed youth, all embarking on travels in this new-fangled mode of steam-powered transportation. This unique place would make a terrific setting for a time-travel romance.

A new lobby connects the station with the hotel and melds contemporary style with period features—the space is roofed with a high glass ceiling spanning two gorgeous Victorian exterior walls, which gives one the feeling of being outside. One of the prettiest restored rooms is the Ladies' Smoking Room (named such because it was the first place where ladies could smoke in public).

Lodging here will have all the comforts Americans expect, although the rooms are European-sized tiny. With the exception of the Royal Suite, there are no four-poster beds here, and the rooms are modern—the only period features in my room were Gothic arched windows. The lavish Chambers Suites, housed in the original part of the hotel, do have more period features (including 18-foot-high ceilings) and come with Chambers Club access and free food/drink, but cost a King's Ransom. However, many hallways and public spaces retain a wonderful period feel, and you can stay here in a basic room for a much more reasonable price. So, if American-style comfort will put you at ease for a good night's sleep, you can have the best of both worlds here.

HISTORICAL OFFERINGS: The Booking Office Bar features Victorian-era cocktails, carefully researched from such books as the 1869 *Cooling Cups and Dainty Drinks* by William Terrington and W.R. Loftus's *New Mixing Book*. The Gilbert Scott Restaurant, specializing in traditional English cuisine, offers another option for dining in Victorian ambiance.

The hotel also offers "Gothic Masterpiece Revealed" — 75-minute tours that bring the hotel's history to life and showcase the meticulously

The Midland Grand Coffee Room, c.1880, and today's Gilbert Scott Restaurant

restored Victorian features throughout. Here's the kind of interesting fact you may learn—the hallways were built noticeably wide to allow for two ladies in Victorian dress to pass each other. (Must reserve tour in advance +44 20 8241 6921; £20pp; max 15 people per tour.) If you're lucky enough to take this tour, remember to imagine this place through the eyes of a Victorian lady, someone who's never seen the immense scale and glitzy opulence of today's Vegas or Disney wonderlands—then you may feel the extraordinariness of the place as she surely did. Features: Mobility accessible rooms with roll in showers.

DETAILS: 207 rooms/38 suites. Check-in: 3pm/Checkout: 12pm. **ROOM:** WiFi (fee), robes/slippers, coffee/tea maker, free bottled water, free overnight shoeshine (request from concierge), lighted makeup mirror, iron/board, soundproof windows, evening turndown, free newspaper upon request, free portable child's crib/play-yard, pet friendly (fee). **FOOD:** Gilbert Scott Restaurant (celebrated chef Marcus Wareing), Booking Bar & Grill (sometimes live 3-piece jazz bands), Hansom Lounge in lobby (serves afternoon tea), 24-hour room service. **HOTEL:** concierge, currency exchange, luggage storage, bellman, beauty salon, Melogy Barber, indoor basement pool (small but distinctive, feels like part of a pasha's harem), sauna, steam room, fitness center. **STARS:** 4½

TAKE HEED! Full American Breakfast is pricey (over $30pp). There are minimum charges for the Hansom Lounge and other dining areas (+$15pp), which annoys some online reviewers; however, I believe this is an effort to keep the crowds at bay due to the museum-like interest this hotel attracts. Some rooms in the Barlow Wing are near the nightclub with blaring music till late at night; if you're a light sleeper request a room away from this and from the lifts when making a reservation. While the majority of reviews rave about the place (one bar patron mentioned being called the next day after she'd lost her purse; they had it and all contents were still inside), there are also reports about a too busy, abrupt, perhaps undertrained staff. Also, keycard problems seem common (Free advice: don't ever put keycards near your cellphone, it can wipe them clean.)

TIP: The aforementioned historical tour, and you don't have to be a hotel guest to take it. Booking Office Bar & Grill is a happening hotspot (i.e. noisy and extremely popular); dining reservations are a must as well as at the Gilbert Scott Restaurant. Menus with prices for both restaurants, including drinks, can be found on the hotel's website. The Restaurant's 3-course "set menu" is a bargain, but check for restricted serving times.

Another Fun Fact: did you know that ordinary people couldn't easily purchase bottled wine in Victorian times, not until the passage of

William Gladstone's 1861 Single Bottle Act! In a way, the St. Pancras pays homage to this by offering a large number of wines by-the-glass, which are great for the single lady that could not possibly down a full bottle. Even better, a glass of Veuve Clicquot champagne can be had for the bargain price of £13.50. It's a Marriott, Category 9: see Marriott County Hall for more brand savings tips.

*H*ow Olde: ♔ ♔ ♔ ♔ ♔
~ *authentic, but with mostly contemporary decor*
Tube: Kings Cross, St. Pancras | www.StPancrasLondon.com
+44 20 7841 3540 | Euston Road

*G*overness on Holiday ~ *under $200*

◇❧————————————————•

CRANLEY HOTEL

Est. 1980s in 1869 building ~ ££

Situated in two 19th Century town houses, this still somehow feels like you're approaching an actual hotel. Perhaps the uniform appearance and larger facade proclaims hotel rather than private residence. But that hotel-y feel ends once you walk through the door and foyer into a pleasant Drawing Room with Regency décor. Clean lines. Wedgewood Blues. Chandeliers. With no doorman or hotel staff apparently around to offer greeting, you could just go ahead and make yourself at home in one of the fireside chairs. But look again and you'll spot a desk with elegant chairs in the back corner. Head over and take a seat for a genteel registration process. And, for a moment, pretend you're the owner of this gracious Victorian mansion and the clerk behind the desk your House Steward at the ready.

THEN: The earliest record of this area in what is now the Royal Borough of Kensington and Chelsea, dates to the 16th Century when it was part of a land holding called Courtfield. Fruit orchards and vegetable gardens were all you would find here. Earl's Court manor and its various owners eventually controlled much of this area, until 1779 when a large portion was sold to a Yorkshire landowner, James Gunter.[37] Yes, that Gunter—confectioner and the inventor of "ices" sold in the famous Berkeley Square shop. The family used this land for growing ingredients for their sweets until the 1860s when the ever-expanding London city, combined with the removal of tollgates and the addition of the world's first underground railway, changed the economics. It was now more profitable to build houses on it. 670 homes were built on their sixty acres, and the area came to be known as Gunter Estates.

The Cranley Hotel occupies three houses—No's 8, 10 and 12 Bina Gardens. The original owner of No. 8 was Matthew Moggridge, a Welsh magistrate, and one of his two sons, Robert, started a small but successful perfumery business in Notting Hill Gate. Robert eventually sold his business to William Penhaligon, a Cornishman whose company went on to become the quintessential English perfumery (holder of two Royal warrants today). Not surprisingly, the Cranley Hotel uses Penhaligon products in its bathrooms.

Is there a princess in the house? No, nor any US connection. A six-degrees-of-royal association could be claimed in that Queen Victoria simply adored Gunter's ices—a bit of a stretch, of course.

The Drawing Room in the Cranley

Among other residents who lived in these three houses were generals, barristers, and spinsters. During WWII, one of the houses served as a church hall and temporary shelter for the locals who'd lost everything in the Blitz. Afterwards, one of the houses was converted into individual apartments ("flats" in the English parlance) and another continued to be used for local community meetings and amateur dramatics, until all three houses on this quiet, tree-lined side street were purchased and combined into the privately-owned Cranley Hotel in the 1980s.

NOW: What you'll find today: décor that is period, with antique furniture and artwork, but it's a simpler, less-fussy version of Victorian. Not over-ornamented. Pale colors like lemon yellow. High ceilings, tall windows with floor-to-ceiling drapes, Bennison fabrics (English hand-printed textiles reproduced from 18th and 19th Century patterns), and mahogany writing desks add to the luxurious feel. The simple lines and muted colors will make your prince happy too.

HISTORICAL OFFERINGS: Sleep like a princess! In Four Poster King and Four Poster Deluxe category rooms that come with hand-pleated fabric canopies of Frette linen over handmade Beaudesert beds. For less, sleep like a lady-in-waiting in half-tester luxury in Superior rooms. Also, you'll be treated like visiting country gentry. Offered a welcome drink upon arrival and a glass of champagne and canapés

Fussy-free Victorian luxury at the Cranley

every evening in the drawing room (7–8pm only). Complimentary of course! And best of all, breakfast in bed, just like the ladies of *Downton Abbey*—although you do have to answer the door to accept the tray, unless you've brought your lady's maid.

DETAILS: 39 rooms. Check-in: 2pm/Checkout: 12pm. **ROOM:** Free WiFi, Irish hand-stitched luxury linens, turn-down service, Penhaligon toiletries, bathrobe/slippers, towel heater, antique writing desk, iPod docking station, minibar, safe, newspaper, umbrella, and upon request: DVD player, hotpot. **FOOD:** Full English Breakfast (spendy) or Afternoon Tea in the lobby drawing room or terrace, 24-hour room service. **HOTEL:** Honesty Bar in the reception area (meaning, help yourself anytime to a beverage and note it on a card for billing later), concierge service, luggage storage, guest computer and business services. **STARS:** 4½

TAKE HEED! The usual—rooms are small by US standards, although some suites are larger or come with terraces (the best has a rooftop balcony overlooking the city). There are 8 steps and no doorman, so you'll be hauling your luggage inside yourself. Some reviews note heat too hot, worn drapes, and bathrooms needing work. They are refurbishing the lobby area as this goes to press, so there may be some changes to policies. Some rooms are not mobility accessible so make your needs known if this is an issue. No in-room coffee/tea facilities, but free upon request. Lastly—important—there are old fashioned locks on the doors; just remember to turn the knob from the inside to secure it.

TIP: Choose the free Continental Breakfast option when booking; it's a better deal than buying separately. Book directly for free local calls, priority room upgrade, early check-in (11am) or late checkout (2pm) if available, and a 5-night stay includes free Afternoon Tea for two (£50 value). Watch for other specials and do the math: Romance Package is great value for 1 night, a good value for 2, but after that you'll be paying more for the extras than they're worth. Best Rate Guarantee: if you find a lower rate elsewhere within 24-hours of booking directly from hotel, they'll match it plus discount 10% more (rules, click on "Best Rate Guarantee" on website, bottom left).

How **OLDE:** ♜♜♜♜♜ ~ *the clean lines in the decor give it a more modern feel*
Tube: Gloucester Road, South Kensington | Map: A
www.CranleyHotel.com | reception@cranleyhotel.com | +44 20 7373 0123 | 10 Bina Gardens, South Kensington

THE GAINSBOROUGH

Building c.1850 ∽ £½

A Kensington address at an outer-borough price! Same white-stone town house, same British flag as the nearby Gore, but no portico. Pretty flower boxes on the window. Entering, you'll find period décor and furniture, but at such a low price I wasn't surprised to find it a bit faded and worn. The check-in process is nicely genteel—one sits on a comfortable period-reproduction chair facing the clerk, but the desk he sits behind is jarringly modern. Still I felt excited to be in a real South Kensington town house, wondering what it must have been like for the first residents of this area.

THEN: Research reveals they were farmers until the mid-19th Century, supplying fruits and vegetables to London residents. Following the 1851 Great Exhibition in Hyde Park, the area was developed into mansions in Italianate stucco for wealthy patrons of the many museums, schools, and theatres being built for Albertopolis (nickname for the neighborhood). By the 1870s, most houses had been completed and occupied in South Kensington.[38]

Royalty? Well, lots of lords and ladies of lesser rank. However, on the block of Queensbury Place, where The Gainsborough is located, lived for a while H.R.H. Prince Murat (son of the Napoleonic marshal who was elevated to King of Naples before being executed there) and his son Prince Murat while they were in exile during the Franco-Prussian War (1870-71).[39] So a Prince may have resided in this very building, but his exact address is unknown. As for US connections, the H.R.H.'s elder brother Prince Achille emigrated to America, dropped his titles, became a naturalized citizen, and was even elected mayor of Tallahassee, Florida (www.TallahasseeMuseum.org).

NOW: The neighborhood is some of the priciest real estate in the city and home to many wealthy foreign émigrés. Don't be surprised if you hear a lot of French spoken. So many French folk live in South Ken that it's been nicknamed "Paris' 21st Arrondissement." It's also a cultural center with some of London's most iconic museums: The V&A, Natural History, and Science. Besides the Royal Albert Hall, there is The Drayton Arms, a small fringe theatre that mounts quality productions.

The hotel itself has changed ownership many times and is *slowly* undergoing some refurbishment. Rooms not yet updated may be in poor condition—don't be afraid to request a better room if yours is unacceptable, but during the high season they might not have one free. This place will be… Basic. Historical. Meets your needs…*most of the time.*

HISTORICAL OFFERINGS: 1 Four-poster canopied bedroom—Room 208 with flowered fabric canopy and tasseled draping is the best. Other Double Deluxe rooms come with princess canopy. Features: The Triple (with a twin bed for 3) or Family Room (sleeps 4) are a good price.

DETAILS: 47 rooms. Check-in: 2pm/Checkout: 12pm. **ROOM:** Free WiFi (guests report spotty), toiletries, hotpot & tea/coffee, safe, newspaper, and upon request: iron/board, electrical adapter. Food: lounge, buffet breakfast room converts to bistro for lunch/dinner (mostly sandwiches), 24-hour room service. **HOTEL:** luggage storage. **STARS:** 2 ½ While they claim a four-star rating, reviewers give it just 2½, with some negative comments.

TAKE HEED! 2-night stay minimum in summertime. Most rooms are tiny and some are in the basement. Rather than shabby-chic, think shabby-Vic. The faded/worn condition of the property is reflected in the inexpensive price, but I found the staff to be friendly and helpful and you can't beat the location. It's here because I found it okay, but there are risks in booking this hotel. If you need everything spic-and-span and in perfectly working order then this would *not* be the hotel for you.

TIP: I recommend contacting them directly to reserve Room 208 or one of the remodeled rooms, and getting it back in writing. Do not accept a basement room. Continental breakfast buffet is a little cheaper if booked directly. There are many fine cafes in the neighborhood for other meals; however, a glass of sparkling wine in the lounge is a nice way to cap the day.

---

*H*OW OLDE: ♟♟♟♟♟
 ～ *Victorian property but some modern furnishings*
Tube: South Kensington | **Map:** A | www.TheGainsboroughHotel.
com | reservations@thegainsboroughhotel.com
+44 20 7957 0000 | 7–11 Queensbury Place

THE GLEBE HOUSE LONDON
(AN AIRBNB LISTED LODGING)

Est. 2012 in 1825 building ～ £½

A WORD ON AIRBNB: This is a fine avenue into period lodging at a reasonable price with the added benefit of friendly hosts that can give you the inside scoop on the local neighborhood and the city. This

The Glebe House London offers period B&B lodging

author has used it in Paris and London and both were excellent bargains. Although I didn't get to stay in Glebe House, I did tour it and meet the wonderful owner, and I feel confident in recommending it. Plus, you can check out her good reviews on AirBnb as well as view other listings. As with any period lodging, there may be quirks associated with the older buildings (no lifts or a/c), so please inquire if you have special needs. Lastly, for safety and social comfort, my preference as a woman traveling alone is to only book in places run by women or couples.

THEN: The Glebe House London is a detached Grade II listed Georgian converted coach house dating from 1825. Located in historic Clapham Old Town in South London, it stands nestled against the grounds of St. Paul's Church and opposite a small chapel. The rest of the small corner is a row of stately Georgian houses. The area is steeped in history, the coach house sitting on the site of the original Manor House of Clapham. There has been a church next door since the 12th century, and it is said that some of Oliver Cromwell's army are buried in the grounds. Clapham began life as a Saxon village and appears in the Domesday Book as Clopeham. Lavender was grown in the fields around the village. The Clapham Sect were instrumental in the abolition of slavery, and many distinguished people lived in Clapham, including Samuel

Pepys. American Connection: scientist Benjamin Franklin stayed in the village for a while in the 18th Century, conducting his experiments on Clapham Common's ponds.

What is today a B&B began life as a livery stable. By 1895, part of it was demolished to make way for Iveley Road and building Victorian houses. In 1903, the original house and attached stables were sold to the Church next door, with the intention of knocking them down and building a vicarage. The house, however, had a sitting tenant, who lived there until 1927 before dying "in indigent circumstances," so only the stables, wash house, cart sheds, dung pit and harness room were demolished, and the house remained. With its Grade II listing, it's today secure from demolition.

NOW: Glebe House is a boutique bed and breakfast run by Alix Bateman, an interiors writer, gilder, and former antiques dealer. The beautiful double rooms are awash with period style, furnished with Georgian antique furniture. Original 19th Century paneling and shutters and fireplaces adorn many rooms. Guests take breakfast in the striking kitchen diner, in front of an original cast iron range, with gilded framed Edwardian prints and antique portraits lining the walls. Glebe House also hires out for film and photo shoots (a BBC period drama was filmed here).

A Glebe House guest room

HISTORICAL OFFERINGS:

Glebe House runs a program of events, including Georgian dinners, where guests dress the part and enjoy parlor games of the period, and workshops in traditional crafts, such as embroidery led by expert tutors, or gilding on glass. Inquire when booking if any are happening while you visit. An antiques and history buff, Alix can direct guests to, or occasionally guide guests on, wonderful days out, from tours of the locations of *Downton Abbey* episodes, to sprawling antiques markets, afternoon tea on a London Bus, East End flower markets, or vintage tea shops. Features: Family/kid friendly (travel crib or toddler mattress, highchair, stair gates, and microwave use). Parking permits for next-door are a bargain £5 per day.

TAKE HEED! No lift and 1 flight of stars. Not wheelchair accessible due to its Grade II listing. Also no a/c. Payment is by Paypal or Bank transfer. No credit cards, hairdryer, or TV. The owner has a friendly dog. Smoking is not allowed inside, but may be done in the garden. **Details:** 2 rooms. Check-in: 4pm onwards/Checkout: 10:30am. **Room:** Private bathroom, FREE WiFi, coffee/tea making facilities. **Food:** FREE continental breakfast and biscuits (cookies). Other: Maps and guidebooks available to borrow, luggage storage, outdoor patio.

---

*H*OW OLDE: ♟♟♟♟♟
Tube: Clapham Common (ten min walk) | **Overland Station:** Wandsworth Road (3 min walk) | Bookings direct or through AirBnB | www.Airbnb.co.uk/rooms/1175819 | www.TheGlebeHouseLondon.com | +44 20 7720 3844 | 6 Rectory Grove, Clapham

---

THE ROYAL PARK

1842 building ～ ££

Walking up to this small hotel on Westbourne Terrace, just north of Hyde Park, it looks like a quintessential London neighborhood. Street after street of white stucco 1850s town houses with pillared porticoes, and the only thing that makes it stand out as a hotel is the British flag hanging from the roof.

THEN: First mention of the area was as Bayard's Watering Place in the 1380s, presumably a place for travellers to water their horses. By 1646, there was a small hamlet called Bayswater, adjoining Westbourne common fields (shared farming land). In 1733, Lord Craven bought some of the land in this area, and by 1776 some speculative building was happening on Uxbridge Road. By 1818, there was substantial building, and Paddington Fields was leased for more. Westbourne development went up in the early 1840s, and by 1842 residents were living in these big four-story houses. They built in the now ubiquitous "Terrace" architecture, which means houses built in a continuous row in a uniform style. Considered the grandest and most beautiful of the new streets, Westbourne's wealthy inhabitants included East India merchants, civil engineers, statesmen (such as the Lord Chancellor), an Admiral, and a Field Marshal.[40]

NOW: The Royal Park Hotel comprises three Grade II houses connected together. It straddles the price categories, but if you're willing to advance purchase it will be a relative bargain four-star hotel in a great neighborhood with some extra niceties—a welcome drink upon

Sleeping like a princess doesn't cost an arm and a leg at The Royal Park

arrival—fancy a glass of sherry or ~ *for the guys* a whiskey on the rocks. (If for some reason the staff forgets, be sure to ask for it.) Also, evening turndown service with homemade cookies and mineral water (arranged between 5–8pm nightly).

The bedrooms feature antiques selected by Jonty Hearnden of the BBC's "Antiques Roadshow." The décor in both the public and private rooms is a pleasing blend of classic contemporary and period, with pale yellows, sky blues, and melon greens—more hint of Victorian, than full-blown immersion. There's a drawing room, library, bar, and garden. The guest rooms feature handmade beds, limestone bathrooms, antique furniture, and original period oil paintings.

HISTORICAL OFFERINGS: Four-poster beds! The Four Poster Suite has a canopy in hand-pleated silk, and a separate sitting room. Lower-priced rooms have handmade dark-wood half-testers. There's also Afternoon Tea, a gourmet version in bespoke bone china. Features: Private garden terrace in the summers. For a fee, continental breakfast or full English is served in a small dining room or in your room.

Stats/Food/Amenities: 48 rooms. Check-in: 2pm/Checkout: 12pm. **ROOM:** Free WiFi, US electrical shaver outlets, Nespresso coffee & tea, evening turndown, minibar, bathrobes and slippers, 100% Irish cotton linens, Penhaligon toiletries, newspaper, tiny safe, DVD player upon request. Food: Afternoon Tea (£42, daily 2:30–6pm), The Hyde (intimate cocktail bar with small plates menu, cozy sofas, fireplace). **HOTEL:** Concierge, fully stocked honesty bar, business services, 24-hr room service, and most unusual, onsite parking (fee), just outside the fee-inducing congestion zone. **STARS:** 4 ½

TAKE HEED! Lower priced rooms are tiny and some oddly shaped. Some rooms are in the basement, and there are some stairs. Limited hours for bell staff.

TIP: Some of the suites come with their own balcony terraces overlooking the street—the perfect place to enjoy a morning coffee, so be sure to request one, in advance, if the weather's going to be warm. The Romance Package with free breakfast, champagne, flowers, and cocktails is a very good deal, but, as always, do the math (available only on weekends). The Heathrow Express train from Paddington Station, just 3 blocks away.

How OLDE: 🎴🎴🎴🎴
~ *you'll get your Victorian fix, with a dose of the modern*
Tube: Paddington (also a train station) | www.TheRoyalPark.com | info.RPHL@roseatehotels.com | +44 20 7479 6600 | 3 Westbourne Terrace, Lancaster Gate, Hyde Park

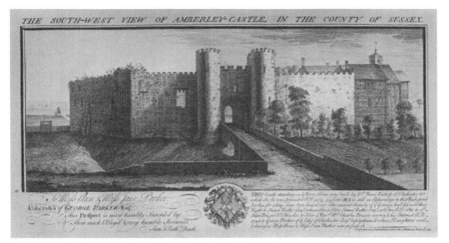

Amberley Castle
in 1737,
as ruins in the 1890s,
and restored today

Stay Like a Princess or English Lady in the Country

AMBERLEY CASTLE

~ *Play fairytale Princess overnight in a medieval castle*

Est. 1989 in 1103 fortress ~ *££* to *££££££*

A castle! I'm going to stay in a—'scuse my English—bloody castle!

About to spend the night in 900-year-old Amberley, I was all but bouncing in my seat. However, it was dark, and we missed the turnoff, and instead took the road to the village, a mere speck of a place, where we arrived at an ancient church and its gravel parking lot. We stared up at more than three stories of thick stone wall to the castle, but no entrance. A cold wind blew and the bare branches of trees waved their moonlit shadows upon the stones like scraggly arms clawing at the base of the fortress. Tingles shivered up my arms and crawled up my neck. Perhaps we'd arrived at a haunted castle.

But we'd still no way to get inside.

After rereading the directions and backtracking a couple of miles, we finally landed at the front of the citadel and drove over the dry moat, between the gatehouse towers, under the portcullis, to arrive in the bailey (a quaint word for a castle's courtyard). While it wasn't nearly as big as I'd imagined from the photos, it was indeed haunted (more on that later).

Anyway, at the moment I had greater concerns. Our lack of maps, lack of data coverage for our cellular GPS, and other delays, had made us very late for our dinner reservation. We hurried toward the arched stone doorway, pushed open the thick wood door—like something out of Hansel and Gretel—and approached the registration desk. Apologizing profusely, we offered to check in later if we could just get a bite to eat before the restaurant closed. Just 60 miles from London, Amberley felt like it was in the middle of nowhere and for us there would be no other food this evening.

Here, then, was my first real impression of the hotel—relaxed friendly staff and top-notch service, where the guest's needs always come first. With only 19 guest rooms, I guess it's possible to offer such truly individual care. That night, we were assured it was absolutely no problem and were escorted to our room and told to come to the Great Room whenever we were ready. We still moved quickly and found that there were a few diners still finishing up. But soon we had the place to ourselves—our chance to play lord and lady of the manor—and no one rushed us, and we enjoyed a lovely, if spendy, dinner. My first feast in a real live castle!

Etiquette Note: Though the keep is medieval, it is no longer *de rigueur* to throw your bones on the floor or pound on the table for more food. The service and amenities are first-class modern here all the way. So we felt we should live up to that standard too.

THEN: How did this place, hidden away in the South Downs, come into existence? In truth, it's not really a castle, but a fortified manor. It is, however, truly ancient. It's listed in the Doomsday Book (Ch. 3) where it was recorded that Amberley had 37 villagers and 38 smallholders in 1086.[41] Its history, of course, goes even farther back—prehistoric man lived here. Their burial places, low mounds called tumuli, are scattered along what is now the South Downs Way. Late Bronze Age/early Iron Age people lived here around 1100 BC; excavations have revealed two large circular huts and the remains of horses. Because of Roman burial sites and pottery shards, it is believed there was also a Roman settlement in the area, possibly just a large farmstead. A Roman glass phial (vial) found at Amberley is reported to be in the British Museum.[42]

And what of the place's ancient name? There is no definitive answer, but Amberley Parish Council of West Sussex believes it might derive from the old English word for amber—not the yellow stone but a measure of volume, roughly equivalent to four bushels of liquid measurement or 32 gallons.[43] The suffix "ley" could mean field, so Amberley might possibly refer to how much agricultural yield would come from one field.[44]

This long-ago fertile field was gifted to Bishop Wilfrid in 683AD by Caedwalla, King of Wessex, who for about three years ruled a whole chunk of southern England. Although unbaptized until just before his death, Caedwalla sought counsel from Wilfrid and later sent him to the Isle of Wight to forcibly convert the pagans to Christianity. While promised half of the Isle as spoils, Wilfrid had to settle instead for the parcel that is now Amberley. This land was to stay in the hands of the church for more than 800 years, passing at some point to the Bishops of Chichester. The seven holders of this title building the estate over the centuries into the stronghold it is today.

Circa 1103, Bishop Luffa constructed a timber-framed hunting lodge and the parish church that still stands outside the castle walls. Seffrid I tore the lodge down in 1140 to build a more elaborate stone hall, which still stands today with its Norman entrance leading to the hotel's reception area. Circa 1200, Seffrid II added the East Wing, and during his reign, John of Langton (1305–1337) added a larger Great Hall for the

*Still defending
Amberley's castle walls*

"Bishop of Chichester's Summer Palace," as it was then known.

The next Bishop knocked that down and built an even larger hall (c.1370). Reede was also the one who received permission from King Richard II to fortify the manor house. While his petition stated a need to ward off pirates, many believe it was to show off his great ecclesiastical power. Building was completed by 1382, and the features we still see today were added: crenellated battlements, two gatehouses, and an oubliette—*for those pirates, ya know.*

What's an *oubliette?*

Leave it to the French to have such a lovely-sounding word for something so evil. From *oublier*—to forget—we get *oubliette* or the "forgotten room." Worse than a dungeon, it's a dark, dank shaft in the ground where prisoners were dropped and usually left to die. Sometimes food was tossed down, often not. There was no ladder and the only light came from the trap door at the top. In the worst of them, the shaft was too skinny to allow sitting or spikes awaited their falling bodies at the bottom (see Ireland's Leap Castle). It can be seen in action in *Outlander* (episode 1.11)—it's where Claire and Geillis were tossed before the witch trial, but theirs is much nicer than Amberley's.

And it's still there today, but bring a flashlight because not much can be seen peering through the iron grill down the deep black hole. One wonders if any pirates were actually tossed within?

Which brings us to the question of ghosts. Amberley has one, however, it's not a grizzled pirate, but a pretty village maiden who is thought to haunt the ramparts. Young Emily, who worked at the manor, fell in love with the reining Bishop at the time and became pregnant by him. As a Catholic priest, he denied, of course, any alliance, and the heartbroken girl threw herself from the battlements. This happened sometime between 1382, after the battlements were added, to the 1530s, when the Bishops lost control of Amberley. Today, fortunate ghost hunters—*I was not so blessed*—can see Emily walking the grounds at dusk or sense her presence in the Herstmonceux Room, which accesses the battlements. But does Amberley really have one? The housekeeping staff would think so and consider Emily troublesome, finding cushions on the floor in the haunted room *after* it's been cleaned.

We'll never know if it was Sherborne who seduced Emily—he was Chichester Bishop from 1508 to 1536—but it is known that King Henry VIII visited Amberley to seek his advice in 1526. Henry, as we might recollect, did not like the response he got to his most pressing concern—procreation—and shortly after separated from the Catholic Church, taking all the church's wealth for himself. Amberley then became property

The house that John built

of the crown. After that, the fortress changed ownership many times, until its eventual downfall in 1643.

Here we have the castle's only notable political footnote. During the English Civil War, the pro-monarchist owner Sir John Goring refused to pay taxes to parliament and turned Amberley into a royalist stronghold, encouraging the villagers and other nobles to place their valuables out of reach of the Parliament within Amberley's stone walls. Lacking a drawbridge, I would guess this was the only time the portcullis was used in defense. A portcullis is a thick, iron, grilled gate, virtually impervious to attack, which was lowered to block the single entrance into the fortress. This forced Oliver Cromwell's hand, and General Waller was sent to destroy Amberley's defenses, pulling down some 20–30 feet from the curtain walls and demolishing the Great Hall. In the long years that followed locals took stones from the ruins and the castle fell into disrepair.

In the late 17ᵗʰ Century, parliament sold the property to Mr. John Butler, a prosperous cloth merchant, who became the first commoner to own it. He built a manor house out of the ruins of the Great Hall. But following the restoration of the monarchy in 1660, King Charles II visited Amberley and decided to give it back to the Bishopric. It seems that Mr. Butler was not reimbursed for this seizure but managed to negotiate a long lease, enabling a further two generations of Butlers to grow up there. During this time, a floor was built halfway up the Small Hall, dividing it into the Great Room below and the Queen's Room above. Murals of Charles II and his wife Catherine of Braganza, in tribute to his returning the castle to the church, can still be seen high up on the wall of the Queen's Room.

In 1872, the church sold Amberley to private ownership, where again it changed hands many times: first to the 15ᵗʰ Lord Zouche (a Curzon, of Curzon street fame) who used it as a hunting lodge. Then in 1893, to the nearby 15ᵗʰ Duke of Norfolk, who used it to entertain guests over a 15-year period while his main abode, Arundel Castle, was being modernized. (Arundel can be visited too, see Ch. 9). The Duke also invested in Amberley, including repairing parts of it destroyed 200 years prior. In 1926, the Emmett family bought it—the husband was a baron, and the widowed baroness remained there until 1982, when she sold it off in pieces. So, after nearly a thousand years as one estate, the farmland was separated from the castle grounds.

Over the last 100 years, each successive owner has made improvements and modernizations. Norfolk repaired the stonework over the portcullis. Later, Hollis Baker reinstalled the 2.5-ton portcullis gate, but the next owners took it even farther, buying the castle in 1988 with the

goal of turning it into a business. The Cummings launched Amberley
Castle hotel in 1989.

As always, we must ask, is there a princess in the house? These days,
maybe, sometimes, but they'll keep that firmly under wraps. In the past,
most definitely. *Both* Queens Elizabeth have stayed within these walls.
QE I leased the place from 1588 to 1603. QE II stayed here in 1945, the
princess visiting her friends the Emmett's daughters.

American connection: From 1982–1988, Amberley was owned by
Hollis Baker, an American WWII veteran who took over his father's
furniture business, Baker Furniture based in Grand Rapids, Michigan.
As his obituary notes, "In mid-life he became an enthusiastic researcher,
historian, collector and renovator of medieval castles in England, France,
and Italy."[45] All together he owned a total of seven châteaux before he
was done.

Fiction connections: Romance author Lauren Royal used Amberley
as the inspiration for her Greystone Castle in the novel *Amethyst* set in
1666. **TIP:** It's sometimes free on the author's website.

NOW: Amberley is both a working hotel and a living museum
where contemporary décor blends with medieval architecture. The
roughly 60–foot-high curtain walls are mostly intact but some parts of
the fortress—most of the parapets and one interior structure—have been
left in a state of charming ruin. It will seem smaller than you'd expect of
a castle, but that is because this was essentially a hunting lodge for the
nobility, both ecclesiastical and royal.

Amberley Castle hotel receives 4½ stars from online reviewers, and
in 2004, it became a member of Relais & Châteaux, an exclusive collection of fine restaurants and lodging. R&C's philosophy is the 5C's—
courtesy, charm, character, calm, and cuisine. I can say firsthand that
Amberley meets these requirements and then some.

While most of the tragic or romantic stories of past Amberley inhabitants have been lost to time, this is your chance to make new ones as
you walk in the footsteps of such romantic real-life characters as Henry
VIII and Queen Elizabeth I. Or stay out late at night and you might
meet Emily.

HISTORICAL OFFERINGS: You're staying in a 900–year-old
castle! Dining in a 12th-Century Queen's Room restaurant with bar-
rel-vaulted ceiling and c.1680 murals. There are arched doorways,
three-foot-thick stone walls, and antiques everywhere: historical paintings, armaments, suits of armor standing at attention. Walk the 14-acre
grounds and English garden. Peer down the oubliette and up at the

---

† *Technically there are three Queens Elizabeth, but to my knowledge the Queen Mother
never stayed there.*

Amberley is a charming mix of ruins and restored buildings. Guests are housed in the buildings with roofs.

portcullis. Visit the village with its ancient buildings, thatched cottages, old pubs, and a quaint working pottery shop. Visit or attend services at St. Michael & All Angels Church[46] built by then Amberley owner Bishop Luffa, c.1100. Enjoy, that quintessential of English customs, Afternoon Tea, served in a drawing room or on the terrace.

And there are white peacocks.

For the day-tripper, a "History Tour with Lunch" is offered on six Tuesdays throughout the warmer months. Beginning at 9:30 with coffee and homemade biscuits in the lounge you can meet your guide and fellow travellers. From 10–12:00 local historian Keith McKenna leads the history tour, and the event concludes with a 3-course lunch and glass of wine (£55pp; see Events Diary for dates; very popular, pre-booking essential).

To Sleep Like A Princess requires a major investment here. Four-poster beds are the Deluxe and Premiere Deluxe categories and include these rooms: Chichester, Lewes, Luffa, Wilfrid, and Sherborne (but the last has a modern metal frame bedstead). Medieval décor and antique furnishings are limited to the Chichester and Wilfrid. On the bright side staying in a Classic level is a relative bargain, sometimes as low as £200.

Each room, many named after former bishops, is unique and maybe located in the Tower House Mews, the 17th Century Manor House, or outside the castle walls in the 17th-Century Bishopric (the former dairy). The majority of the rooms have contemporary décor, however there are various period features—arched doorways, exposed wood beams, or 14th Century lancet leaded windows, for example—and views might include the interior keep or the dry moat. Pevensey and Herstmonceux have shared access to a 14th Century Gate Tower with viewing of the portcullis and its machinery. All the bathrooms are modern and some are utterly sumptuous. Read the website carefully and make your room request directly to the hotel so that you aren't disappointed upon arrival.

Features: Complimentary homemade biscuits (cookies) and mineral water in your room. Full English Breakfast included in every rate.

DETAILS: 19 rooms. Check-in: 3pm/Checkout: 11am. **ROOM:** Free WiFi, L'Occitane toiletries, slipper/robe, Vispring bed, hotpot with coffee/tea, free bottled water/biscuits, heated towel rack, iron. Food: Queen's Room restaurant (3-course £67 or 7-course £85), Drawing Room Lounge (serves pantry menu, £10–20), Full Afternoon Tea (£30), room service (limited hours). **HOTEL:** professional-standard 18-hole putting green, tennis court, croquet, luggage storage.

TAKE HEED! Smart casual to dressy for the dining room (no sneakers or jeans). Children 5+ are welcome in hotel, but must be 8+ to dine in the restaurant. Saturdays have a two-night minimum stay. Non-UK travellers must present passport upon arrival. No A/C but a fan is supplied. A few reports mention small meal portions and slow service, although by American standards many European meals seem small. And while no one wants their food to arrive cold, slow service can also mean relaxing and taking one's time while dining. Really, what else is there to do in the middle of nowhere at night?

No elevator! The restaurant and public ladies room are located on the 1st floor (that's one flight up in England; would be our 2nd floor here in the US). However, the hotel makes every possible accommodation for those with disabilities (such as offering the ground floor room at the lowest available rate and providing meals in the downstairs lounge). See "Accessibility" on the website (among the list at the bottom) and call the hotel in advance to arrange necessary accommodations.

TIP: The Classic rooms are a bargain at £200; book them early for summer as they go quickly. Or stay for much less in Arundel and just visit for afternoon tea or dinner.

Note: see Easy Excursions in Ch. 9 for more information on itineraries and arrival by train.

𝓗OW OLDE: ⚜⚜⚜⚜⚜
www.AmberleyCastle.co.uk | info@amberleycastle.co.uk
+44 17 9883 1992 | Nr Arundel, West Sussex, BN18 9LT

ARUNDEL: THE NORFOLK ARMS
Est. & built 1785 ∼ £

THEN: It was purpose built to be a coaching inn by the 10th Duke of Norfolk in 1785. Walking through the large arched entryway, you can almost feel the ghosts of horses and carriages past. It was constructed of red brick, and the stables and coach house were behind the hotel on Mill Lane. By 1799, it was the main coaching inn in Arundel and popular with visitors from Brighton. By the 1850s it offered a railway carrier and omnibus service (horse-drawn bus), and the ballroom opened as a place for public meetings, concerts, and other events. As late as 1980, the hotel still belonged to the Norfolk estate.[47]

NOW: Today, the Norfolk Arms Hotel offers affordable lodging and inexpensive meals in a genuine Georgian coaching inn. While carriages no longer transport guests here, it is only a short distance to the train station and Arundel Castle, making this a super-easy overnight. And if you've more time in the area, you'll enjoy the antique shops, restaurants, and atmosphere in this quaint town. And, of course, there's Arundel Castle, but know that it's only open for half the year (see Ch. 3). You can also make this your low-cost home base to visit Amberley castle for a look-see and meal.

The décor of the hotel is English Country meets shabby chic—fun, eclectic, exuberant. From the grandfather clock in the corner to the mix-matched furniture and the happy mint walls that decorate the restaurant—it works. The pub features period patterned ceilings, wood paneling, and stone fireplaces combined in a funky way with modern purple furniture. The Inn has added a beer-garden courtyard for outdoor dining and drinking in the summer. They go local too, with locally-sourced farm-to-table foods and ales from nearby breweries. Along with reasonable food prices, the wine list even has sparkling wine at £4 a glass and full bottles that don't gouge the customer! The guest room décor is all about simple, clean lines, bare walls, and modern furniture. There are some period features left in the bedrooms, such as original windowpanes and leaded glass.

HISTORICAL OFFERINGS: Four-poster bed! The "Feature Double" comes with an antique carved-wood canopy bed and a sitting area. This summer it ranges a bargain £165-219 (2017).

DETAILS: 33 rooms. Check-in: 3pm/Checkout: 11am. Room: Free WiFi, hotpot with coffee/tea from local teashop & a little jar of cookies, White Company toiletries, iron/board upon request, room service (limited hours). **FOOD:** Castle Room Restaurant (English cuisine with

a modern twist, mains £12–18), The New Bar (with pub food, £8–17).
HOTEL: can provide a variety of extras for a small charge (champagne, flowers, fruit, etc.), onsite parking (£5), or the train station is just a half-mile away. **STARS:** 3½

TAKE HEED! No elevator, so if there are mobility issues, request lower floor. Poor shower water pressure. They still have that original ballroom complete with a minstrel's gallery, and it's popular for weddings, which might mean loud music late at night or busy staff.

TIP: Vintage Afternoon Tea is a bargain—just £21 for two people. It won't be gourmet or super fancy, but it's got all the elements and cute mismatched china too! Book hotel online and get the best rate plus free breakfast. Rooms in the rear are quieter, especially on weekend nights. If you're tall avoid the attic rooms.

How Olde: ♔♔♔♔♔ ~ *a real Coaching Inn, but it'll feel more like trendy times than historical romance*
www.NorfolkArmsArundel.com | reservations.norfolk@sjhotels.co.uk
+44 33 0102 7230 | 22 High St, Arundel BN18 9AB

◇~✐~━━━━━━━━━━━━━━━━━━━●

CLIVEDEN HOUSE & SPA

~ *A chance to play Lady of the Manor at a country estate*

Est. 1984 in 1666 mansion ~ ££££½

Driving up to the hotel entrance is impressive, but not nearly as much as taking a walk out into the garden to look back at it. From this vantage point, I feel transformed into Jane Austen's Elizabeth Bennet gazing at Pemberley, taking in the extraordinary Italianate façade and feeling a sense of longing to be a part of this ancient story. The stone building is stunning with twin balustrade staircases gracefully wending down to the manicured lawn. It sits regally on the green in three graceful layers: a wide arcaded terrace, then the ground floor with a long line of elegant arched windows, and lastly a two-story square edifice that sits atop the manse, like the top layer of a tiered wedding cake. The tall, square, clock tower standing off to the side draws my eye left, the late afternoon sun glinting off its 24-carat gilded face, and I'm reminded that it's time to go back inside—to experience, however briefly, the life of a lady in a country manor house.

THEN: This place has had three lives. And each of them has left notorious tales of romance, lust, and sometimes love. Historical romance authors, get your pens ready…

Cliveden, then (c.1720) and now

First, we have a story of lust with George Villiers, 2nd Duke of Buckingham, 20th Baron de Ros, KG, PC, FRS. *He was titled and entitled.* This might have something to do with the fact that from seven months old, he was raised in the royal household of King Charles I, playing with the royal offspring, including two future kings. George grew to be a very handsome, popular man, and it was said that "a young lady could not resist his charms...all his trouble in wooing was, he came, saw and conquered." Seems true, given that his wife, Mary Fairfax, threw off her betrothal to the Earl of Chesterfield (twice were the banns read) in order to marry gorgeous George.

Anyway, now at age 38, he was a wealthy, married, passionate man in need of digs for his pleasures. He built the first Cliveden to be a fox-hunting lodge for entertaining his friends, but, more importantly, for assignations with his mistress, the married Lady Anna Talbot, Countess of Shrewsbury. They enjoyed each other's company at Cliveden, which was an easy boat ride down from London, but to be clear, George didn't sully her—she'd already had at least two affairs, one duel fought over her, and acquired a reputation as a nymphomaniac. When her husband could take it no longer, he challenged the Duke to a duel by the sword and lost. Wrote Samuel Pepys—who seemed to be everywhere with his busy pen—"…my Lord Shrewsbury is run through the body, from the right breast through the shoulder." Her husband died from his wounds after lingering for two months, but her love for George lived on. He was a debauched lothario, but it seems there might have been some true affection, because offending everyone, especially the king, he continued his affair with Lady Anna, even bringing his mistress to live with him and his wife in London, and there she birthed him a son. But there's no HEA here—they were forced by Parliament to separate after she baptized the illegitimate child at Westminster Abbey, which angered many. They were never reunited, and Anna departed for a convent in France for a while, *presumably to do penance?*

Compounded with his continued court intrigue, the affair hurt George politically, and in the end he died a greatly reduced man. As for his duchess, Pepys had, of course, something to say about the "most virtuous and pious lady," recording earlier how she was "patiently bearing with those faults in him which she could not remedy" and "had complaisance enough to entertain his mistresses, and even to lodge them in her house; all which she suffered because she loved him."[48] Mary outlived George by many years, and one hopes it was a peaceful time for her.

The second owner, George Hamilton, 1st Earl of Orkney by order of Queen Anne, was the opposite of gorgeous George. Hard-working, a court favorite, and famed soldier, he greatly expanded the house, and added the still standing Blenheim Pavilion and Octagon Temple (1727–35). Brief American Connection: he was Governor of Virginia from 1710–1737, although he never visited our fair land.

Frederick, Prince of Wales, leased the property from 1737–1751, and during this period it was second only to Hampton Palace as the center of royal life. Frederick is less known, historically, probably because he died before his dad, George II, so never became king. He did leave a cultural contribution, however. Like his father, he was a big fan of Handel and made Cliveden the sight of many musical events featuring Handel's music. It was the place that Thomas Arne's *Rule Britannia* premiered in 1740. Because Frederick never became king, the succession passed to his son, George III, who had grown up at Cliveden.

Over the next 142 years, Cliveden passed through two lives, burning catastrophically to near total loss and being rebuilt and burning down again. Now owned by the Duke of Sutherland, he selected renowned architect Charles Barry (of Big Ben and Houses of Parliament fame) to rebuild the mansion for a third time, resulting in the Italianate villa that remains today. In 1861, Henry Clutton added the impressive 100-foot-tall Water Tower hidden inside a Watch Tower. And the gardens were transformed to what we see today.

Now we come to a mini-romance. In 1868, Hugh Grosvenor, 1st Duke of Westminster, bought the estate because it had earned a special place in his heart after enjoying his honeymoon at Cliveden. He lived there happily for 25 years, with his first wife Constance and later with his second, Katherine. It must have been a happy time at the manor. It was during this period that Queen Victoria also grew fond of Cliveden, leading us to…

Is there a princess in the house? Many! The earliest records of royal visits were George I in 1724 and Queen Caroline in 1729. And, of course, while Prince Frederick lived here, many royals visited. Later, Queen Victoria was fond of Cliveden, travelling here by boat from Windsor for tea or to stay over. She visited Cliveden eight times, one time bringing an entourage of 90 people. The widowed Queen always brought two portraits of her beloved Prince Albert with her, one placed at the foot of the bed on an easel and the other miniature placed by her pillow.

But the Duke of Westminster was also a great philanthropist and gentleman horse breeder, and in 1893 was forced, reluctantly, to sell Cliveden, and remove his family to their principal residence at Eaton (the family seat, not the college called Eton). He needed more funds for his many horses and for the five hospitals and eight or so other charities he supported. The Queen was famously "not amused" and wrote to him in April 1893: "*The Duke must excuse the Queen if she says she thinks he has built too much at Eaton and that if that had not been so, Cliveden, might have been retained.*"

Transportation at
Cliveden, Then and Now

American Connections: Cliveden's golden age was just around the corner—and two more stories of tragedy, then love. The new owner was the wealthiest man in the US, William Waldorf Astor, who paid $1.25 million (by contrast, the Duke had paid just £30,000 for it less than 50 years earlier). Astor had relocated his family to England in 1891, and bought Cliveden in 1893. Tragically, his beloved wife Mamie died just one year later at the age of 36. He became a recluse, filling the mansion with European art, including buying and installing the entire Louis XV ballroom from the Chateau d'Asnières in 1897. For his extremely generous contributions to English charities, he realized his dream of becoming a member of the peerage, being made a Baron in 1916 and a Viscount in 1917, titles that passed to his sons, thereby transforming his first generation American children into English aristocracy.

Now for the love story: in 1905, his eldest son met and fell in love with another American transplant, Nancy Langhorne. Upon their marriage in 1906, dad gave the entire Cliveden estate and all its contents to the groom as a wedding present and to the bride a magnificent tiara featuring the 55-carat Sancy diamond (now in the Louvre). The new Viscountess Astor restored Cliveden to a place of great entertainment and popularity, and she later became the first woman Member of Parliament in 1919.

Among Cliveden's notable guests entertained in lavish style were King George V and Queen Mary, Princess Marie of Romania, Winston Churchill, George Bernard Shaw, Charlie Chaplin, female aviatrix Amy Johnson, and American President Roosevelt and his wife. The Astors were also charitable, allowing the estate to be used as a hospital in WWI, serving as many as 600 wounded soldiers.

*The Great Hall c.1890s
and today*

And Lord and Lady Astor were treated like royalty wherever they travelled. It was a HEA for a while. Just as I sometimes wonder what would really happen down the road in some of the more convoluted romance novels I've read, this story doesn't end as happily as it starts. So, we'll just end this particular love story here.

Lastly, ➤ **for the guys**, we need to jump ahead to 1961 for Cliveden's most scandalous tale, one of lust, intrigue, tragedy, and perhaps murder. Known as the Profumo Affair, it's a convoluted story, but here goes.

One hot weekend in July, two country house parties were taking place at Cliveden. In the mansion, the Astors welcomed many guests, the most prominent of whom were Lord Mountbatten of Burma, the President of Pakistan, and John Profumo, British Minister of War—and a married man. A second party, led by Astor family friend, Stephen Ward was going on at the Summer Cottage (a pretty second house on the property). Among his guests were the beautiful Christine Keeler, a call-girl of just 19 years of age, and Captain Yevgeny Ivanov, a Soviet Embassy attaché…and a spy…and also married. Quite a mix to bring together on one estate, and it was possibly all the fault of the sweltering weather, because John brought his guests to the main house swimming pool (the one guests still use today), and there, John Profumo met young Christine for the first time. Supposedly she was swimming naked in the Cliveden pool while Ward and Profumo watched. John and Christine began an *affair de coeur* that lasted for months before becoming England's biggest sex scandal of the century.

So here's how it ended. John was enjoying his extra-marital liaison, but Christine was two-timing him with Yevgeny...and then sold her story to the press. Now it wasn't just a moral issue, and Parliament stepped in over concerns of national security. Under siege by the press, John made a second disastrous mistake—giving false testimony to the House of Commons.

Again, there is no HEA here. John's career was in ruins; he was forced to resign his post. Yevgeny's wife left him, but reports are that in the late 1980s he was awarded the Order of Lenin...for his work in England in 1963.[49] The Tory government lost power, partly because of the mess, in the 1964 elections. Stephen Ward was made a scapegoat; tried for trumped-up charges of immoral earnings (supposedly pimping). On the night of his conviction, he killed himself by taking an overdose. (Recent claims purport that an MI6 freelance operative murdered him.) Perhaps most tragic of all is Christine. She may have been at the center of it all, but there's plenty of evidence to suggest she was a young, beautiful pawn, not entirely innocent but still used by powerful men for their own needs. She spent 9 months in prison for perjury, fell into obscure poverty, and as late as 2013 referred to herself as "a dirty joke."

American Connection: The story doesn't quite end there. In a 2015 book, *Near and Distant Neighbours: A New History of Soviet Intelligence*, Cambridge Professor Jonathan Haslam makes a case that the damage to national and international security was much bigger than thought, reporting that as part of the debacle, Yevgeny was able to use his tiny Minox spy camera to photograph highly classified US documents, including specifications on a top-secret X–15 spy plane and our tactical nuclear weapons, among other things, all of it highly valuable at the time to the communists. Even more interesting, the 1990s English translation of Yevgeny's memoir, *The Naked Spy*, deleted the passages about his spying on Profumo (the publishers were afraid John's widow would sue), and it took Haslam studying the Russian version more than 20 years later to find out this new information.[50]

But back to Cliveden—because of the mounting expense of maintaining this grand estate, the 3rd Viscount Astor had already given Cliveden House to the National Trust in 1942, under an arrangement that allowed the Astors to continue living there until he died in 1966.

NOW: After 300 years as a country retreat, Cliveden House opened as a country retreat for the general public. At the same time, the National Trust operates the parklands, also open to the public. Thirty years later and following a major refurbishment, the hotel is continuing to garner high praise. Online reviewers list such attributes as absolutely first-class and anticipatory service. The staff remembers your name as if you are really a guest of the family. It's a honeymoon-worthy, five-star, Relais & Chateaux branded hotel that made the 2016 top five lists in both *Condé Naste* Readers' Choice and *Travel & Leisure UK/Ireland*. And, for the romance fan, it's the chance to try out the country-house-party lifestyle so often described in our romance novels.

However—playing Lady of the Manor doesn't come cheap, and as always the four-poster beds are found in the higher-priced rooms. The least expensive Club and Classic Rooms tend toward modern decor, but some retain period ceilings, elegant window treatments, or other special features. Consider the Kipling (east wing, patterned ceiling, pretty drapes) or Langhorne (Clutton Wing, princess canopy, views of the rolling hills). Some Deluxe Doubles feature romantic four-poster canopied beds and views of the grand drive: Asquith (main mansion, beautiful furnishings), Chinese (east wing, oriental décor and golden colors), and Gibson (main mansion, decorated for a Gibson Girl, who was, by the way, Nancy Astor's sister). If you can spring for a Junior or Deluxe Suite—your king will have to take out a second mortgage—request these gorgeous honeymoon-worthy suites: Queen Charlotte (princess canopy, feminine décor), and Sutherland (princess canopy over Louis XV style gold bed, grand marble chimney, ornate ceiling), Canning (east wing, four-poster bed, stunning carved fireplace, and oak beam ceiling), and Shrewsbury (west wing, marble fireplace, four-poster, sitting room). All rooms have handmade beds and antique furniture. You can see them all on their website.

There are two restaurants overseen by the Michelin-starred gourmet chef André Garrett. The elegant Terrace Restaurant with velvet drapes and chandeliers overlooks the lawn and Thames in the distance. The Astor Grill is housed in the old stable (some alcoves are old stalls and the wood floor is original) and offer simpler fare in a casual setting.

HISTORICAL OFFERINGS: the chance to play lady of the manor is what it's all about. The house is like a museum from the oil paintings to the ornate marble fireplaces, 16th Century Tapestries, Suits of Armour, and Burgundian fireplace. Look for John Singer Sargent's portrait of Nancy Astor in the Great Hall. Also, historic boat launches, Afternoon Tea, and Cliveden's Butler Tour. Be sure to take a peek at the Louis IV dining room, reserved for private functions but stunning.

DETAILS: 34 rooms/9 suites. Check-in: 3pm/Checkout: 11am. Room: Free WiFi, desk tablet with hotel information, welcome amenities, turndown service, free Hildon bottled water, free newspaper, luxury Asprey toiletries, bathrobes and slippers, heated towel rack, safe, refrigerator upon request. Food: André Garrett Restaurant (3-course Market Menu dinner £55, coffee extra), Astor Grill (American/British, mains £16–32, with fair priced beers/wines by the glass), Afternoon Tea (2:30–4:30pm, 1.5 hour seatings, £37, book min 3 weeks in advance for weekends/holidays), room service ordered by tablet. **HOTEL:** private guests only lounge for cocktails, honor "butler's pantry" with snacks/drinks, complimentary tea, babysitting by reservation, fitness center, pool, spa, 9 hole golf course, tennis, squash, croquet. Note: old building but they do have elevators. **STARS:** 4½

TAKE HEED! A gorgeous and unique venue for weddings/special events, but that means rooms or the entire place can be reserved and closed to hotel guests; inquire to avoid disappointment. Also, there are some reports of slow dining service.

TIP: Winter brings lodging deals; check website for such promotions as "last minute booking" (£300 per night for Club rm) or 3 nights for the price of 2. The Heathrow Stopover Package (listed under rates when booking but not on the main website) is a very good deal for one night, less so for multiples (do the math). Dining at Andre Garrett's is more expensive on weekends, and his Market Menu lunch served Mon-Sat is a bargain (£33 and nearly the same food as served for £55 at dinner). Be sure to check website "Offers" for dining specials (for example, sometimes a complimentary springtime shared river cruise is offered). Lastly, the National Trust has dining/activities for less (See Cliveden Ch. 9). Dress: smart casual (no shorts or sneakers in the Terrace Restaurant).

*H*OW OLDE: ⚜⚜⚜⚜⚜
www.ClivedenHouse.co.uk | reservations@clivedenhouse.co.uk
US 800 344 5087 | Taplow, Berkshire SL6 0JF

◇-◛◞————————————————————◦

THE GRAND BRIGHTON

~ *Visit Prinny's Regency Playground at Brighton-by-the-Sea*

Est. and built 1864 ~ ££

From the outside, this beachfront hotel only hints at its Victorian age—ornate wrought iron Juliet balconies, a cupola tower anchoring one end, and some dormer windows at the top that probably offered accommodation for the wealthy guests' servants. However, once you're greeted by the top-hatted doorman and step inside you're transported back to a Victorian delight. All the public spaces are wonders of period décor, from the decorative and structural ironwork to the Corinthian marble pillars to the ornate plasterwork ceilings, and the splendid sweeping spiral staircase. A time-traveling Regency heroine written to arrive inside The Grand Brighton wouldn't, at first, notice that anything is wrong. She might even make it through Afternoon Tea on the Victoria Terrace, a fanciful glassed-in conservatory, before confusion sets in when the waitress wants to swipe a credit card through a little hand-held box. From there, our Regency beauty will need a modern hero to guide her through all the 21st Century conveniences that make the place a first-class hotel.

THEN: Brighton has a pre-historic past, somewhat similar to Arundel Castle (Ch. 3). The biggest difference is that the economy here has always been based on the sea—first fishing and now tourism. By 1086, the Domesday Book documents a settlement called "Bristelmestune," and records that 4,000 herring was the rent to be paid to the king. This Old Town was a warren of tight alleyways and ancient buildings (now nicknamed "The Lanes"). It's full of quaint dining and shopping today. When the town spread outward, the streets became a more orderly grid that faces the ocean. As for the name, there are reportedly 40 variations on it. By at least 1660 it had been shortened to Brighton, although the official name remained Brighthelmstone until 1810.

Through its early history Brighton was attacked by Anglo-Saxons and French invaders. To secure the town, defensive gun batteries were placed along the coast, and in 1793 the West Battery was built on King's Road just west of West Street. The battery held eight muzzle-loaded cannons that could fire 36-pound balls. Behind it was a crescent of houses referred to as Artillery Place, and the Royal Navy Lieutenant in charge of it lived in one. Although the battery was never used in defense, it was fired to salute royalty, often causing nearby windows to shatter. In 1858, it was removed in order to widen and straighten the King's Road. Look for a flagpole on the beach that marks the exact spot. Today only a few "crescents" of Georgian-era homes remain, and the ones here were demolished when The Grand Brighton was built—the hotel's curving driveway is on the old King's road.[51]

By the Georgian period, sea bathing to cure illness was becoming fashionable, and this early tourism business was greatly increased thanks to the patronage of Prinny and the building of the Royal Pavilion (Ch. 3). Then came the steam train in 1841, leading to

―――――❧◇

The Grand Brighton's curved driveway is the former Artillery Place crescent.

an explosion of tourism. The new Grand Brighton was built to serve upper-class travelers, and offered the finest in services and "modern" conveniences. For many, it would be their first time experiencing the marvels of an elevator for its seven floors. Called a "Vertical Omnibus," the lift was hydraulically powered with water from cisterns on the roof. It was the third lift in the UK, and the only one outside London.

The hotel has remained open ever since with one exception. In 1984, a bomb was hidden in a bathroom in an attempt to assassinate Prime Minister Margaret Thatcher while she was there for a political conference. While she survived, five people close to her died in the explosion that left a gaping hole in the façade where a portion of the building's midsection collapsed into the basement. Firemen later reported that many more would have died but for the fact that the well-built Victorian structure remained standing. In defiance of the terrorists, Thatcher opened the conference the next day, winning widespread approval for her stand. The hotel was then closed for extensive repairs, and Thatcher returned two years later to speak at a reception celebrating the re-opening. The IRA terrorist was found in Glasgow a year later and arrested; he served only 14 years in prison before his release.

NOW: The 150-year-old Grand Brighton continues to sparkle, and even more so with the ongoing multi-million-pound refurbishment which has polished up the place but, luckily, kept the period features that make this hotel so special. It's not full Victorian immersion here, but the carefully-chosen modern furniture blends well to create a pleasing whole. And you get top-hatted doormen! The guest rooms are all contemporary, with only a nod to the hotel's past in the shape of the chair

The Grand Brighton today

or mirror. One welcome addition in the remodel was air conditioning, and it should be noted that the lifts are no longer powered by water (although maybe that's not a plus as one reviewer has noted needing to walk down the stairs during a rare storm-related power outage).

HISTORICAL OFFERINGS: Afternoon Tea by the Sea. They offer the Grand (£30) or Terrace (£17), the higher being full Afternoon Tea menu versus a Cream Tea (see Ch. 5 for the difference). They offer a glass of champagne too for £13, but the Prosecco's a bargain at £7. Seatings are 12:30pm, 2:30pm, and 4:30pm. Ask for Terrace seating when making reservation.

Features: Beach! Just across the street, so bring your swimsuit if it's summertime. Free full buffet breakfast daily 7–10am. Live jazz-trio music on Friday and Saturday evenings in the Victoria Lounge from 8–10pm; no cover but arrive early to get a seat. 11 accessible rooms. 'Green and Grand' conservation program earned them Gold Status with the Green Tourism Business certification program, plus they support local charities.

DETAILS: 201 rooms. Check-in 3pm/Checkout: 11am. Room: Free high-speed WiFi, US outlet adaptors, free still/sparkling bottled water, hotpot with coffee/tea, bathrobes and slippers, luxury toiletries, Egyptian cotton linens, black-out curtains, iron/board, 24-hour room service, safe. Food: GB1 Seafood Restaurant (2AA Rosette award, British/seafood cuisine), Victoria Lounge, Bar, and Terrace (ocean facing). **HOTEL:** Concierge, bellhop, free newspaper in lobby, luggage storage, full-service spa with lovely relaxation room (sauna, but no pool or jacuzzi), gym, laundry facilities, parking/valet too (both pricey), 24-hr business center. **STARS:** 4

Reports of helpful, friendly, above-and-beyond service. **TAKE HEED!** The façade is undergoing major refurb, scheduled to last until fall 2017. Expect scaffolding view and drilling noise for ocean front rooms until it's completed. This is an old hotel; while the rooms won't be as small as in London, they are not uniformly sized, so be sure to inform hotel if you have special needs (for instance not all rooms can accommodate rollaway or crib). **TIP:** Sun-Thur, 5–7pm, Happy Hour with selected drinks at £5.

How OLDE: ✿✿✿✿✿
～ *Victorian public spaces, contemporary bedrooms*
www.GrandBrighton.co.uk | reception@grandbrighton.co.uk
+44 12 7322 4300 | 97–99 King's Rd, Brighton, E. Sussex, BN12FW

BRIGHTON MARINA HOUSE HOTEL

Building 1814 ～ £

This B&B is super cute, both outside and in. In summer, hanging baskets overflowing with flowers greet you, and during the holiday season you get festive decorations. Inside it's country French—because the English owners hail most recently from France where they lived for many years.

THEN: Kemptown, the neighborhood where this B&B is located, is to the east of the old town center, and feels like its own little village. The name came from a residential development of 105 expensive houses built by former MP, Thomas Read Kemp. While the hotel's building predates this development by ten years, today the entire area is considered part of Kemptown. Kemp's project had the most modern technological developments at the time—no more tossing the foul contents of chamber pots out the window. Instead, each house's wastewater and rainwater was carried underground to a central sewer under the street that carried the effluence out to the ocean. To make the system work, there was the advanced technology of pressurized water piped into each home's kitchen sink and basement WC, however it was only for 2 hours a day initially (c.1834). Family cisterns or individual wells helped supplement, and by 1853, water was pumped 24/7. Heating that water was done in a small tank inside a modern, coal-fueled, cast-iron kitchen range. To get the water to bedrooms it was carried up back stairs.[52] It may have been state-of-the-art at the time, but for servants it still sounds like back-breaking work.

Charming Kemptown has thrived and is popular with actors and artists, creating a flamboyant, fun atmosphere that continues today, with an array of bustling High Street shops, cafes, and pubs. In short, Kemptown has prospered, which can't be said for Thomas Kemp. The project wasn't initially successful, and overwhelmed with debt—in the age of debtor's prisons—Thomas fled to Paris in 1837 and by 1844 had died there.[53]

NOW: The inn's hosts, Susie and Telly, proudly opened their little gem in 2011. They'll give you a warm, friendly welcome, because they seem to truly enjoy running their boutique hotel. The décor they've created is a shabby-chic delight. The breakfast salon is charming with large vintage crystal chandelier, fireplace, and period artwork. Even better is the luscious chef's kitchen just behind the buffet cabinet, where you can see chef Telly in action. Free cooked-to-order English/French breakfast is included, with locally-sourced ingredients. They offer vegan, gluten-free, and dairy-free options. Located in Kempton, Marina House is an 11 minute walk to The Lanes or Royal Pavilion.

HISTORICAL OFFERINGS: Four-poster beds! Most rooms have them, some in white country French, some in dark wood. Features: Four minute walk to the beach. Garden in summer.

DETAILS: 9 rooms. Check-in 2pm until 8pm/Checkout: 11am. **ROOM:** Free welcome treats (chocolates/candies), hotpot with coffee/tea, free bottled water upon request, mini-refrigerator (except small rooms), free toiletries, hairdryer. **FOOD:** Breakfast room with free buffet continental and cooked to order from 8:30–10am. **HOTEL:** Free high-speed WiFi in public rooms, ironing facilities, luggage storage, photocopy/fax machine. **STARS:** 5. Positive reports include friendly service and above and beyond help, such as the owners quickly mailing personal items left behind by accident.

TAKE HEED! No elevator in this five-floor boutique hotel and no ground floor rooms, so not accessible, but they will carry your luggage up for you. Can request one flight up rooms. The least expensive rooms are very simple and small with bathroom in the hall (less than £100, so if possible spend a little more for a bargain four-poster bed and en-suite bath). Rooms are European sized. Minimum 2 nights on weekends.

TIP: Room #4 in white French provincial has a small balcony and partial ocean view (1st floor/US 2nd floor). #9 is the most romantic in deep red with a dark-wood canopy bed (3rd floor/US 4th). #10 with a king four-poster and #7 have side sea view. Sometimes 2 or 3 night bookings come with free afternoon tea (inquire to be sure).

*H*OW OLDE: ♟♟♟♟♟ ~ *a bargain vintage experience*
www.Brighton-mh-hotel.co.uk | rooms@brighton-mh-hotel.co.uk
+44 12 7360 5349 | 8 Charlotte St, Brighton, East Sussex BN21AG

Piccadilly Circus, c.1890

CHAPTER 7

Walk, Float, or Dance in the Footsteps of Your Favorite Heroine

While some London sites are long gone, sadly—no more weak lemonade at Almack's—there are still many Victorian activities to experience. Try rowing or picnicking in Hyde Park, taking a carriage ride near Windsor Castle, attending a 700-year-old ceremony at the Tower of London, dancing at a 200-year-old ball, or watching a Shakespeare play in a reconstructed Elizabethan theater. Museums are included here as well, because that is something Victorians liked to do, and they're great places to see period furnishings, paintings, and clothing.

Although these may be a patchwork of activities, when combined with period lodging and an authentic Afternoon Tea, you can make your own Regency or Victorian story where you're the starring heroine. See our **MUSEUM QUICK GUIDE** in Ch. 4 for details.

Chapter 7 Activities by Category:

◇❦◦————————————————————————•

BOATING

Until the advent of the steam train in the 1830s, sailing on the Thames was one of the most comfortable ways to travel. Queen Victoria did it often on her way to Cliveden House (Ch. 6). Prior to the building of Westminster Bridge, most Londoners took boats to get to Vauxhall Gardens. It was necessary transportation then, but now it's a chance to see the London sights from a different perspective. You've many options to get on the water, however almost *none* of them are period.

TOURIST CRUISES ～ From modern sightseeing cruises to canal trips, there are many offerings.

CITY CRUISES ～ Hop-on/off, with commentary, and specialty round-trip cruises like the lunch, tea, or sundowner, which offer 1.5-hour trips with meals. £17 for hop-on; £32 for meal. 2015 Certificate of Excellence from TripAdvisor. www.CityCruises.com

JASON'S TRIP ～ The original London canal trip in a 108-year-old canal boat that was originally used to haul cargo. Take a leisurely 45-minute ride down London's canals from Little Venice (Warwick Avenue Tube) to Camden with commentary (reverse trip *sans* commentary). You won't see the major sights, but you'll see old water-based neighborhoods, animals at the zoo, and learn some interesting history of the canals from 1800 to now. £9.50 Cash only. Closed in the winter. www.Jasons.co.uk/index.html

FERRIES ～ Are an economical way to get on the water, and a fun way to go on an excursion to the Greenwich-based Fan Museum. Or take a shorter route, but don't forget to download the app in:flow for a FREE audio guide www.ThamesClippers.com/visitorapp but you'll need an international data plan.

RIVER BUS ～ To see most of the sights, take the Blue or Green lines from Westminster (short walk from the Tube station) with direct service to Greenwich. Roughly 1 hour ride. £6.50 one-way. Tip: £16 River Roamer tix have unlimited hop-on/off; not a bad deal if you return on it too. Travelcard, buy-in-advance, and other discounts at www.ThamesClippers.com.

TATE TO TATE ～ For visiting the Tate Modern and Tate Britain art museums. This express route covers a nice chunk of the river, but

Room enough in the Serpentine for rowboats and swans

ends before the Tower of London. £8 one-way. Bonus: the museums are FREE. Check out discounts at www.Tate.org.uk/visit/tate-boat.

WOOLWICH FERRY ～ FREE ～ The quick ride is too far east to see London sights, but one can get a distant view of Canary Wharf and the Thames Barrier, the moveable flood-control pier. And it's FREE! The return trip can be done through the foot tunnel—not exactly a bucket-list item, but who else can say they've walked under the Thames. www.Greenwich.co.uk/useful-information/woolwich-ferry

BOATING ON THE SERPENTINE ～ From early April till October 31, you can play Regency heroine and let your dashing hero row you around this man-made lake in Hyde Park. Extra historical points if you bring a parasol. There are also pedalos (we call them paddle boats). Although these are modern plastic versions, the earliest mention of such craft was c.1488, by Leonardo de Vinci. So you're, *like*, totally medieval if you go this route. Or flip futuristic and ride the SolarShuttle, a 40-passenger craft that runs completely on solar power. www.SolarShuttle.co.uk £12 pp an hour for rowing. Make it even better with a picnic hamper from Fortnum & Mason (£55-400, see shopping Ch. 8); they've been providing London's upper crust with such delights since 1707.

RIVERBOATS ON THE THAMES ～ Operating out of Windsor by the French Brothers since 1978, the Thames is much skinnier here and more scenic, offering charming views of riverside buildings and sights, and impressive views of Windsor Castle (make it part of Ch. 9 day trip to see the castle). The basic is a 40-min or 2-hr ride (£7.50 or £13), and they have Cream Tea steamboats (2.5 hrs, £42), or you can take the boat from nearby Runnymeade all the way to or from Hampton Court Palace, which has its own dock (that's a 4 hour cruise so you'll need to train home from there or Uber back to Windsor).

www.FrenchBrothers.co.uk, sales@boat-trips.co.uk,
+44 17 5385 1900, Windsor Promenade.

CEREMONIES

CEREMONY OF THE KEYS (c.1340s) ∿ FREE

Here's your chance to participate in a medieval ceremony dating back more than 700 years. However, before proceeding further, it must be noted that this free event inside the Tower of London is so extraordinarily popular it must be booked a year in advance. Also, it's short, about seven minutes.

And, don't expect to see inside any rooms—it's just a chance to be a tiny part of a long history that will go on nightly until...*I guess...* the end of time. Makes me wonder if a future historical romance fan, like myself, will take this tour in another 700 years—say in 2717. Will there be flying cars buzzing overhead? Will she require an individual breathing apparatus because the air is so polluted or will such problems be solved? Will the Tower guards, called Beefeaters, still wear those cute tunics and fancy hats, a style leftover from the Tudor era? And will they recite the same queries while a small band of smiling tourists gives witness?

"Halt!" Who comes there?" calls the sentry.

"The keys," responds the Chief Yeoman Warder.

"Whose keys?"

"Queen Futura's Keys." (*Made the name up, 'cause, obviously, it won't be QE II in 700 years.*)

The sentry continues...

"Pass Queen Futura's Keys. All's well."

The brief ceremony begins at exactly 9:53pm, when the Chief Yeoman Warder is met by a military escort. We watch as they secure the main gates of the Tower and then follow them back down Water Lane, only to be challenged by the sentry, as above. After, we are led through the archway of the Bloody Tower just inside the fortress and watch as the Chief Warder salutes, "God preserve Queen Futura." A little more pomp and circumstance, along with the playing of the *Last Post* bugle call, and the Chief takes control of the keys. All's well for another night, and we fortunate folk are escorted out a side door.

The Ceremony of the Keys goes on nightly, rain or shine, war or peace. It has only been interrupted once, during WWII, when there was an air raid on London and bombs fell on the old Victorian guardroom just as the Chief Warder was coming through the Bloody Tower archway. Reports are that they actually carried on—after dusting themselves off.

And, lastly, why is one tower called bloody and why a fancy ceremony when the monarchs no longer live within? The Bloody Tower earned the name because it's believed to be where two young princes were murdered in 1493, although their mysterious disappearance has never been solved; the elder prince would have been crowned King Edward V, but his uncle Richard III is accused of stealing the throne instead. While monarchs haven't lived in the fortress for hundreds of years now, the Crown Jewels have been stored here since 1303. Hence the reason for the high security, although one can be sure the priceless treasure is today also protected by much higher-tech methods.

Booking information: It's limited to 40–50 guests. Must be booked online a year in

Formal attire for Yeomen of the Guards, c.1890

advance; the tickets are released monthly and are gone within weeks. Nontransferable. Tour is free but £1 to cover booking administration costs.

www.hrp.org.uk/tower-of-london/whats-on/ceremony-of-the-keys

OTHER CEREMONIES OF THE KEYS ⌇ At Edinburgh's

Holyrood Place in late June if one is lucky enough to be one of the 700 invitees. In Gibraltar it's performed free every September by the Royal Gibraltar Regiment and every Saturday at noon in an unofficial reenactment that is open to the public

(www.VisitGibraltar.gi/ceremonyofthekeys).

CHANGING OF THE GUARD (c.1660) ⌇ FREE

While I can't imagine the "quality" standing outside in the cold to watch this type of event, I'm sure any young lady of lower birth, new to the city, was thrilled to see such a spectacle here or in other royal parades. I haven't found the scene in a novel yet … so if you have, please let me know … but I can imagine the storyline, the innocent heroine on tiptoe, eyes wide at the sight of such hitherto unimagined pageantry, only to find, some years later that she's now a princess herself, waving back at the crowd.

The Household Regiments have guarded the sovereign palaces since 1660 and have been stationed at Buckingham Palace since 1837 when Queen Victoria moved in. Grab yourself a spot early (10:30am) near the railing of the Victoria Memorial—even earlier in the summertime. In their scarlet tunics and fluffy bearskin hats, accompanied by a band, it's a colorful, regal, and fun 45-minute ceremony as the "New Guard" replaces the "Old Guard," with a detachment marching on to St. James's Palace. 11:30am daily from April-July and alternate days during rest of year.

The biggest such event is the annual Trooping of the Colour to celebrate the Queen's Official Birthday. While her actual date of birth is April 21, the parade is held, by longstanding tradition, on a summer's day in June that is the day of Elizabeth's accession to the throne, her anniversary of becoming Queen. Mucho pageantry with hundreds of marching guards, bands, horses, gun salutes in Green Park and the Tower of London, and even a Royal Air Force fly-by. If you're lucky, you'll spot the Queen on the balcony of Buckingham Palace too. Tickets are sold to this event but if you arrive early enough you can grab a free spot along the route.

There are multiple guard changings, including St. James's Palace, Horse Guards Parade—both in London—and at Windsor Castle. For Trooping of the Colour tickets: www.Changing-Guard.com

◇─❡ℓ⌷───────────────────────────────⌷

CROWN JEWELS AND OTHER PRETTY STONES ～ *History with Bling*

Many romance novels feature the acquisition of jewelry. Sometimes as part of the heroine's marriage. Sometimes as booty for a courtesan. The most romantic is when it's a surprise gift from the hero. He has noticed she lacks any jewels at a ball or some such thing. As the trope goes, his gift is then rejected for being too personal or expensive or intimate. But in the best HEA fashion the couple is ultimately united and the lady proudly wears his jewels. Take a look at these collections to see firsthand what one of your favorite historical heroines might wear.

And, don't forget to take a moment to imagine your own hero placing one of these priceless pieces around your neck. Which would make you swoon? Which would be just *too* much? Pick your fav and post a pic to my FB—I would love to see them!

CROWN JEWELS (from 1160)
～ Tower of London

FUN FACT: Until the monarchy of George IV, the jewels worn in the Coronation Regalia were mostly "rented" and returned afterwards. Paste fakes filled the gaps until the next coronation. However, the Prince Regent wanted a magnificent coronation, spending a whopping £243,000 in 1821 on his regalia and the event— that would be more than $26 million today. After that, renting became passé and today every gem you'll see is real.

Now head to the Tower, where you'll be dazzled by the 23,578[1] gems that make up the Crown Jewels collection, including the world's biggest, most famous stones—the Sceptre's 530.2 carat Cullinan I diamond (Great Star of Africa) and the 105.6 carat Koh-i-Noor (Mountain of Light) set in the Queen Mother's Crown because it's said to be unlucky for men to wear due to its long, bloody saga. The oldest piece, a spoon, dates to the 12th Century, and the saga of the collection over the past 900 years makes a fascinating lesson in British history.

ANOTHER FUN FACT: For a small fee you could at one time touch the jewels! The collection first went on public display in 1669 in the Martin Tower. All that was required was to hand the Jewel House

Keeper a few coins. This less than perfectly secure system ended when Colonel Thomas Blood stole St. Edward's Crown in 1671. The items were recovered (although damaged), the perpetrator was pardoned and given land in Ireland—go figure—and the beaten custodian lost this added source of income.[2] †

But not for long. The collection was put behind iron bars in 1690, a guide-sheet was created, and visitors were locked inside the tower during their visit. But for a small donation, one could still reach through the bars and touch the jewels. And so it goes. This ended in 1815 when a woman, later deemed insane, pulled apart the arches of St. Edward's Crown—that coronet has really taken a beating.

Some may remember that in 2012 someone broke into the Tower of London and stole keys; although never caught and the locks quickly changed, the public was assured that no simple set of keys on a hook would ever allow access to the Crown Jewels. Trust me. They're locked up tight![3]

Today only the appointed Crown Jeweler is allowed to handle these exquisite items and is on call 24/7. Said William Summers, who held the post from 1962-91, "Where the Crown goes, there go I." The current fortress inside Waterloo Barracks has the highest level of high-tech security (including two-ton, six-inch-thick steel doors, bombproof glass, and some 100 hidden cameras)—important because the Crown Jewels are rumored to be uninsured. How could they be? They are officially…"priceless."

You'll find this amazing collection under armed guard in the Jewel House. Be aware that lingering is not possible. Unlike the Hope Diamond at the Smithsonian in Washington, D.C., where the last time I went it was a huge crush of unmovable bodies, to view the Crown Jewels one rides a moving walkway and only gets a few moments in front of each item. However, when I was there, no one stopped me from riding it again. Other items include robes, orbs, jewelry, and a silver bowl so big you could bathe in it.

YET ANOTHER FUN FACT: the British constitution prohibits the removal of any of the Crown Jewels from the UK. As a result, when George V visited Delhi in 1911 to be proclaimed Emperor, a new crown had to be made. Watch for it on your sidewalk ride—it's silver gilt with emeralds, rubies, sapphires, and 6,100 diamonds!

---

† *Apparently, I've been told by a friend, this makes perfect sense in the history of the English in Ireland. Today, it's a standing joke that when a UK government minister falls out of favor with his party, he gets the job of Secretary of State for Northern Ireland. King Edward may have started a tradition, although I think Ireland is so pretty and magical, I'd take banishment to there anytime!*

Victoria & Albert Museum (1852)

~ William and Judith Bollinger Gallery ~ FREE

What the V&A doesn't have in crowns, it makes up for in jewelry. The William and Judith Bollinger Gallery displays 3,500 jewels from the V&A's collection, one of the finest and most comprehensive in the world. With pieces dating from 1,500 BC to today, the majority represents the last 800 years of European jewelry. And you'll get to see rare items from other monarchs—pendants from Queen Elizabeth I, diamonds from Catherine the Great of Russia, bracelets from Marie Antoinette, the famous Beauharnais Emeralds (gifted by Napoleon to his daughter), and Empress Josephine's tiaras. Fabergé eggs. Diamond tiaras by Cartier. Bling and more bling! Plus some oddities that could only come from the fussy Victorian period: the Lover's Eye Brooch (a painted eye surrounded by pearls) or The Canning Jewel (a merman pendant) and, of course, the ever popular hair jewelry made from the locks of a deceased beloved. V&A also has period clothing and decorative arts.

◇⟋⟋⟋⟋⟋⟋⟋⟋⟋⟋⟋⟋⟋⟋⟋⟋⟋⟋⟋⟋•

Dancing and Balls

The Victorian ladies enjoyed endless balls in private residences during The Season. For the time-travelling adventurer, there are a few options these days for playing princess. Here are a couple balls where one can don a floor-length gown and dance the night away.

Royal Caledonian Ball ~ Believed to be the oldest charity ball in the world, 2017 marked the 169th gathering of Scots in London. Held in Grosvenor House's Great Room (Ch. 6), the men sport kilts and the ladies a sash in their lover's tartan. More than 650 reelers dance the night away—literally till 3:30am—but break for breakfast at 12:30am. Royal Patronage: Her Majesty the Queen, HRH Duke of Edinburgh, HRH The Princess Royal, and the Duke and Duchess of Kent (this doesn't mean they'll be there, but given the number of upper crust on their committees, there are likely to be some nobility present). Features: Bagpipe and Drums marching band and a set reel that opens the ball. Dress: Men, Highland evening dress, Black Tails, military uniform. Women, formal floor-length gowns. Both, Mess dress, if entitled. Stats: usually held in April; £155 includes whiskey and "breakfast" at 12:30am or £245 plus dinner & reception. www.RoyalCaledonianBall.com.

Other Regency Dances ~ These are held occasionally in historic venues in London and annually in several towns within an hour of the city. Some come with a day's or weekend's worth of Regency activities and lectures. So plan your trip to coincide with any one and don't forget to pack your Regency attire. www.RegencyDances.org has a list of regency balls around the world (including ones near London) and Mrs. Bennet's Ballroom does a week long Jane Austen Regency Week festival each June that starts with a dance (www.JaneAustenRegencyWeek. co.uk, www.facebook.com/MrsBennetsBallroom).

VIENNESE BALLS ～ This is also on my bucket list. Sadly there are none in London, but www.VienneseBall.org has a list of them all around the world, including 11 in the US! I'm going to need to start practicing the waltz.

◇~~~━━━━━━━━━━━━━━━━━━━━●

FAN MUSEUM ～ Est. 1991 in 1721 building
Beautiful, exotic, rare.
With 3,000 fans, something is sure to catch your fancy.

This small museum in the heart of Greenwich is a must for anyone who loves fans or period dress. This outing can be combined with a bargain Afternoon Tea at the museum (Ch. 5) or make a day of it (Ch. 9). Expect the exhibits to take from 30 minutes to an hour, depending on how in-depth you go.

FAN HISTORY: Did you know that Greek, Etruscan, and Roman pictorial records show that fans were used as far back as 3000 BC? And the usage of fans in China probably dates back further. In Europe, fancy folding fans—often ornamented with precious metals and stones—were initially reserved for Royalty, but we all know that by the Georgian period, proper skill with a fan was something all debutantes needed to master. Functional, ceremonial, and decorative, their history is brought alive at the Fan Museum with permanent and temporary exhibits on two floors.

BUILDING HISTORY: The museum is housed in two Grade II listed town houses. However, when they were purchased in 1985, these two fine examples of Georgian architecture were abandoned and in bad disrepair, their interior period features crudely remodeled. It took five years to maneuver through the permits process for a listed building and complete the work, at a cost of £1.5 million. In addition, an Orangery reproduced in the Georgian style was built that overlooks a 'secret' Japanese garden (the garden is not accessible). Finally, in 1990, the two buildings were ready, carefully restored to their original character along with necessary improvements needed for use as a public museum.

MUSEUM HISTORY: The museum owes its existence to Hélène Alexander. Born in 1932 in Alexandria, Egypt, she earned degrees in theater design and art history. By the 1980s, Hélène had amassed a collection of 3,000 fans. With her husband, they decided to bequeath the collection to a new museum dedicated to fans, and they were instrumental in laying groundwork for this, including overseeing the acquisition of the buildings and the remodel. Today, the museum is an independent charitable trust, run by a board of trustees, and the current holdings include more than 5,000 objects. There are fans from all over the world, and the oldest fan dates to the 11ᵗʰ Century. They've an extensive collection of 18ᵗʰ and 19ᵗʰ Century fans, including ones painted by Paul Gauguin (1887), Walter Sickert (c.1890), and even Salvador Dali (1978). HRH The Duchess of Cornwall is a Royal Patron of the museum.

Features: Afternoon Tea in the Orangery. 3-hour fan-making workshops on the first Saturday of the month (limited to 6 people; book in advance, tea/coffee and biscuits included, £25). Terrific little gift shop with reasonable prices. Free returnable guide. Cloakroom. There is a ramp and elevator for the disabled. **TIP:** Tuesday is free for seniors/disabled. Their website has a searchable database with photos. Fun to look at and great for research. Academics and researchers can make appointments to visit the onsite archive.

◇❧⌐──────────────────────────────────•

FINERY AND FRIPPERY AND FIGHTING
⌐ Museums with period attire

Ever wonder if Elizabethan dresses were as wide as they appear on television? Question what Regency and Victorian attire really looked like? Contemplate the difference between a morning dress and a ball gown? Well wonder, question, and contemplate no more. Cause here's where to see what people wore in different periods. Plus, what the menfolk wore or used for war. Fun! (A reminder: visiting info/websites in Museums Quick Guide, Ch. 4.)

HOUSEHOLD CAVALRY MUSEUM (1750)
⌐ for the guys into military history

There's no better place to see gorgeous historic military uniforms than this museum, which is also a working stables, dating to 1750. The Grade I building in the Palladian style is striking. This royal horse regiment has provided security for England's monarchs for more than 350 years, and you'll learn the history and get a "behind the scenes" look at all the work that goes into it. Besides uniforms, there are swords, royal standards, even Fabergé silverware and musical instruments, and if

─────────────────❧◇❧─────────────────

*⌐ for the guys at Wallace Collection and
Household Cavalry museums*

you're lucky you'll see the horses being groomed. A glass wall makes the stables always open for viewing. Plus there are two daily ceremonies: Horse Guards Parade at 11am (10am Sundays) and the Daily Inspection at 4pm in the courtyard. The first is a smaller "changing of the guards" than the Buckingham Palace one but much less crowded. The second supposedly got its start as punishment. One afternoon in 1894, Queen Victoria found her guards drinking and gambling while on duty and proclaimed a "four o'clock" inspection would take place for the next 100 years; that expired in 1994, but Queen Elizabeth II kept it going for the sake of tradition. There is disabled access, and a free audio-guide tour.

MUSEUM OF LONDON (Est. 1976) ~ FREE

With more than 6 million objects, the museum documents the history of this city from prehistoric to modern times. Among topics from this Guide there are exhibits on Roman times, the Great Fire, an interior of Wellclose debtor's prison, and even the Lord Mayor's gaudily-impressive coach. The adjunct Museum of London Docklands (Est. 2003) in a 19th Century Grade I warehouse on the Isle of Dogs tells the city's trading history on the Thames.

Fashion is covered from the Tudor period to present day, however their core focus is attire for the wealthy and pieces worn by the royal family from mid-17th to mid-20th Century. While they aren't "fashion" exhibits per se, the museum uses period dress throughout their various exhibits to offer extra context on the subject matter. For example, check out the Vauxhall Pleasure Gardens exhibit in the basement for an atmospheric introduction to male and female Georgian and Regency attire. They also have almost 4,000 fashion plates from the 1600s until 1830.

NATIONAL PORTRAIT GALLEY (Est. 1856 and moved into 1896 bldg.) ~ FREE

Want to see princesses? You'll see them *all*, albeit in two-dimensional form. Interested in period attire from different eras? You can't do better than here, and while only paintings, some of these masterpieces are so detailed, the lace or velvet so lush, the colors so vibrant, that they look almost three-dimensional. The museum has more than 4,000 paintings, sculptures, or miniatures. It's the oldest museum dedicated to portraits, and the newest portrait is of the newest Royal Highness, Catherine, Duchess of Cambridge. It was unveiled in 2013, and she is now the museum's royal patron. American Connections include portraits of Yanks such as George Washington, Thomas Jefferson, Pocahontas, and Consuelo, Duchess of Marlborough. Born a Vanderbilt heiress, she was reputed to have coined the phrase, "heir and a spare," which is what she needed to produce before she was allowed out of the unhappy marriage. The groom got to keep her $2.5 million dowry. I gleaned this tidbit (then verified elsewhere) from the NPG's useful online 'Search the Collection,' which has thousands of works available to view and even download.

VICTORIA & ALBERT MUSEUM (1852) ～ Textile and Fashion Collection ～ FREE

Spanning five millennia, the collection of more than 75,000 attire-related items is one of the largest and most comprehensive in the world. Particularly strong in European fashion from the 18th Century on, highlights include the earliest surviving wedding suit worn by King James II in 1673 (prior to his coronation), a super-wide 1755 Mantua court dress (almost 8 feet across), and an utterly divine, flat straw hat with strawwork flowers from Italy, c.1760.

WALLACE COLLECTION (Est. 1900 in 1776 bldg.) ～ Arms and Armour Galleries ～ FREE

One wonders if the blood-red walls in some of these galleries are a statement about these objects' use. Regardless, this colossal collection of fierce fighting kit is impressive. With items dating from the 10th to 19th Centuries, there are Indian, Persian, Turkish, and of course European par-

aphernalia. Highlights include a gorgeous Mughal Court Dagger and Scabbard (pure gold hilt inlayed with hundreds of small diamonds, rubies, and emeralds, circa early 1600s), one of only two of this quality in the world (the other in Kuwait). Then for pure evil, there's a 19th Century German

◇❧

Period fashions abound in London museums. Gorgeous reproduction by Victoria Vane.

Parrying dagger—beautifully etched steel with gilding in gold, this wicked knife has a switch that opens it into 3 blades-in-one. Ouch. Most fantastical is an entire room of horse mannequins and riders wearing various styles and periods of equestrian armour. All it would take is a little "Night at the Museum" magic and we'd have a full-on battle royal through these halls.

ALSO CHECK OUT ∿ Buckingham or Kensington Palace for occasional exhibits on royal fashion.

IMPERIAL WAR MUSEUMS ∿ *for the guys*
The IWM is really 5 museums that explore modern war and conflict, of which three are in London. Visiting details in Museum Quick Guide, Ch. 4.

IWM LONDON (Est. 1917 in 1815 bldg.) ∿ FREE
Housed in the former Bedlam hospital, the IWM tells the story of people's experiences of modern warfare from WWI to today. The collection contains more than 32 million objects—everything from weapons and uniforms, to early fighter aircraft, to diaries and trinkets—so obviously not all are on display. Among the notables is the life preserver that saved L. Sharpe's life (an American) when 1,198 others perished in the German submarine sinking of the Lusitania in 1915. Another Yankee connection: because 128 US citizens perished, the resulting anger helped spur America's entrance into WWI. 3D exhibits are especially powerful, such as walking through a full-scale model of a WWI trench with the sounds of bullets whizzing overhead.

CHURCHILL WAR ROOMS (built in 1939; museum from 1984) ∿ fee
This secret underground bunker under the streets of Westminster is where Winston Churchill and his cabinet worked to win WWII. Now opened to reveal its secrets, you'll see the labyrinth of rooms where people worked and lived while bombs exploded above ground. The highlight is the Map Room, left exactly as it was the day the war ended 1945—literally, workers switched off the lights and closed the door. For 35 years these abandoned artifacts lay right where they'd been, collecting dust and beginning to decay, until Margaret Thatcher spurred the government to restore everything and open the bunker to the public. The second half of this institution is the Churchill Museum, which tells his life story.

HMS BELFAST (built in 1938; museum from 1971) ∼ Fee
This Royal Navy warship, in service from WWII until 1963, has been restored, and today visitors may explore its 9 decks to learn what life was like for the crew.

◇◦◈◦◦────────────────────────•

THE SHERLOCK HOLMES MUSEUM
∼ for the guys... that are Holmes fans

This "museum" is really for the avid fan, and more specifically for the fan of Doyle's stories—there's no connection to the modern television show. And it's quite expensive for what takes about 20 minutes. So...some thoughts. You can go for free to take a selfie in front of 221b Baker Street and of the blue plaque recognizing that Sherlock Holmes once lived here. Then take a look around the gift shop next door also for free. If you do want to go inside, buy the ticket in the shop first, and while in the display make sure to have someone take your photo sitting in Sherlock's chair by the fireplace. As for location, it's easy to find with the big green sign and the queue of tourists waiting to get in (they limit the numbers because it's tight in there), but if you're a real stickler for numbers, you won't find it because 221b is actually located between 237 and 241. It took until 2005, but the Royal Mail now officially recognizes this address, and fan mail from around the world is delivered here. Please know that it's not disabled-accessible, and there are several flights of stairs.

◇◦◈◦◦────────────────────────•

HORSEBACK RIDING

To be a lady of quality, one must also be a horsewoman. How else to lead the hunt? Thankfully the sidesaddle is a thing of the past, and modern riders with two X chromosomes may ride in britches with nary a second glance. On the other hand, wouldn't you rather be wearing a gorgeous handmade riding habit with a cute little hat perched upon your coiffed head?

RIDING IN HYDE PARK ∼ beginners welcome, believe it or not...English saddle.
Riding in royal Hyde Park dates to 1536 when Henry VIII created it for hunting. Later it became the place to be seen during the 18th and 19th Centuries, especially on Rotten Row. Today, there are five miles of well-maintained trails in two designated routes open to commoners on

Riders from nearby Hyde Park Stables visiting The Royal Park Hotel

rented hacks—well, even the nobility could ride there, but you're not likely to see them. **FUN FACT:** Queen Elizabeth's carriage horses are still exercised daily in the park—in the morning watch for a liveried coachman driving a team along Rotten Row.

HYDE PARK STABLES ∼ Open daily 7:30am-6pm and offers group or private rides for riders of all abilities, including complete novices. *Really.* To be clear, these are really trail rides—you're tethered to a guide by a lead. Unless they know you well, you'll not be allowed to ride independently, even if you tell them you're an experienced rider. But for a once-in-a-lifetime thrill, take a jaunt through Hyde Park on the back of a horse and know that you'll be safe with an instructor escort. This isn't a bad thing: I was once given a difficult horse, Mozart, for a ride in NY's Central Park, back when there was still a Manhattan stable. Mozart decided he wanted to go home, and despite repeated attempts to school him back onto the riding path, he made a break for it, charging onto Central Park South. Lucky for me, there was no oncoming traffic, or…you get the idea.

That said, if you are truly an experienced rider, you'd find this tethered ride unacceptable. Starting at £95 for a 1-hour group ride, including guide, hats, boots. www.HydeParkStables.com

ROSS NYE STABLES ∼ Open Tue-Fri 7am-6pm and Sat-Sun 9am-6pm. Established in 1965, it's the oldest riding school in Central

London. While they take beginners, this is the stable for more advanced riders. You'll still have a guide, but if you're experienced you can trot and canter off lead and have that Regency Rotten Row experience. Starting at £75 for a 1-hour group ride, including guide, hats, boots. www.RossNyeStables.co.uk

RICHMOND PARK OPERATION CENTAUR ∼ For the experienced horseman, this is an inexpensive subscription for a weekly 75-minute hack starting at just £50 per week. A bargain. www.OperationCentaur.com/horse-sharing

◇❧———————————————•

HORSE DRAWN CARRIAGES
∼ *Ride like a Princess*

If hunter seat or dressage equitation is not your idea of a fun time, consider the more sedate option of a carriage ride. However, unlike NY's Central Park, carriage rides in London proper are not a common thing. Doable, but pricey and requiring advance planning. Consider one for something truly special, like a proposal. Or consider taking a ride at Windsor Castle with these highly regarded tours.

WINDSOR CARRIAGES (1849) ∼ Add a carriage ride at Windsor to your easy day trip (Ch. 9). These won't break the bank— only £50 for a 30 min trip up the long walk. Lots of options, including

————————❦◇❦————————

A "Barouche and Six" at Cliveden House, c.1890
You won't find that, but how about a coach and two!

a 60-min evening tour of the Royal Windsor Great Park for £100. Runs April to October. Make sure to clarify what type of conveyance will be used. www.WindsorCarriages.co.uk

ASCOT CARRIAGES (2009) ~ Similar prices with discounts on weekdays for tours of the park. They offer a £125 Romantic Wedding Proposal Ride with champagne. Runs year round. Make sure to clarify what type of conveyance will be used. www.AscotCarriages.co.uk

RICHMOND PARK ~ London's largest Royal Park has offered carriage rides in the summer and December as a fundraiser for Operation Centaur. If there are any in the offing, these are reasonably priced (£125 for 2 for 60 minutes). www.supporttheroyalparks.org/events/horse_carriage_rides

HORSEMAN'S SUNDAY ~ not a ride but a horsey spectacle

A cavalcade of horses and riders from Hyde Park and beyond gather outside St John's, Hyde Park Crescent. After a church service inside—two-legged believers only—the vicar appears before the congregation on a horse for the traditional blessing of the horses, followed by a ride-past with some 100 horses and ponies, plus horse-drawn buggies. There is also a Village Fete with bake sale, music, and more. This annual event, celebrating its 50th year in 2017, takes place on the penultimate September Sunday from 10am-2pm. Search on "horseman's Sunday Hyde Park," but to clarify, this takes place at Hyde Park Crescent, a smaller park a few blocks north of the big one.

◇～～━━━━━━━━━━━━━━━●

THEATERS

Historical romance fiction often sets scenes in theaters. The heroine might be snubbed there or the hero might grasp the opportunity for clandestine caresses in their box. And everyone is there to see and be seen, which was as true in real life as in fiction. After the demise of the medieval theaters due to the Puritan closures, entertainments were again small private events in homes. Then during the renaissance many new theaters were built, some of which still exist and continue to hold performances. Here's a list of a few notable ones.

OLD GLOBE THEATRE ~ see 'Globe' in Ch. 3

'OLD VIC' OR THE VICTORIA THEATRE (1818–present) ~

Near Waterloo Station, this pretty period theater was rebuilt in 1871 and features plays. There are also unaffiliated Young Vic and New Vic (not in London) venues offering plays. www.OldVicTheatre.com

ROYAL OPERA HOUSE (1732-present) ~ Often called just

Covent Garden because of its original location, this theatre was rebuilt two times after devastating fires. Rebuilt in 1858, the current Grade I listed auditorium is beautiful inside, like a jewel box. Perfect for its permanent residents: The Royal Opera and The Royal Ballet. Note: don't be discouraged by the rather jarring modern entrance that's been tacked onto it; once inside you're in the Georgian era. www.roh.org.uk

SADLER'S WELLS (1683–1998–present) ~ In Islington, it's the

sixth theater on this site, and this one is thoroughly modern in décor, having opened its doors in 1998. It's renowned for dance performances of all kinds. www.SadlersWells.com

THEATRE ROYAL DRURY LANE (1683–present) ~ The

oldest theater in London, having been rebuilt a few times. The current one is 200 years old, Grade I listed, and is gloriously period. And it has theater 'boxes' lining the sides just like you find in our romance novels, including two Royal ones. Near Covent Garden, it offers theater and musical comedy. Ironically, it's never been situated exactly on Drury Lane. www.ReallyUsefulTheatres.co.uk/our-theatres/theatre-royal

THEATRE ROYAL HAYMARKET (1720–present) ~ Originally

called The Little Theatre in the Hay, it is a small, Grade I listed venue in the West End for plays with 893 seats. Gorgeously authentic, both inside and out. www.trh.co.uk

◇⌒⌒⌒⌒⌒⌒⌒⌒⌒●

VISITING VICTORIAN HOMES
~ museums with period furnishings and décor

Here's a list of places where you can learn the difference between a 'veilleuse' and a 'veilleuse.' Or the many uses for a commode.

CHARLES DICKENS MUSEUM ~ This museum is in the

beautifully decorated Georgian town house where he lived from 1837-39, complete with antiques and his personal possessions. See Chuck's office where he wrote *Oliver Twist*, *Nicholas Nickleby*, and more. **TIP:** Café with quite charming Victorian-style courtyard serving tartlets,

See parlours from four centuries at The Geffrye, Museum of the Home

teas, and homemade cakes—and a £6 bargain glass of sparkling wine. Researchers may apply for access to the full 100K collection of research on Dickens. Mostly mobility accessible, but requires staff to access elevator; free for carer; see website for details.

THE GEFFRYE, MUSEUM OF THE HOME ∼

This museum recreates rooms of London's merchant class in four different distinct periods from 1700s to 1900s. See full listing in Ch. 3.

HANDEL HOUSE MUSEUM ∼ Located in George Frideric's Georgian home of 36 years in Mayfair, where he composed his *Messiah*. The house has period furniture, paintings, and the restored rehearsal/performance salon where Handel debuted some of his most famous work. **FUN FACT:** Jimi Hendrix lived here too in the 1960s and you can see his restored bedroom. **TIP:** Very popular; book in advance. Weekly concerts Thurs at 6:30pm, including baroque recitals in the very room where Handel rehearsed his musicians and singers. Accessibility: reduced fee, carers free; lift access behind building in Lancashire Court walkway.

18 STAFFORD TERRACE / THE SAMBOURNE FAMILY HOME (Est. 1980 in c.1870 bldg.) ∼ Step back in time to 1899 in the former home of Edward Linley Sambourne (famed *Punch* cartoonist) where he lived with his wife Marion, two children, and live-in servants. It's a rare example of the 'Aesthetic interior' or 'House Beautiful' style, a 19th Century movement that featured exotic decorations from Japan,

China, and the Middle-East. The house has been preserved almost exactly as it was, and tours include the standard rooms found in a home, plus the maid's room, a Victorian bathroom, and his studio where Linley experimented with early photography. You'll also see examples of his drawings and photographs. For added fun, book a 'costumed' tour with either Mrs. Sambourne or her parlour maid Mrs. Refell. Tours are 75 mins and cost £10. Open access (no tour) £7. Limited hours, and advance tour booking essential. A second property in the neighborhood is the 1830 Leighton House Museum, which is described as a 'Private Palace of Art.' A purpose-built art studio/home, this building does not have furnishings but the structure and décor is an extraordinary example of the aforementioned 'Aesthetic interior' style. £9 with free tours on Wed & Sun. Neither is wheelchair-accessible and both have multiple staircases.

DENNIS SEVERS' HOUSE (Est. sometime during Severs' life in c.1724 bldg.) ∿ A privately run establishment in a Georgian era Spitalfields town house, this is more a theatrical experience than a museum. **AMERICAN CONNECTION:** The creator, Dennis Severs, was from California, and he called his creation "still-life drama." You're visiting a tradesman's home circa 1724-1914 where the occupants are always just around the next corner (I know, but it's "theatre" and as one walks through each room you jump foreword in time). In *British Heritage Travel*, Sandra Lawrence calls it "part stage set, part art installation, part game, and part historical essay."[4] This is a multi-sensory experience with sounds of inhabitants in the next room and the smells of cooking and it's all done in silence. Dennis Severs, himself, was a character with a unique perspective on life and history—check out his story for background into how this place came about. The experience is about 45 minutes and is not wheelchair-accessible. For safety concerns, children are not allowed. Very popular, so book in advance. Some report it feels staged, but many others just love it. The evening candlelight visits are especially popular but the daytimes are cheaper. My advice—go with an open mind and let yourself float free into the past.

SIR JOHN SOANE'S MUSEUM ∿ Sir John's former home, now Grade I listed, has been left untouched since his death 180 years ago. Travel back to Regency period in the heart of Legal London to see his curiosity-filled home and art collection, which includes many architectural models. **TIP:** 1st Tuesday of the month they run very popular candlelight tours; limited to 200 so queue early. Website has 15% discount vouchers for the nearby Field Bar & Kitchen café. Extensive online archive for research. Disability accessible but requires pre-scheduling.

MUSEUMS WITH EXHIBITS OF HOUSEHOLD ITEMS:

THE BRITISH MUSEUM ∿ The Waddesdon Bequest features some exquisite pieces such as the 800-year-old Palmer Cup (a beautiful stained-glass challis); plus Clocks and Watches in Room 38-39, Medieval items in Room 40, Europe 1400–1900 in rooms 46-47.

VICTORIA & ALBERT MUSEUM ∿ This is the place to go to see it all, from china to chairs and everything in between. Dauntingly immense but since it's FREE you can break it up into sizable visits. Highlight: The Dr. Susan Weber Gallery tells the story of furniture making over the past 600 years all laid out in one fascinating timeline of outstanding examples from each period.

THE WALLACE COLLECTION (Est. 1900 in c.1776 bldg.) ∿ Go here to see French furnishings. Although other European masters are represented, the majority of pieces are from across the channel, including Louis XV period furniture, some owned by Marie-Antoinette, and one of the finest museum collections of 18th Century Sèvres porcelain in the world. The museum is housed in the beautiful Hertford House, worth seeing just for the mansion, but there's also a world-class painting collection of Old Masters as well as the exhibits described herein.

As for a veilleuse, both versions can be seen at the V&A. The ceramic one designed to keep your tea warm is in Room 138, Case 8, although they don't use the French word for it, ostensibly preferring Beverage Warmer since this example is English. Veilleuse also means daybed—an ornate 1750s model can be seen in Room 3. Regarding commodes, it also derives from a French word—in this case for "convenient"—and the museum owns all three types. Dating to 1700, the term originally meant a handy cabinet or chest of drawers; there are gorgeous examples throughout the V&A's furniture galleries in various hardwoods with decorative veneer, gilding, or marquetry. The second meaning is a taller cupboard that holds a porcelain washbasin, perhaps with a mirror attached (see Room 122, case 6). As for the more American meaning—a portable toilet—the V&A's antique loos are either in storage or on loan, but there's a child's version in the adjunct Museum of Childhood in Bethnal Green neighborhood (FREE).

However, you can visit Queen Victoria's personal 1850s loo at the V&A—a pretty Victorian space behind a modern brown-wood door at the far end of the V&A cafe. Once inside the hallway, look for the original crown and monogram tiles decorating the walls.

CHAPTER 8 ✧

Shopping in Merry Old England

Most of these establishments hold "royal warrants." This custom, which denotes royal patronage, began with Royal Charters to trade guilds—the first granted by Henry II in 1155—and by the 15th Century this practice had evolved to 'The Royal Warrants of Appointment.' Today, they remain greatly prized, demonstrating that the establishment sells to the current royals and that they offer the highest "service, quality, and excellence." There are currently about 800 warrant holders. Watch for their warrant to be displayed proudly on the wall inside the store.

Some of these shops will reek of olden times—well not really reek, of course, but the floors may be uneven or the walls adorned with historical mementos. The department stores, however, have been updated countless times. Know that if they are here, they're old! Lastly, the prices in many will seem exorbitant, but I did find souvenir bargains (Best Bets). And don't feel intimidated—you've as much right as anyone to visit these stores, but also maybe it's not the day to wear that ratty t-shirt.

Have fun!

How OLDE: ⚜⚜⚜⚜⚜ ∼ *for all of them...*

YE OLDE DEPARTMENT STORES

FORTNUM & MASON (1707) ∼ Founded by William Fortnum and Hugh Mason, this upscale department store was already one hundred years old by the time our Regency heroines were gadding about town. It seems young Wills was a royal footman to Queen Anne and she demanded new candles every night. The enterprising young man resold the slightly used candle wax at a profit, and thus an iconic

English brand was born. Prices here are less steep than in the nearby arcades but still pricey. Fortnum's sells fine foods, gifts, perfume, and some housewares. The Piccadilly flagship has delicious chocolates in its confectionary, and everything from caviar to cake. They're known for extravagant picnic hampers and for delicious picnic lunches. **TIP:** Ask for extra plastic shopping bags with your purchase—the pretty mint branded sacks make great gift bags for the souvenirs you buy there. FYI—thanks to a new UK law they may have to charge for them now, but it's only about ten cents, so still the cheapest gift bag you'll ever find. Lastly, they have restaurants, offer afternoon tea, and more, but I recommend trying out their new, clubby cocktail lounge on the 3rd floor serving iconic martinis at a good price. **BEST BETS:** Candies, branded tea towels, jars of Piccalilli— an English relish and a bargain! (Avoid chocolates in the hot months.)

Hours: M-Sat 10am-8pm | Sun 11:30am-6pm | **Tube**: Green Park, Piccadilly Circus | **Maps**: B & C | www.FortnumAndMason.com +44 20 7734 8040 | 181 Piccadilly

HARRODS DEPARTMENT STORE (1849) ～ This may be the most famous department store on the planet. It's huge, with seven floors and more than 300 departments. It debuted the world's first ever "moving staircase" in November, 1898, offering customers smelling salts and brandy after the traumatizing ride. A.A. Milne's *Winnie the Pooh* was inspired by seeing his son, Christopher Robin, playing with a teddy bear bought in Harrods in 1921. The store's motto is "Omnia Omnibus Ubique," Latin for "All Things for All People, Everywhere," and while some items will give you sticker shock, there's merchandise here at all price levels. **TIP:** Don't wear risqué clothing or anything with offensive logos, or you'll be asked to leave. *Of course, I know you'd never do that!* No large backpacks or luggage. Certain departments are by appointment only (e.g., fine jewelry), and you'll be escorted out, so check store guide first. **TIP:** You can book one-on-one makeup lessons and consultation, but do it at least a month in advance. **BEST BETS:** Level four for Harrods' branded merchandize at more reasonable prices, such as crown key chains, branded chocolate coins, baby bibs, and their annual Harrods bear.

Hours: M-Sat 10am-9pm | Sun 11:30am-6pm | **Tube**: Knightsbridge **Map**: A | www.Harrods.com/visiting-the-store | +44 20 7730 1234 87–135 Brompton Rd, Knightsbridge

SELFRIDGES & CO. (1909) ∽ The story of this high-end department store has been told in the PBS show starring Jeremy Piven as Harry Gordon Selfridge, a scrappy American that built a wildly successful empire only to lose it later in life and die destitute. His store was groundbreaking with all the modern conveniences and, most importantly, the novelty of letting shoppers handle the merchandise themselves rather than waiting for items to be presented by a clerk. He made shopping fun and provided another place—besides tea parlors—for ladies to go in public un-chaperoned. It's unclear whether Harry or Marshal Fields (his previous employer) coined the phrase "The customer is always right."—but Selfridges made it known worldwide. Oh, but I wish that saying were still true, especially every time I hear, "I'm sorry but we can't do that," or worse, "The computer won't let me do that." I've no doubt that if Harry were alive today, he'd never let a mere computer stop a sale.

Selfridges is the second-largest department store in the UK. Inside, it's still go big or go home, but sadly not many period features remain. It could be any fancy mall in the US. **TIP:** A hallmark of early Selfridges was providing amusements within the store to lure shoppers—he famously displayed the first plane ever to cross the channel and hosted the first public demonstration of a rudimentary television. That practice continues today with monthly in-store events, everything from psychic readings to photography shows to celebrity chefs guesting in their fine dining restaurant. **BEST BETS:** Branded jams and foodstuffs, exclusive liquors, and this adorable little bottle called "The Bubble" by Gray and Feathers, billed as the world's smallest bottle of champagne (just wrap them carefully in plastic and put in your checked luggage). For gifts that can't be had elsewhere, there are exclusive liquors and champagnes or the Ted Baker Aracon icon small shopper bag in patent-plastic—it's so glamorous it could double as a purse.

Hours: M-Sat 9:30am-9pm | Sun 11:30am-6pm | **Tube:** Bond Street, Marble Arch (5-7 min walk) | www.Selfridges.com +44 11 3369 8040 | 400 Oxford St

PICCADILLY SHOPPES ～ 1707-present

This entire area is chock-a-block full of historical shopping and lodging, and it borders the St. James's Street shops below. Perhaps start with a walk up old Bond Street and imagine the Victorian ladies alighting from their carriages to make their purchases. Both Brown's Hotel and The Ritz are nearby and you can discreetly enter and look around the lobbies, perhaps giving your feet a rest with a drink in their hotel bars (The Ritz's Rivoli is my fav). Likewise, Fortnum & Mason has a café inside, The Parlour, but I found it's often too busy and bustling to be relaxing—although they're famous for their hot chocolate. Just the thing on a cold winter's day. I suggest plotting your route ahead of time to save on walking, because negotiating the New-York-City-level crowds along Piccadilly can wear one down.

Tube: Piccadilly Circus or Green Park (both on Piccadilly)

BURLINGTON ARCADE (1819) ～ What's a shopping "arcade"? It's like a street of small shops but covered with a glass roof. This arcade came about because Lord George Cavendish, then living in Burlington house—now the Royal Academy—wanted to stop "ruffians"

Burlington Arcade in 1828 . . .

BURLINGTON ARCADE, PICCADILLY.

from throwing garbage down his alley, but officially it was commissioned "for the sale of jewellery and fancy articles of fashionable demand, for the gratification of the public and to give employment to industrious females." Almost 200 years later, it still serves all these purposes—although men also clerk here now as well. This charming period arcade is similar to an American mall except that it is one long tunnel open at either end with 40 quaint—and expensive—stores lining the way. Great for window-shopping, people-watching, and crossing to the next street over when it's raining. This one connects Piccadilly and Burlington Gardens thoroughfares. **TIP:** Watch for the Burlington Arcade "beadles" in top hats and Edwardian frockcoats—cutest security guards ever! Guarding either entrance, today they continue to enforce "proper" behavior—no whistling, singing, playing of instruments, running, open umbrellas, or perambulators—and their charming period livery also looks great in photographs. **BEST BETS:** Ladurée Swiss macaroons, Penhaligon soaps. (Avoid the £175 7-inch wood sparrow in Linley, but FB-me a pic if you find it—there might be a prize for you.)

Hours: M-Sat 9am-7:30pm | Sun 11am-6pm | **Map:** B
www.BurlingtonArcade.com | 51 Piccadilly

. . . .and today

PICCADILLY ARCADE (1910) ～ This much smaller cousin opened at the end of the Edwardian era. While only a little over one hundred years old, this arcade retains its charming, period feel. This one connects Piccadilly with Jermyn Street. The building is Grade II listed, and inside you'll find about 16 very high-end brands, mostly English. One unusual shop worth a look is "The Armoury of St James," with World Order medals and hand-painted toy soldiers. **BEST BETS:** Maille (fancy French mustards & vinegars), Piccadilly Vaults (art deco jewelry), and Santa Maria Novella (perhaps world's oldest pharmacy, est. 1612—branded bubble bath, compotes, honeys).

Hours: Vary by store but generally 10am-6pm | Sun 12-4pm
Maps: B & C | www.Piccadilly-Arcade.com | +44 20 7647 3000
enter between Duke and St. James's streets

FLORIS (1750) ～ Nine generations of the Floris family have run this exclusive perfumery established to serve "to the court of St. James." They are the second-oldest such establishment in the world (the other's in Germany). Their first royal warrant from King George IV is still on display along with the sixteen others they've been awarded. Previous customers have included Florence Nightingale, Mary Shelley, and, of course, the arbiter of Regency fashion, Beau Brummell. Even James Bond wears Floris. **BEST BETS:** This is a great place to grab a special and "relatively" inexpensive gift—Floris perfumed soaps. Or splurge on the truly extraordinary—a ninety-minute consultation and fragrance made just for you for £195.

Hours: M-Sat 9:30am-6:30pm | Closed Sun | **Map**: C
www.florislondon.com | +44 20 7747 3612 | 89 Jermyn St

HATCHARD'S BOOKSHOP (1797) ～ Founded by John Hatchard, it is the oldest bookshop in the UK, and feels like it with dark wood paneling, Georgian reproduction chairs, and books cluttering every available surface. Bought in 1990 by the Waterstones chain, happily Hatchard's still retains its period charm. Holder of three Royal Warrants, they sometimes have book signings with famous authors—J.K. Rowling or Diane Von Furstenberg—or nobility, such as the current Duchess of Devonshire. By the way, they have perhaps the largest selection of books on England's history and royalty you'll ever find in one place. ～ *For the guys* there's even a wall of books dedicated to Winston Churchill and a section on military history. When you tread these five ancient floors you are walking in the footsteps of Queen Charlotte (wife of King George III), Rudyard Kipling, the Duke of Wellington, Oscar Wilde, Lord Byron, and even Jane Austen. **BEST BETS:** Everything! And it's the perfect place to pick up a new romance for your flight home.

Hours: M-Sat 9:30am-8pm | Sun 12-6:30pm
Map: B&C | www.hatchards.co.uk
+44 20 7439 9921 | 187 Piccadilly

INNS OF COURT SHOPPING

EDE & RAVENSCROFT (1689) ～ The oldest tailor in the city, they had the honor of making the coronation robes for Their Majesties William and Mary in 1689. They have several stores now, but the original is near the Inns of Court, where they primarily make the legal robes and those old-timey white wigs UK judges wear (which we Yanks find amusing). While unlikely that you're in the market for English legal attire, if you're in the neighborhood it's a chance to see this stuff firsthand, and they have some antique wigs and hats on shelves. **BEST BETS:** Window-shopping, although they do have these super cool, sterling silver, Vintage Car Cufflinks for £85.

Hours: M-F 8:45am-6pm | Sat 10am-3pm | Closed Sun
Tube: Chancery Lane | **Map:** D | www.EdeAndRavenscroft.co.uk
+44 12 2386 1854 | 93 Chancery Lane

ST. JAMES'S STREET SHOPPES
～1676-present

A mere two short blocks down from White's, this once infamous neighborhood of gentlemen's clubs is now the height of gentility. It is quite safe for a young lady to walk along un-chaperoned, which was certainly not the case when Georgette Heyer's Regency heroine Sophy was chastised by her upstanding but uptight companion for driving them down it in an open phaeton.

> *...Miss Wraxton demanded: "Tell me at once where you are taking me!"*
>
> *"Down St. James's Street," replied Sophy coolly.*
>
> *"What?" gasped Miss Wraxton, turning quite pale. "You will do no such thing! No lady would be seen driving there! Amongst all the clubs—the object of every town saunterer! You cannot know what would be said of you! Stop this instant!" ... "I will never forgive you! Never!"*

Of course, feisty Sophy does not stop—it's not her way to worry about what people might say when she's on a mission. While the scurrilous reputation of St. James's Street is long gone, the gentlemen's clubs and their venerable neighbors remain. Lucky for us!

Tube: Green Park for all these shops
All closed Sundays

BERRY BROS. & RUDD, WINE & SPIRIT MERCHANTS (1698) ～ Initially founded as a grocers specializing in coffee by the Widow Bourne (not much else is known about her, not even her first name), she had the serendipitous good luck of St. James's Palace—mere steps from her store—becoming that very year the principal residence of King William III and Queen Mary II after the Palace of Whitehall was destroyed by fire. Thus began a family business that has been highly successful over 315 years and is still run from the original shop at No. 3 St. James's Street. Their colorful history includes hiding Napoleon III in their cellars, having 69 cases of their wines sunk on the Titanic, and supplying alcohol to American smugglers during Prohibition. Sounds like the plot to a thrilling romance to me! *Hmmm...*

Open the front door and one is immediately struck by the fact that this isn't your local mom and pop liquor store. Worn hardwood floors, dark-wood paneling, and relatively few bottles of wine on display are what greet you. No cash register, no sales person, just an open space— that and the very large wooden scale hanging in the corner that was used initially to weigh the coffee. Because scales in the 1700s were rare, this device quickly became the fashionable place for the well-to-do to weigh themselves. Today you can't sit on it, but you can take a photo. Walking farther in there are small rooms branching off with wines ranging from £5 to £5000. **TIP:** Head to the Spirits Room for free tastings of their specialty liquors. **BEST BETS:** I bought their miniature branded King's Ginger liqueur (£5) as terrific little souvenirs to bring home (wrapped carefully and in checked luggage).

Hours: M-F 10am-6pm | Sat 10am-5pm | www.bbr.com
+44 20 7022 8973 | No. 3 St. James's St

LOCK & CO HATTERS

(1676) ∿ The oldest hat shop in the world. Still popular among the upper crust, many guests wore Lock hats to the wedding of Prince William to Catherine Middleton. Past famous customers include the Duke of Wellington and Charlie Chaplin, and their paper patterns are displayed on the wall along with their two royal warrants. Also the Duke of Sale was a customer. Never heard of him? Then I suggest you read Georgette Heyer's *The Foundling*. "*He was a gentleman of high breeding. His hat bore the name of Lock upon the band.*"

The prices are well out of my range, but I found the staff pleasant, and I enjoyed looking at all the antique hats on display as well as the ultra-high-fashion ladies' hats on the upper floor. On a side note, their website's History section under Heritage is one of the most complete I've found online, and includes a brief chronicle of hats, where I learned the origins of the phrase "Mad as a Hatter." Sadly, it was a 19th Century mental disorder afflicting factory hat workers caused by inhaling toxic mercury nitrate fumes. **TIP:** Look for Sir Winston Churchill's and Admiral Lord Nelson's hats in the curated Heritage Room mini-museum. **BEST BETS:** Canvas bag with the storefront on it for £10 or gloves for £95.

Hours: M-F 9am-5:30pm | Sat 9:30am-5pm
www.lockhatters.co.uk | +44 20 7930 8874 | No. 6 St. James's St

TRUEFITT & HILL (1805) ⌣ *for the guys*

This "Gentlemen's Barber Shop," established by William Francis Truefitt, quickly became the Court Hair Cutter and official wigmaker by Royal Appointment to King George III. Listed as the Oldest Barbershop in the World in the 2000 *Guinness Book of World Records*, it has existed at various Mayfair addresses, with the current location dating only to 1994. Visit here and you'll receive the same Royal Warrant service as every male English royal since George III. Other notables include Charles Dickens, Oscar Wilde, Laurence Olivier, and, of course, the all-time arbiter of Regency fashion, Beau Brummell. Famous past American customers include John Wayne, Frank Sinatra, Fred Astaire, and Cary Grant.

Your guy, too, can receive the royal treatment with a hot lather shave or haircut, but be warned the prices are not for the faint of heart (£45 for the basics to 100 minutes of pampering service for £160). I must admit that my hubby has not tried it...yet, but they do get good reviews, including the mention of a glass of champagne being offered to the waiting wife. *I like the sound of that!* Be sure to make a reservation. **TIP:** Guys should wear their wingtips or other leather shoes because a FREE shoeshine comes with each service. **BEST BETS:** A sample pack of their different colognes £6.50, horn combs £11, or—because it's just so cute—the red, white, and blue Churchill Dog stuffed paperweight £15.

Hours: M-F 8:30am-5:30pm | Sat till 5pm
www.TruefittAndHill.co.uk | info@truefittandhill.co.uk
+44 20 7493 8496 | 71 St. James's St

CHAPTER 9 ✤

The Country Life

Easy day or overnight trips to experience nearby castles and charming villages

Castles and country estates are an essential element of historical romance fiction. Rare is the plot that doesn't strand a heroine at a country inn at some point or send her to a weekend country house party or have her held hostage in a tall round tower only to be rescued when she throws down her golden... *oh, yeah,* that's a children's story, but you get the idea.

These overnights or day trips are selected because they're easy and, more important, with a little effort can be done without needing to drive—or driving on the wrong side of the road. And over there the right side is the left side. Even the traffic circles (called roundabouts) go in the wrong direction, opposite of counter-clockwise. And then there's the heavy traffic along tourist routes. Don't get me started on the traffic! But if still undaunted, renting a car can also be an adventure—it only took us three hours to drive 62 miles, but that's another story

Easy Day-Trip Excursions

FAN MUSEUM AND GREENWICH
∼ Make a day of it!

Start with a River Bus ride to see London from the water. ∼ ***For the guys***, once in Greenwich, they can visit the 19th Century Cutty Sark sailing ship and National Maritime Museum while you take in the Queen's House. Quick stop at Royal Greenwich Park, for picturesque views of London. Notice the Royal Observatory up on the hill—time may stop for no man, but here with Greenwich Mean Time it's where the world's time starts. Quick lunch with a Thames view at the 200+-year-old Cutty Sark pub or dine in Regency splendor at The Trafalgar Tavern. Then tour the Fan Museum and finish with Afternoon Tea in the Orangery. Return by overland train for a pass-through view of the modern high-rises at Canary Wharf.

Learn more about the Royal Museums Greenwich at www.rmg. co.uk. **TIP:** Join mailing lists for a FREE drink at www.CuttySarkse10. co.uk or 10% off at www.TrafalgarTavern.co.uk. **WHEN TO GO:** Tuesday or Sunday when reserved tea is offered; reservations required. For Afternoon Tea see Ch. 5 and for Fan Museum history, Ch. 7. Ferry service, Boating, Ch. 7.

◇◈◈───────────────────•

WINDSOR CASTLE ～ Make a day of it!

This amazing edifice has survived civil wars, world wars, and most recently a devastating fire. It's the largest and oldest inhabited castle in the world, with more than 500 people living and working there. With turrets and towers a plenty, it's the stuff fairytales—or romance novels—are made of, although sadly, even with some 1,000 rooms, Windsor Castle doesn't take overnight guests, at least not the paying kind. It does, however, make a great day trip or easy overnight if you stay in one of the Windsor village inns. This is a lot of walking so comfortable shoes are a necessity. For history and hours, see Ch. 3.

ITINERARY 1 ～ DAY TRIP

AM: Early train to Windsor. Buy your coffee and breakfast pastry in the station for the 30–40 minute trip. Aim to arrive by 9am.

Arrive: Walk to castle up a steep hill (10 min) with pre-booked ticket in hand to save time and money. Remember: if the Royal Standard is flying, the Queen is in residence. There's no food/drink allowed in the castle (only bottled water). You can get a re-entry permit to return. At entrance, get in line for the airport-style security check-point. Luggage and backpacks must be checked, complimentary.

❋**AM Highlight ～ Windsor Castle:** To get your bearings, start with a free 30-min Precincts Tour from Courtyard led by a war-den (every 30 min). Then comes the free multimedia tour lasting 1½ hours. Plan to see:

✦ State Apartments

✦ Semi-State Rooms (winter only)

Lots to see gliding on the Thames near Windsor Castle

- ❖ St. George's Chapel (closes 4pm, but you can attend evensong service at 5:15pm; Sun only for worship)

- ❖ Queen Mary's Doll House (from the 1920s with running water and even wine in the miniature bottles)

- ❖ Drawings Gallery with works from the Royal Collection

- ❖ Changing of the Guard ceremony (11-11:30am Mon, Wed, Fri, and Sat usually).

NOTE: For safety/security the route is one-way along the tour. Want a quieter visit—go in the afternoon after most tour operators depart, but you'll miss the Changing of the Guard. Average time to see everything is around 3 hours. When to go: State Rooms have opening dates all year; additional 5 Semi-State rooms only open in winter; Sunday's Chapel is limited to worship. **TIP:** See website for provisional closings, and check again just before departure for unexpected closings. Price: see Museum Quick Guide, Ch. 4.

Lunch: Eat at a historic pub in the village—there are many. I recommend Gilbey's or Two Brewers Windsor (below). For more: www.Windsor.gov.uk.

✳**PM Highlight** ⌇ **Afternoon Carriage Ride:** Give your feet a break with a ride though Royal Windsor Great Park (see Ch. 7).

Late Afternoon: Walk the quaint cobblestone streets to see the village. Have a drink on The Brasserie terrace overlooking the Thames.

Dinner: Eat here or catch train back to London.

ITINERARY 2 ⌇ DAY TRIP TOUR

If time is an issue, the easiest way to visit Windsor Castle is to book a bus tour from London, but you'll be on the operator's schedule. Some full-day tours include Hampton Court Palace or other sights, but avoid tours that take you to three places; there really isn't time for that and you'll just be rushed about.

EASY OVERNIGHTS IN CASTLE COUNTRY

There are many other things to do here, so a list of activities follows. Here are two itineraries, with details listed at bottom.

ITINERARY 3 ⌇ 2-DAY OPTION WITH WINDSOR HOME BASE

DAY 1 ◇·◉✐⚬⚬⚬⚬⚬⚬⚬⚬⚬⚬⚬⚬⚬✦

AM: early train to Windsor.

Arrive: Store luggage at hotel (I suggest taking only 1 carryon and storing the rest at 'Left Luggage' in London train stations; see end of chapter).

✳**AM Highlight** ⌇ **Choose Your Activity:** Suggestions include Blue Guide walking tour, pre-booked Eton College tour (limited dates), or Thames River cruise (fab views of Windsor Castle from the water).

Transfer: Catch noon-ish Shuttle Bus to Hampton Court Palace.

Lunch: Enjoy a Palace Picnic from the onsite Tiltyard Café—reasonable sandwiches, soup, and you can finish with authentic English tarts from the 16th to 18th Centuries. Eat outside in the Wilderness Gardens on benches or the grass, or in the 20th Century Garden on picnic tables (there's indoor seating if the weather's not cooperating).

✳**PM Highlight** ⌇ **Hampton Court Palace:** Built by Cardinal Thomas Wolsey but enhanced by Henry VIII. 5 min walk to main entrance. Have your pre-booked tickets to save money and time. For Palace history/details, Ch. 3. Plan on 3 hours to see it all:

Hampton Court Palace, in 1827 and today

✦ Great Hall

✦ Kitchens

✦ Maze and Gardens

✦ Royal Chapel with Henry's recreated crown

✦ Cumberland Art Gallery with some Old Masters.

Late Afternoon: Uber back to Windsor (30–40 min depending on traffic, UberX is cheapest at £22–30). As above, stroll the village or have a drink by the Thames.

Dinner: Try out a local pub.

✳**Bonus Activity:** See a show in a pretty Edwardian-era theater.

Sleep: See lodging below.

DAY 2 ◇❧⟶

Breakfast: Hotel breakfasts are spendy unless included; eat nearby for better deal. Check out of hotel but leave luggage there.

❋**AM Highlight** ∽ **Windsor Castle:** As in Itinerary 1, get there early with your pre-booked tickets to avoid the queue.

Lunch: Historic pub. Afterwards, stroll the village.

❋**PM Highlight** ∽ **Afternoon Carriage Ride:** Royal Windsor Great Park (Ch. 7)

Dinner: Eat here or catch train back to London.

ITINERARY 4 ∽ 2-DAY OPTION, BACKPACKER STYLE

Cheaper option and less transfer time, but leaving luggage in London rail station is absolutely required.

DAY 1 ◇❧⟶

AM: early train to Hampton Court.

Arrive: Leave small overnight backpack in lockers at Palace's Clock Court (for more info, see www.hrp.org.uk/hampton-court-palace: FAQ's in "Visit Us"). The park opens at 7am, but the castle not until 10am. Aim for arrival at park by 9:30am.

❋**AM Highlight** ∽ **Hampton Court Palace:** Same as Itinerary 3. **Special Options:** pre-book a tour to the Royal School of Needlework (limited dates £16–22). ∽ *For the guys,* if he's tired of castles—*How can anyone be tired of castles?*—then let him play golf, 18 holes to be exact (reservations required; weekday green-fees are reasonable, but weekends are higher (£20–32.50 versus £32.50–70; clubs rental £25; there's also a driving range).

Lunch: Picnic at Hampton Court Palace (as above). Then retrieve overnight bag.

Transfer: Shuttle Bus to Windsor Village (in summer pre-book the 1:45pm or 2:30pm shuttle; pickup is 5 min walk from entrance; ride is 30–45 min).

Arrive: at St. John Baptist Church, then walk to hotel to drop overnight bag (5–7 min).

❋**PM Highlight** ∽ **Choose Your Activity:** as above.

DAY 2 ◇❧⟶

∽ *from here the plan's identical to Itinerary 3.*

WINDSOR EATS

GILBEY'S ∽ Cross the bridge to check out Eton and dine brasserie style in an old butcher's shop. It's a mix of French and 'Modern British'— both food and décor—and they serve wine from their own English vineyard. And if you don't like the lodging listed below, Gilbey's has a Studio Suite complete with continental breakfast in your room. **TIP:** Mon-Thur they have a good set menu for cheap (£22.50 for 2 courses).

Price: a la carte mains £18–25 | www.GilbeyGroup.com/restaurants/ gilbeys-eton | +44 17 5385 4921 | 89–83 High Street, Eton

THE BRASSERIE ∽ This is the place to go on a warm night for romantic terrace views of the Thames, but for food go with simple basic choices (e.g. choose a burger over the grilled halloumi).

Price: mains £12–25 | www.SirChristopherWren.co.uk/food-drink/ the-brasserie | +44 17 5344 2400 | Thames St, Windsor

TWO BREWERS WINDSOR ∽ 17th Century pub with small menu but good food. Reservations a must because this low-ceilinged two-room place has only 9 tables. Traditional Sunday roast gets high marks. Limited hours for food; closed for dinner on Fri-Sat; check website. Due to the tiny space, no children allowed inside but can dine outside at picnic tables.

Price: mains £13–26 | www.TwoBrewersWindsor.co.uk/services/din-ner | +44 17 5385 5426 | 34 Park St, Windsor

TIRED OF PUB FOOD? There are several ethnic restaurants immediately around the castle.

WINDSOR SLEEPS

CLIVEDEN HOUSE ££££½ ∽ is an option if you've a rental car (see listing later this chapter).

MACDONALD WINDSOR HOTEL ££ ∽ 4 star contemporary hotel in Georgian building, 5 minute walk from Windsor Central station and 10 from Windsor Riverside station.

www.MacdonaldHotels.co.uk/our-hotels/macdonald-windsor-hotel +44 17 5348 3100 | 23 High St

CASTLE HOTEL WINDSOR—MGALLERY BY SOFITEL

££ ∼ 4 star contemporary hotel in Georgian building, directly across from the castle (5–10 minute walk from both rail stations).

www.Accorhotels.com/gb/hotel-6618-castle-hotel-windsor-mgal-lery-by-sofitel/index.shtml | +44 17 5325 2800 | 18 High St

CHRISTOPHER WREN HOTEL AND SPA, SAROVA HOTELS £

∼ Best deal here and some rates include breakfast. Mostly contemporary décor in a 1700s building with some lovely period features (the Oak Room is particularly nice). Riverside location by Eton Bridge with pretty Thames-view dining on patio and in restaurant (5–10 from both train stations). As with many lower priced hotels, there's usually something a little off; service and food are raised as issues on online review sites. **TIP:** Their feature rooms (££) have extras and at least one has a **four-poster canopy bed** that is a bargain; make sure to confirm availability at booking. Same contact info as The Brasserie.

TRANSPORTATION

THE WINDSOR-HAMPTON SHUTTLE ∼ £10 one-way. This runs only at lunchtime, with daily departures from either royal abode at 12:15, 1:00, 1:45, and 2:30pm for the 35–45 min ride. Wintertime just 12:15pm departure from Hampton and 1pm from Windsor. Does not run Dec 24–26 and when either sight is closed to the public. **MUST** be pre-booked. www.SurbitonCoaches.com

TRAINS

TO WINDSOR ∼ They run about every half hour. Discounts for buying early, travelling off-peak, and round-trip (called return). Southwest rail line (www.southwesttrains.co.uk).

From London Paddington (change at Slough) to Windsor & Eton Central: 35 min for £10.10 one-way; £14.20 for return.

From London Waterloo (direct) to Windsor & Eton Riverside: about 55 min for £10 one-way; £19 return.

TO HAMPTON COURT ∼ Oyster Card holders may use it to get to the Hampton Court (Zone 6), but not to Windsor.

From London Paddington (change) to Hampton Court: 1 hr 12 min for £10 one-way; £17 for return.

From London Waterloo (direct) to Hampton Court: about 36 min for £7 one-way £14 return.

WINDSOR ACTIVITIES

WINDSOR & ETON TOUR GUIDES ～ Blue Badge guides offer tours of the area. Learn more at www.WindsorEtonTour.com.

CARRIAGE RIDES ～ see Ch. 7.

RIVERBOATS ～ French Brothers 40 minute or 2 hour river cruises out of Windsor Promenade offer great views of the castle. See Ch. 7.

ETON COLLEGE TOURS ～ Just across the bridge is Eton town and college. Public tours of the school can be taken when classes are not in session and the town can be visited anytime. www.etoncollege.com

THEATRE ROYAL WINDSOR (1910) ～ The only unsubsidized professional producing company that operates year-round in Britain presenting classical theater to musical comedy. The current building dates to 1910, but theatricals in Windsor can be traced to 1706 and probably earlier. Around 1597, Shakespeare supposedly wrote *The Merry Wives of Windsor* in the local Ye Olde King's Head inn (c.1525 and apparently just closed).1 Check out the interesting history of the theatre in their "About" at www.TheatreRoyalWindsor.co.uk.

GUILDHALL & ROYAL BOROUGH MUSEUM ～ Designed in 1690 by Sir Christopher Wren (famed architect of London's St. Paul's Cathedral), today it's a small museum telling the history of this area from prehistoric times to present day. Royal connection: Prince Charles and Camilla Parker-Bowles married at Guildhall in 2005, and the first ever same-sex marriage in England took place here in 2005 between Elton John and Canadian David Furnish. www.FriendsofWindsorMuseum.org.uk.

FUDGE KITCHEN ～ An American Connection and a two-degrees-of-separation to me! In the heart of Windsor is a confectionary (est. 1983) that gives credit where credit's due—noting that fudge was invented at Vassar College by accident, giving rise to the dismayed call of "Oh fudge." On their website, the Fudge Kitchen owner notes that the US is still the fudge-making leader of the world, and they give recognition to a place near where I grew up: Mackinac Island in northern Michigan. This quaint little island with no cars has some 14 fudge shops along two blocks, some dating to the 1800s. Back in the UK, Fudge Kitchen makes American-style fudge by hand on traditional marble slabs, but a purist may take issue with their use of whipping cream instead of butter. You can sample it at their store and make up your own mind. www.FudgeKitchen.co.uk or +44 17 5386 2440. Located at 20 Thames Street.

PRINNY'S REGENCY PLAYGROUND
~ Brighton-by-the-Sea

The ancient seaside town of Brighton, formerly Brighthelmstone, is renowned as a seaside playground for royalty and also for the smuggling that took place along this Southern coastline—popularized in romance novels when the heroine either discovers smuggling in action or is kidnapped by pirates that later turn into princes.

This excursion by train includes a tour of Prinny's favorite retreat (the extravagantly and exotically-decorated Royal Pavilion), shopping and dining in "The Lanes" (a quaint historic district of twisting alleyways), and a visit to the boardwalk for a breath of that romance-famed salty sea air. Spend the night in a historic Victorian seaside inn or return the same day to London—either will make for a fine getaway to Regency England.

ITINERARY ~ DAY TRIP

AM: Early train to Brighton in East Sussex (see below). Buy your coffee and breakfast item in the station and enjoy a leisurely 1–1.5 hour breakfast.

Arrive: Brighton Railway Station (1840), a cavernous Grade II* listed space. While the original station has mostly been obscured by additions and modernizations, take a quick gander at the double-spanned

The Royal Pavilion today

glass and iron roof—pure Victorian elegance. Look for the Travel Information booth inside the station for a large local area map and for takeaway maps/coupons (There are Visitor Information Points all around the town, called VIP).

❊**Bonus:** Brighton Toy & Model Museum ∽ Just outside the entrance, literally, it's built under the Victorian arches that support the station. Thousands of antique toys, some to the 1750s, but most 1900–1950. Note: model trains only run on special days; see website. Hours: Tue-Fri 10am–5pm; Sat 11am–5pm. Fee: £6.50. Duration: at least 1 hour. **TIP:** The FREE-entrance lobby has a VIP (if the station booth is closed), plus "Glamour of Brighton" display cases worth a peek even if you don't want to visit the toys. www.BrightonToyMuseum.co.uk

Then walk to Royal Pavilion (about 15–30 minutes; the prettiest but not shortest route is along the gardens).

❊**AM Highlight** ∽ **Royal Pavilion:** Tour this exotic, opulent oriental palace built by King George IV. For its history, see Ch. 3. Duration: at least 1 hour. **TIP:** Tickets 10% less if bought online. Bargain 2-day "History Pass" includes palace, Brighton Museum, and Preston Manor (open only Apr-Sep) for £15. **Freebie:** An extra £2 audio guide rental is needed for touring or you can access FREE audio guide with your smartphone. One needs to connect to 'Link Free' network and create an account—worthwhile because this will give you city-sponsored FREE Wi-Fi at various spots throughout Brighton. **TAKE HEED!** Only the first floor is wheel-chair accessible.

Price: £12.30 | **Hours:** Daily Oct-Mar 10am–5:15pm | Apr-Sept 9:30am–5:45pm | Closed Dec 25–26
www.BrightonMuseums.org.uk | +44 30 0029 0900

Lunch: Eat at a historic pub. There are many old pubs here (check www.VisitBrighton.com for more), but for Victorian splendor I recommend **The Cricketers**. There's been a pub and inn here since 1547, and this place is steeped in history. The original owner, Derrick Carver, was burnt at the stake, a martyr for his religious beliefs, and its most famous "guest" was possibly Jack the Ripper. Robert D'Onston Stephenson, one of the many men believed to be the Ripper, lived in what is now the Greene Room in 1888 (check it out before leaving). But, I suggest you try for a seat in the uber-Victorian red parlor. Dine there on real ale and elevated English dishes, such as Barfields garlic & fennel sausages and mustard mash with ale gravy or roast beetroot tart tatin. All meats and seafoods are locally sourced. **TIP:** In summers, there are sometimes "Ghost Walk of the Lanes" tours that end at The Cricketers with the option of a bargain 3-course set meal. Reservations advised at the pub, unless you're going in the dead of winter like we did.

Price: mains £12–20 | **Hours**: Sun-Thur 12–10pm | Fri-Sat 12–8pm
www.CricketersBrighton.co.uk | info@cricketersbrighton.co.uk
+44 12 7332 9472 | 15 Black Lion St

PM: After lunch, take a walk through "The Lanes," an ancient part of town that now houses fancy little boutiques, and while none of the buildings date from the Middle Ages, the twisty-turny layout is a genuinely medieval warren of narrow lanes, twittens and catcreeps. What are those? A twitten is an old Sussex corruption of "betwixt" and "between," and means a small passageway between two buildings. If a twitten has steep steps, then it's a catcreep (formerly cat's-creep). Finish your walk along the seaside promenade heading north to see Regency Square and the Grade II restored 1884 Victorian Birdcage Bandstand (concerts here on summer Sun afternoons), and finally Adelaide Crescent. The promenade section is 1 mile.

Seafood Dinner: One can't go to this ancient fishing village and not dine on seafood. My recommendation is to head back to The Lanes for **English's of Brighton** (est. 1850, bldg. c.1700s). The restaurant is housed in three very old fisherman's cottages. This is a 150-year-old restaurant with history—look for old photos of Charlie Chaplin, Vivien Leigh, and perhaps Archduke Franz Ferdinand because he used to dine there too. There's even a top-hatted ghost who likes to stroll the kitchens from time to time (again, we didn't get so lucky). But I promise you the fish is as fresh as the "catch of the day." English-supplied seafood and local bakery and ice creamery. Lacking a reservation, we considered ourselves lucky to get a spot at the marble-topped oyster bar, where we dined on lobster bisque with Cognac cream and gruyere glazed fish pie with buttered garden peas. Sometimes there is live jazz or opera music. **TIP**: Sign up for their email and you might get a freebie starter or dessert. 5-course Menu Èpicurien for £39.

Price: mains: £15–50 | **Hours**: Daily 12–10pm | Closed Dec 25–26, Jan 1 | www.Englishs.co.uk | book@englishs.co.uk
+44 12 7332 7980 | 30 East St

Eve: Catch train back to London. 1–1.5 hour ride.

"The Lanes" from Brighton's ancient past

BRIGHTON OVERNIGHT OPTIONS

HOTELS

BRIGHTON MARINA HOUSE HOTEL (In a 1814 bldg.) ~ This small B&B is located in the Kemptown neighborhood and has four-poster beds at a bargain price. See Ch. 6 for details.

THE GRAND BRIGHTON (est. 1864) ~ This grand dame hotel has glorious Victorian features in the public spaces and contemporary guest rooms. Or enjoy an afternoon tea in their Victorian Terrace. See Ch. 6.

HOTEL DU VIN & BISTRO (est. 2006, bldg. 1934) ~ This fun hotel is situated on the edge of The Lanes and has a hip, contemporary feel. It's as if 'modernity' were dumped into a Tudor inn owned by a salty old sea cap'n—in the coolest possible way. From £224. Worth a stop for a drink in their lobby bar. This late addition does not have a full Ch. 6 description, but check it out at www.HotelDuVin.com.

OTHER MUSEUMS AND ACTIVITIES ~ Starred ones are

owned by Brighton & Hove City Council (www.BrightonMuseums.org. uk).

BRIGHTON MUSEUM & ART GALLERY* (1861) ~ eclectic collection of decorative, costume, natural sciences, world, and fine art. Highlights: Bronze Age Amber Cup and George IV's breeches.

HOVE MUSEUM* (est. 1927, bldg. 1870s) ∾ Housed in a Victorian villa, this is a FREE family-oriented craft museum with added focus on film pioneers.

PRESTON MANOR* (est. 1933, bldg. 1738, estate prior to 1086) ∾ Open only Apr-Sept, this Grade II* listed historic manor is furnished in Edwardian style from the servants quarters and kitchen to the elegant reception rooms to the master's bedroom. Located 2 miles north of Brighton. Fee: £6.60 or "History Pass."

BOOTH MUSEUM* (est. 1874) ∾ FREE natural history museum focusing on birds, butterflies, and bones, plus rocks; got its start from a Victorian naturalist.

VOLKS ELECTRIC RAILWAY (1883) ∾ Britain's oldest electric railway runs every 15 min for 1¼ miles along the beach from Aquarium Station (near Brighton Pier) to the Marina. Fee: roundtrip £3.60 Hours: generally Apr-Oct; reconstruction ongoing, so see website. www.VolksElectricRailway.co.uk.

HISTORIC WALKING TOUR ∾ by Jackie Marsh-Hobbs (est. 2000) ∾ Periodic tours led by a local historian and guide: 33 Palmeira Mansions (Victorian life and house tour), Brighton's Seawater Tour (forgotten histories and stories, seaside architecture, and the history of the seawater cure), and of the railway station only in May during Brighton's Fringe Festival. £8 www.JackieMarsh-Hobbs.co.uk.

TRAINS ∾ Two companies service Brighton: Southern and ThamesLink. Trains depart from these stations: Victoria (roughly 1 hr travel time), St. Pancras Intl (1.5 hrs), and London Bridge (1.25 hr). There are about 7 trains an hour. Prices for a round-trip standard fare (not first class) purchased in advance range from £23 off-peak to £54 for peak travel times. Easy to use booking website for small fee: www.TheTrainline.com. Official websites: Southern: www.SouthernRailway.com and ThamesLink: www.ThamesLinkRailway.com.

TRAIN TIP: Buy ticket in advance and travel off-peak (starts 9:30am) to save money; use easy TrainLine website to get routes/fares, but book directly with carrier to save another £.75-1.50.

BRIGHTON TIP: Don't go on Sun-Mon—some museums are closed. Can be massively crowded in summertime, so go on a weekday. If staying overnight, drop luggage at hotel—no storage at museums/pavilion. Great tourist information at www.VisitBrighton.com. Brighton Greeters Scheme offers FREE 2-hour volunteer-led information sessions (like having a local friend to tell you the best places to eat); learn more at VisitBrighton.com. **RESEARCH TIP:** The Brighton Museums' searchable archive, local history, FREE teacher materials, and much more is available at www.BrightonMuseums.org.uk/discover.

Fairytale Princess Overnight

◇◦❧◦

MEDIEVAL CASTLES IN AMBERLEY AND ARUNDEL

This is a one- or two-night excursion to visit two castles and explore a charming village and thriving Arundel town. This can be done by train, but you'll find it easier by rental car. The highlight is staying in the 900-year-old Amberley Castle (see Ch. 6), but if the price is too much, staying in a quaint inn in Arundel is another option.

Arundel Castle can only be visited on a tour. Nearly 1,000 years old, this magnificent working fortress is still the home of the current Duke and Duchess of Norfolk and comes complete with English gardens, gorgeous period decor and paintings, and even Shakespeare theatre performances in August. A two-night itinerary is provided, but it can be pared to one night or even a day trip just to see Arundel.

PRINCESS ITINERARY ∼ 2 NIGHTS BY TRAIN

DAY 1 ◇◦❧

AM: take a mid-morning train to Amberley Railway Station. Grab coffee and breakfast item in the Victoria Station, for enjoying on the train.

Transfer: Have taxi arranged via hotel to bring you to Amberley Castle (about £4). It's only a 20 min walk, but you'll have luggage. At the castle, drop your bags at the reception desk. Enjoy looking about the grounds and gardens; ask if they have a guidebook to the place. Take pictures—you're about to stay in a castle!

Lunch: Early Afternoon Tea at the castle. Ask for seconds—this is lunch. Luxuriate and take your time.

PM: Walk next door to tiny Amberley hamlet—one of the prettiest little villages in Sussex. Check out the ancient church, historic thatched houses, and pottery shop. Please know that there are two neighborhoods to Amberley village—one adorable hamlet by the castle (only food here is the sporadically-open but utterly-charming Amberley Village Tea Rooms at the end of Church Street). The other is by the train station (quaint too, with views of the River Arun, and with two very old pubs).

After checking out the hamlet, walk on to visit the section by the train station (1 mile). Perhaps stop for a pint in one of the pubs (www.

The imposing Arundel
castle in 1633 and today

BridgeInnAmberley.com or www.RiversideTearooms.co.uk which has
a river view and bargain tea for £13). Later walk back (20 mins) and
settle into your room. Dress for dinner; formal attire isn't necessary, but
there is a dress code—plus this is your romantic night!

※**Dinner:** Tonight is the Queen's Room on the second floor of the
great hall. The service can be slow, but that's okay. This fine meal
is your entertainment for the night. Make it last. Afterwards, if the
weather allows, a stroll outside in the moonlight might be nice.

Sleep: See hotel listing for more information, but know that the
four-posters are on the high end and only a few rooms have period
décor. Sleeping like a princess here will cost you, but making it a one-
night excursion is an option that can help.

DAY 2 ◇❧⎯⎯⎯•

Breakfast: Full English breakfast comes with room rate.

AM: Head out for a day in Arundel. You can taxi there for about £20 or walk to Amberley Railway Station (not staffed; ticket machine) to catch the train for a 5 min/£2.50 ride to Arundel. (Yes, this is a lot of walking, but that is the English way, rambling on the moors and that sort of thing...) In the morning there are 2 trains per hour, but not every train stops so be sure you've checked the schedule. Return trains run hourly; same price/5 minute ride.

You'll arrive in Arundel, an old-world river town with Tudor buildings that date to as early as 100 AD. It was a thriving Saxon town by 1086. Walk around and take in the sights: the Catholic, French Gothic Arundel Cathedral (1873), Arundel Museum, and shopping in little stores such as Castle Chocolates, and for us readers, Kim's Books and The Book Ferret, housed in a 16th Century building and carrying some fiction set in Arundel. ～ *For the guys* stop at Antiques & Militaria, a high-end flea market of antique weapons, medals, and a small "military museum" at 18 High Street.

Lunch: Belinda's Tea Room (dating to the 16th Century) or, if driving, head to the historic Black Rabbit, an ancient pub owned by Hall & Woodhouse brewery (est. 1777) on the banks of the Arun with picturesque views of the river and castle. (www.Arundel.org.uk/Belindas-tea-rooms or www.TheBlackRabbitArundel.co.uk). Eat early, for more time at Arundel Castle.

❋**PM Highlight** ～ **Arundel Castle and Gardens:** Its earliest erections date to only about 45 years before Amberley's, but that's where any comparison ends. Amberley is sweet and small. Arundel is massive and majestic. It

•⎯⎯⎯❧◇⎯⎯⎯

Take Afternoon Tea at Amberley Castle, outdoors if weather permits

*Amberley Castle's Queen's Room in the 12ᵗʰ Century Great Hall
The c.1680 mural on the back wall honors the restored
King Charles II and Queen Catherine.*

looks exactly like what you would expect of an ancient royal fortress. This is the kind of place that romance dreams are made of, its turrets and crenelated ramparts set against a background of misty fields, streams, and grazing animals. Rapunzel couldn't do better than to be locked in the splendidly tall round tower. Today, let your imagination float free as you experience this enchanting place.

For a history of the castle, home today to the 18th Duke and Duchess of Norfolk, see Ch. 3. Interestingly the 16th Duke planned to give it to the National Trust, but the 17th kept it, creating a charitable trust to pay for restoration. It was one of the first castles open to visitors, starting in 1854. Today, more than 176,000 visit over the 7 months it's open. During the other months, it's the "principal seat" of Edward William Fitzalan-Howard, 18th Duke of Norfolk, formerly Earl of Arundel, and current Marshal of England.

What you can see when you visit Eddy's country abode:

❧ More than 40 acres of gorgeous gardens and grounds, including rose and white gardens

❧ The Collector Earl's Garden, a recent installation full of playful features including green oak Pagodas and Oberon's Palace with a dancing water crown

✦ Fitzalan Chapel (c.1390), a fine example of Gothic ecclesiastic architecture and burial place of all Norfolk Dukes

✦ Castle Keep where, if you're hearty, you can climb the 131 weathered steps to the top for views of the Downs and River Arun

✦ Main reception rooms, such as the 133-foot-long Barons' Hall that commemorates the Magna Carta, a Regency library with carved Chinese lanterns, and a rather large dining room, each room chock-a-block full of old weapons and gleaming armory, antique furniture, paintings, and tapestries.

✦ Priceless curiosities such as Queen Victoria's coronation homage chair and the rosary beads carried to the scaffold by Mary Queen of Scots, along with landscape masterpieces by Canaletto, Van Dyke, and Gainsborough

✦ Lavish Victorian decorated bedrooms and magnificent four-poster beds, one fit for a duke, the other, in pretty pinks, a duchess

✦ Plus access to the Castle café, fine-dining restaurant, and gift shop in the old Castle kitchens.

In addition, there are special events throughout the summer. If you're lucky enough be there at the right time (check the Arundel Castle calendar) you might see costumed/horsed Norman & Crusader reenactments and living history displays, historic roadster displays, flower festivals, Morris dancing, and pirates & smugglers at play! The pinnacles are two events in May and July—Castle Siege and Joust Week. The tickets are more, the crowds bigger, and the pageantry grandest.

Price: a range, but you'll probably want the £20 Gold PLUS in order to see the bedrooms | **Hours**: 10am–5pm Tue-Sun, April-Oct 29, plus select bank holiday Mon | Some areas close 30 min early www.ArundelCastle.org | +44 19 0388 2173 | Arundel, West Sussex

Dinner: Return to Amberley for a second Queen's Room dinner. For less, eat in Arundel (see www.Arundel.org.uk for ideas or just wander until you find something that calls to you) or stop off after alighting from the return train in Amberley village to eat in one of the pubs mentioned above.

Sleep: Amberley Castle. The next day, after leisurely breakfast (included), take the train back to London.

Advance Booking Checklist: besides hotel reservation, reserve taxi pick-ups, as needed, afternoon tea, and dinner at Queen's Room. **TIP:** If you're going the backpacker route or if you don't feel like lugging all your suitcases for an overnight excursion, use the left-luggage option described at end of this chapter.

TRAINS ∼ Hourly departures from Victoria Station to Amberley for 1 hour 20 minute ride. Prices for round-trip standard fare (not first class) purchased in advance range from £10 off-peak (outbound 10:36–11:55 train; return 7–8:28pm) to £48 for peak travel times.

CAR RENTAL ADVICE ∼ If you choose to drive, here are some tips. 1. Rent an automatic (you'll save considerable money with a standard transmission, but have you ever tried shifting a stick with your left hand? And the car we rented had 6 gears arranged differently!), 2. Rent a car with a trunk for securing your luggage and don't leave anything in view, 3. Have both paper maps and a charged GPS system (your phone or a TomTom, but in case that fails—poor reception or dead battery—having a paper map is essential), 4. Have patience (remember your partner is not your enemy), 5. Again, have patience (you may be 3 hours late, hungry, and stuck in the dark on a one-lane road behind a stalled driver-trainee, in a tiny hamlet where there's not room to even turn around (*yeah, it happens*), but eventually they'll figure it out—or, as happened with us, the teacher will take over and drive the car out of the village center so the seven stacked-up cars can continue on their way. If you think perhaps I'm just spit-balling ideas—nope, these suggestions I learned by hard example.

MODIFIED CASTLE ITINERARIES TO SAVE MONEY OR TIME

The plan above is just a starting point; it can be easily changed to meet your needs. Here are two possibilities:

1 NIGHT AT AMBERLEY

You've two options: 1) if by train, check out and leave luggage at Amberley, returning to claim it before taxiing to station for train back to London, or 2) drive so you can take your luggage in your trunk the next day after checking out; see Arundel, then head back to London.

1 NIGHT STAY IN ARUNDEL ∼ with dinner at Amberley.

This will work better for driving, but is doable by train with some taxi expense. Early departure to Arundel; drop bags at hotel (Norfolk Arms in Ch. 6) and enjoy town. Taxi/Uber to Amberley in the afternoon to visit village and castle grounds before dinner in Queen's Room. Taxi back to Arundel. The next day, visit Arundel Castle before training back to London.

Arundel's Norfolk Arms hotel looks just the same as in the 1890s, but inside they've added all the modern conveniences.

*L*ady of the Manor at a Country Estate

EASY OVERNIGHT AT CLIVEDEN HOUSE & SPA

Cliveden House is both attraction and lodging for this easy overnight. A luxury five-star hotel serving at most 90 overnight visitors, Cliveden is there to "transport you to a different world," says one recent guest.

Make this the last stop of a London tour for your chance to experience for a night or two the English country lifestyle. Breakfast at 10am, spend the day at genteel leisure, dine in regal splendor, and finish with cocktails in the library. Then the next day, all relaxed and romanced, it's a short ride to Heathrow and your flight back to reality—but you'll get to take wonderful memories with you.

So what's a Lady of the Manor like you to do? As little or as much as you want.

LADY LEISURE ⤳ Georgian guests enjoyed the foxhunt. While that's no longer on offer, horseback riding and clay pigeon shooting can be had nearby. Regency ladies visiting Cliveden enjoyed walks, croquet, and picnics—and you can too. Start with a leisurely stroll through the Grade I listed gardens (yes, even gardens can be listed) to see the water fountain, formal gardens, and Cliveden Maze. Or set out on a long hike exploring the 376 acres of National Trust parkland. **TIP:** In summer you'll find more solitude before 10am, when the grounds open to the public. Enjoy an outdoor picnic lunch, snack, or afternoon tea, provided by Cliveden's chefs. Served in Bento boxes, they have vegetarian options as well as English traditional (£10–38 pp, 48 hrs notice). **TIP:** Save money by bringing your own bottle of bubbly.

BOATING ⤳ Topping the list of Victorian activities is boating, and the oldest of Cliveden's vintage flotilla date almost that far back. And you'd be in royal company as it was Queen Victoria's preferred method of traveling to Cliveden. There are several pricey options in their vintage boats that hold 4 to 10 people—from champagne cruises, to jaunts to nearby Henley, to picnic lunches. Or join fellow guests for a 45-minute shared twilight river cruise on the Thames (10 max) in the charming 1911 Suzy Ann while sipping a glass of champagne (£50pp; 5pm & 6pm, April-Oct; deck shoes or sneakers required; no toilet facilities, access requires a steep walk and is not accessible for persons with limited mobility.)

At this point it should be mentioned that the National Trust has owned Cliveden since 1942. The NT offers less expensive boating and daytime dining options in the public areas of the estate. You might as well take advantage of them because you're paying for parkland access whether you use it or not: £12pp for overnight guests and £7 for restaurant guests, but the fees help maintain all those acres of woods and gardens.

NATIONAL TRUST ACTIVITIES ⤳ All located on the grounds, these additional services and dining options are offered to all park visitors (cliveden@nationaltrust.org.uk +44 16 2860 5069). There's a gift shop too.

Dining: the Orangery Café, Dovecote Coffee Shop, and Doll's House Café (takeaway food) are only open for morning coffee, lunch, and afternoon tea (10am–4:30pm). The prices are very reasonable and their menu offers some interesting choices.

Cinema: at the Gas Yard shows a free introductory film, "Cliveden: Camelot on Thames."

Boating: Spend some time on the water in a rowboat (certainly more period) or a small motorboat (less work) and don't forget your parasol or bring a picnic or bottle of bubbly. Prices: rowboats are £16 for ½ hr, £21 for 1 hr; motorboats are £31 for ½ hr, £36 for 1 hr. Cash only, plus £30 deposit. There's also a 45 minute skippered electric boat ride for £11—you'll see more but have company.

CLIVEDEN POOL ∼ Your last option for an outdoorsy-lady-of-leisure experience is the most modern and notorious—you can go for a scandalous swim. The pool was installed in 1961 by the 3rd Viscount Astor to stop his lady wife from swimming in the Thames, and while the water is certainly newer, you'll find it's the same pool that started the Profumo Affair. It's tucked away in the walled garden in The Pavilion Spa. Hotel guests receive complimentary use of the indoor and outdoor heated pools and Jacuzzis (services are extra but reasonably priced for a luxury hotel). Additionally, there are indoor and outdoor tennis courts, a fitness trail, and a fitness room for hotel guests.

RAINY DAY ACTIVITIES ∼ When it's wet outside, Victorian ladies, such as yourself, find enjoyment reading by the fire in the Great Hall, perhaps a game of chess, or get up a foursome and play a game of whist (learn the simple rules at www.Britannica.com/topic/whist). Or take a "**Butler Tour**" to learn the history of the mansion and see behind-the-scenes places, or just wander on your own (there are vintage photos of past guests on the walls downstairs).

✳**Highlight** ∼ **Afternoon Tea:** Taken in the Great Hall, this is quintessential Victoriana. Served on the recreated Astor Tea Service fine bone china, the menu features their famous Cliveden fruitcake, the traditional English Battenberg cake, and the Scottish treat, Tiffin. **TIP:** Their listed champagne is pricey, but ask if they have the less expensive sparkling pink moscato or prosecco which is served elsewhere at Cliveden. **TIP:** They'll box up your leftovers. Also, make sure to note whether you want to take tea in the Great Hall (old world ambiance) or in the Terrace Restaurant (views of the gardens). Lastly, check the website's

Cliveden still has outdoor dining but, sadly, without a butler and footman

"What's On" for memorable experiences: for example, black-tie dinners with Royal Opera performers and talks by noted historians.

Transportation to Cliveden

Cliveden Arranged: The hotel will be happy to arrange transportation for you, including limousine or helicopter...and either will be spendy. Less expensive alternatives include rental car, train with taxi/Uber or just Uber. Once there, take Bourne End Road to the Hedsor Gate, open from 8am–5pm (after hours press intercom for access).

UberX: ranges £37–60 depending on time of day, plus tip.

Train: about 4 departures an hour from Paddington to Taplow: (35 min for £10x2 people); then UberX (£6–8) for a total of about £27, plus tip.

A Final Note

As mentioned in Ch. 6, Cliveden House offers a good package for short stays with tranfers to Heathrow. Check their website for current availability.

◇━✐✐━━━━━━━━━●

Left Luggage Services

Rail stations no longer have lockers, but Excess Baggage Company runs staffed storage services in the following locations (all are 7am–11pm unless noted): Charing Cross, main concourse; Euston platform 16–18; King's Cross, main concourse; Liverpool Street, platform 10; Paddington, track/platform 12; St Pancras Int'l, main concourse (M-Sat 5:30am–11pm, Sun 7am–10pm); Victoria, platform 8. Also at Heathrow and Gatwick airports. The approximate cost is about $12 per suitcase for 1 day; longer periods the rate per day decreases. See website for more information: www.left-baggage.co.uk.

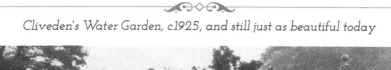

Cliveden's Water Garden, c.1925, and still just as beautiful today

CHAPTER 10

Before you go ~ What would Emma advise?

My dearest friends,

I am honored that you might seek to avail yourself of my prudent counsel on the topic of an excursion to the incomparable London. Using a friend's turn of phrase, it is, perhaps, one of those cases in which advice is good or bad only as the event decides. So, I offer these suggestions, knowing in my heart, as I do, that you will use what is helpful and ignore the chaff.

If I might share a deep secret, I, myself, had the pleasure of visiting London both in my current time and in the future, when, to be sure, the place is much changed yet remnants of the city's great historical past are everywhere. One need only seek them out and if a body were to do that, then opening their mind to the possibilities is all that is required to enjoy an imaginative visit to my time.

As to advice, I know that what I am writing will be of the smallest use to you, but I feel that I must share some for your well-being and future enjoyment. First, and foremost, the acquisition of a <u>detailed map of London</u> of the highest calibre would not be amiss. I cannot tell you how often I popped up from that underground train and found myself thoroughly turned about, and this after spending long moments perusing the station's large neighbourhood map. Yes, this is indeed your most important travel accessory.

Secondly, I would encourage the public carrying of a <u>sturdy umbrella</u>. While in my time, this is just becoming the fashion, in the modern era one would surely be thought strange to be seen walking thus unencumbered during a solid rain, and, as you might know, in London it rains a great deal. Everybody has their level of comfort, to be sure, but to safeguard that you stay dry and do not catch cold, an umbrella is a must.

Thirdly, I must address <u>safety</u>. In the 21st Century it is most certainly acceptable for a lady to go about her business without a maid trailing behind, but I would still caution you to use... well... caution. Every big city has pickpockets and lovely London is no exception. Keep your reticules firmly in hand whenever you're in public, and whatever the inconvenience to holding such upon your lap, do not hang them off the back of your chair in dining establishments. That's the surest way to find they have gone a walking when it's time to depart. Keep small amounts of money handy so that you do not need to pull out your pocketbook on the street, and urge your gentleman friends to keep their wallets in the front pockets of their breeches.

While most parts of central London are safe, especially in daylight, one should take extra care if alone after dark. Generally, if other tourists abound, so may you with a degree of ease; however, if the streets are deserted and it's late at night, then perhaps a hackney would be best. Oh, excuse me, I believe you Colonials use the term, taxi. Lastly, don't forget to deadbolt your hotel room door and never open it unless you are expecting someone. Common sense, really, but if one is a country girl, like myself, such things might not come readily to mind.

Another consideration is which season is best for a London excursion. Spring and summer can be quite nice for the weather, and the gardens lovely, but the city is extra crowded with tour groups and prices are the highest. Winter is less crowded due to the cold and rain, but people from the States find that the sun goes down unusually early here, setting as early as 3:51 in the afternoon. December, with the Christmas decorations, is charming but this also brings with it a surge of my fellow countrymen and international sojourners too! I understand that London is one of the most popular destinations in the world—and it certainly seems like everyone on earth is crowding in, but then again, nowhere else offers quite so much history for the romance novel reader.

Quickly, before my hand grows weary from applying the pen, I offer some additional suggestions ~ take a bus tour of the city when you first arrive to help get your bearings and see major sights from the comfort of a horseless coach ~ read a general London guidebook for an overview of the city ~ buy an Oyster Card, and no, dear reader, this will not entitle the bearer to free oysters whenever they dine; rather it is a card that will allow easy and inexpensive traverse of London via the Underground or "Tube" ~ for those lasting memories, do try to include at least one splurge, that one-cannot-be-missed experience desired most of all. Perhaps an afternoon tea at the Ritz or night in a castle. Whatever takes your fancy, but something so special its remembrance will be forever cherished.

Why all the fuss, you might inquire. "Why not seize pleasure at once?" as another friend remonstrated to me. "How often is happiness destroyed by preparation, foolish preparation!" But I would answer, in this case, and given the great expense, preparation is not foolish but the essential ingredient to ensuring a successful London holiday. One need not undertake it in military-campaign fashion, although personally I often throw myself into my projects thus; rather, everybody should consider their personal needs and budget and allow the appropriate time and energy for planning.

And above all else, my dearest new friends, whether your travels involve only the prose in this book or a real-life adventure, I do hope you have had or will have the most delightful excursion into the London of my time.

Yours affectionately,

~ Emma

APPENDIX I ∼ NOVELS QUOTED IN THE GUIDE

Author's Note: It's my great pleasure to recommend these wonderful histori-cal romance authors. ∼ *Sonja*

Victoria Alexander: *Yesterday and Forever* ∼ A time-traveling modern women meets her hero in London's past. (1995)

Jane Austen: *Pride and Prejudice* (1813) ∼ An Austen masterpiece of manners and mayhem.

Mary Balogh: *The Famous Heroine* ∼ An outsider thrust into *ton* society and wins it all in the end. (1996)

Lynne Connolly: *Temptation Has Green Eyes* ∼ The commoner heiress mar-ries up, but it's a marriage of convenience until the couple fights a common enemy. (2015)

Tessa Dare: *Any Duchess Will Do* ∼ The servant girl wins a duke, if she'll have him. (2013)

Georgette Heyer: *The Grand Sophy* (1950), *The Corinthian* (1940), *The Foundling* (1948) ∼ Fabulous Regency stories from the founder of Regency romance.

Elizabeth Hoyt: *To Taste Temptation* ∼ An American in London tale, but with a twist, the transplant's a man and the ocean is less wide than the gulf between him and his Lady. (2008)

Sabrina Jeffries: *The Forbidden Lord* ∼ When a country girl must masquerade as a Lady, the Lord that wants to unmask her falls for her instead. (1999)

Erin Knightley: *A Taste for Scandal* ∼ A rogue meets his match in a bakery—and she's the baker—which is perfect for a wetting your appetite for one of the Afternoon Teas in this Guide. (2012)

Johanna Lindsey: *The Heir*† ∼ A Highlander in London falls for country girl in her first London season, but their burgeoning love must overcome his duty and her secret past. (2000)

Delilah Marvelle: *Lord of Pleasure* ∼ When a desperate widow offers herself as a courtesan, what's a master rogue to do—send her home safely, but this humorous and sexy story doesn't end there. (2009)

Judith McNaught: *Whitney, My Love* ∼ A sweeping love saga. Also rec-ommended: *Until You*, an American in London tale where the heroine gets amnesia and doesn't know who she is while falling for an English Lord. (1985, 1994)

Historical novels, although contemporary when written:

Daniel Defoe: *The Fortunes and Misfortunes of the Famous Moll Flanders.* (1722)

Sir Arthur Conan Doyle: Sherlock Holmes in *The Hound of the Baskervilles.* (1902)

H. Ranger (pseudonym): *Harris's List of Covent Garden Ladies or Man of Pleasure's Kalender for the Year 1788.*

---

† *Given by permission of the Aaron Priest Literary Agency.*

APPENDIX II ⌇ ADDITIONAL NOVELS AND TRUE STORIES TO ACCOMPANY YOUR JOURNEY

Countess of Carnarvon: *Lady Almina and the Real Downton Abbey: The Lost Legacy of Highclere Castle* ⌇ The true story of Almina's marriage to the 5th Earl of Carnarvon in 1895 and her life. (2011)

Georgette Heyer: *Regency Buck* ⌇ A must if you are interested in visiting Brighton-by-the-Sea (Ch. 9) as the Royal Pavilion is at its entertaining hey-day here. (1935)

Joan Johnson: *Captive* ⌇ In this Pygmalion transformation, a wild American heiress is forced by her guardian/nemesis/future love to learn proper manners so she can enter London society. (1996)

Johanna Lindsey: *A Rogue of My Own* ⌇ Young Lady Rebecca becomes a maid of honor in Queen Victoria's court in Buckingham Palace, a place of intrigue, malice, and seduction. (2009)

Natalie Livingstone: *The Mistresses of Cliveden: Three Centuries of Scandal, Power and Intrigue in an English Stately Home* ⌇ A must if you plan to visit Cliveden. (2016)

Joan Overfield: *Time's Tapestry* ⌇ A modern woman is swept back in time, where she has to contend with a handsome lord with problems while trying to learn to behave like a Regency lady. (1996)

Julia Quinn: *An Offer From a Gentleman* ⌇ A London-based Cinderella story complete with a magical masquerade ball, a midnight return to drudgery, and the hero left with nothing but an article of clothing to find his true love. (2001)

Lauren Royal: *Amethyst* ⌇ Before departing on your own fairytale princess side-trip to a castle (Ch. 9), read this romance partially set in castles modeled after Amberley and Arundel. (2012)

Bertrice Small: *Blaze Wyndham* ⌇ With royal court novels now popular, this one—where a country-bred widow ends up the mistress and confident of Henry VIII—is 25 years ahead of its time. (1988)

Louise Allen: *Walks Through Regency London* ⌇ Not a novel, but a handy companion to the Romance Readers Guide, offering your chance to walk in the footsteps of your favorite heroine in 10 highly-immersive self-guided tours.

APPENDIX III ∼

◇❧────────────────────●

NOTE ON ENDNOTES: To save paper, they're available by request to info@romancereadersguides.com.

◇❧────────────────────●

IMAGE CREDITS

Thank you to the following photographers, hotels, companies, Wikimedia Commons, and picture libraries for their assistance with this Guide. Many of the images are in the public domain and are credited here for informational purposes.

FRONT: "Two Strings To Her Bow" 1882–John Pettie.

CH.3 Pg17: "The Albany" c.1830–Thomas Sheperd. Pg19: drawing 1821–George Cruikshank. Pg24: painting 1827–John Preston Neale. Pg38: painting 1824–Augustus Pugim, Sr. Pg52: Drawing 1766–Edward Rooker, Government Art Collection. Pg53: 2015 Ilya Kuzhekin, Wikimedia Commons. Pg63: Professor John Palmer, University of Hull, and George Slater–Http://OpenDomesday.org. P71: "Rotten Row, Hyde Park" c.1900–Thomas Binks. Pg71: Library of Congress (LoC) Prints & Photographs Division, Photochrom Collection, ppmsc.08575. Pg78: LoC, ppmsc.08569. Pg81: photo–original uploader was Lonpicman at English Wikipedia (CC BY-SA 3.0) https://commons.wikimedia.org/w/index.php?curid=7971798. Pg99: drawing c.1555–Bernardino de Escalante. Pg100: photo–© Bob Collowan/Commons/CC-BY-SA-4.0. Pg104: drawing 1785–Thomas Rowlandson. Pg108: drawing 1903–Brandon Head from *The Food of the Gods: A Popular Account of Cocoa,* (pub. 1903, facing pg87). Pg117: map c.1658–Wenceslas Hollar, The Thomas Fisher Rare Book Library, University of Toronto. Pg118: photo–David Iliff (License: CC-BY-SA 3.0).

CH.4 Pg120: map c.1550–Braun & Hogenberg (Sanderusmaps.com [Public domain], via Wikimedia Commons. Pg120–121: map 2009–MRSC-OpenStreetMap (http://www.openstreetmap.org CC BY-SA 2.0). Pg122–129: *Stanford's Library Map of London and its Suburbs 1862* provided by Anthony Craig, Mappalondon.com.

CH.5 Pg141: "The Palm Court at The Ritz" provided by Angel.S, www.AVictorian.com ©1997-present. Pg158: photo–Ewan Munro, London, UK [CC BY-SA 2.0], via Wikimedia Commons.

CH.6 Pg232: drawing 1737—Nathaniel Buck and Samuel Buck, British Museum. Pg232: drawing 1876—*A History of the Castles, Mansions, and Manors of Western Sussex*–Dudley George Cary Elwes (Illustrations by Thomas Batterbury and William Penstone). Pg256: LoC ppmsc.08577.

CH.7 Pg260: key photo–Bullenwächter–Hamburg Museum, CC BY-SA 3.0, ...curid=29229314. Pg261: LoC ppmsc.08582. Pg263: crown 1919 made by Cyril Davenport. Pg270: period dress & photograph–Victoria Vane (Facebook.com/Renaissance2Regency). Pg280: photo 1904—Bill Nelson collection.

CH.8 Pg283: "The Bubble"–www.GraysandFeather.com. Pg284: drawing 1828–Thomas H. Shepherd. Pg286: perfume bottle photograph–Izzy Rouillard.

Pg287: book–Wellcome Library, London. Pg288: wine bottle–RenseNBM (CC BY-SA 4.0). Pg289: top hat–Nikodem Nijaki (CC BY-SA 3.0).

CH.9 Pg293: photo–Mark Furney, Own work (CC BY 3.0) … curid=5700260. Pg295: painting1827–Henry Bryan Ziegler. Pg295: photo–Duncan Harris, Nottingham, UK [CC BY 2.0 (http://creativecommons.org/licenses/by/2.0)], via Wikimedia Commons. Pg300: photo 2014–Poliphilo (Own work) [CC0], via Wikimedia Commons. Pg303: photo 2007–Stephen McKay, CC BY-SA 2.0, …curid=13180204. Pg306: drawing 1633—*A History of the Castles, Mansions, and Manors of Western Sussex* Dudley George Cary Elwes (Illustrations by Thomas Batterbury and William Penstone). Pg306: photo 2009–Farwestern Photo Gregg M. Erickson–Own work (CC BY 3.0) …curid=8271746. Pg311: photo c.1890–Gravelroots.net photo collection. Pg315: LoC ppmsc.16490.

INSTITUTIONS ∽ **The Fan Museum:** Pg149, 267. **The Geffrye, Museum of the Home:** Pg63: Painting 1906–Philip Norman. Pg63 & 277 photos–Richard Davies.

HOTELS ∽ **Amberley Castle:** 232, 235, 236, 239, 307, 308. **Brown's Hotel, a Rocco Forte Hotel:** 139, 172, 173, 174. **The Chesterfield Mayfair Hotel:** 143, 187, 189, 190. **Cliveden House & Spa:** 12, 243, 246, 245, 247, 274, 313. **Cranley Hotel:** 222, 223. **The Egerton House Hotel:** 145, 177, 178. **The Glebe House London:** 227, 228. **The Gore:** 169, 191,193, 195, 196. **Grosvenor House, A JW Marriott Hotel:** 197, 199, 201. **The Ritz, London:** 141, 182. **The Royal Park:** 230, 273. **St. Ermin's Hotel, The Autograph Collection:** 207, 208, 210, 211, 214, 215, 217. **St. Pancras Renaissance° Hotel London:** 214, 215, 217, 219.

Additional photography by Steven Glapa.

◇⤸⎯⎯⎯⎯⎯⎯⎯⎯⎯•

ADDITIONAL ACKNOWLEDGEMENTS

We would like to offer our additional thanks to everyone who helped make this publication possible, and especially to these helpful folks ∽ Anthony Craig (www.mappalondon.com), Peter Buckman at The Ampersand Agency (Georgette Heyer), romance author and seamstress-extraordinaire Victoria Vane, Bill Nelson, Phil Dixon (Gravelroots.net), Alix Bateman at The Glebe House London, Trevor at The Gore, Howard Hartley, unofficial historian at Grosvenor House, Michael Chaloner at Cliveden House, Joi Izilein at The Ritz, London, and numerous others at Amberley Castle, Brown's Hotel, Cranley Hotel, The Chesterfield Mayfair Hotel, The Egerton House, The Fan Museum, The Geffrye Museum, Hotel du Vin, Marriott Hotel County Hall, The Rookery, The Royal Park, St. Ermin's Hotel, and St. Pancras.

Lastly, I'm also thankful to these SVRWA authors for their excellent beta aid: Linda S. Gunther, Janet Miller, Reina M. Williams, and many others who offered their useful opinions.

INDEX

Bon Voyage!
Whether into a great romance or off to wherever life takes you.

We'd love to hear from you:
www.RomanceReadersGuides.com
Facebook.com/RomanceReadersTravelGuides
Goodreads.com/RomanceReadersGuides
Twitter: @RomGuides

Made in the USA
Lexington, KY
14 June 2017